RAY SANDERSON

Illustrations by the author

ADLARD COLES NAUTICAL
London

To Jackie

Published by Adlard Coles Nautical
an imprint of A & C Black (Publishers) Ltd
35 Bedford Row, London WC1 4JH

First published in Great Britain by
Adlard Coles Nautical 1992

ISBN 0–7136–3455–3

A CIP catalogue record for this book is available from the British Library.

Typeset in 10/11pt Plantin by Tradespools Ltd, Frome, Somerset

Printed and bound in Great Britain by
J. W. Arrowsmith Ltd, Bristol

The chart extracts and tidal stream information are reproduced as examples only and should not be used for navigation purposes.

Figs 50 and 51 are based on Admiralty Chart No. 2045. Fig. 53 is reproduced from Admiralty Tidal Stream Atlas NP 337. Fig. 54 is reproduced from Admiralty Chart 394.

CONTENTS

LIST OF FIGURES

LIST OF PHOTOGRAPHS

· PREFACE ·

The aim of this book is to introduce an outright beginner to sailing offshore by suggesting how to select a sailing school, what should be brought and how it should be stowed, and what will be learnt during a typical five-day introductory cruise. The style of this book is different from other books on this subject since the instruction is given within the context of a cruise at sea. It covers the seamanship aspects of the RYA syllabus but meteorology and first aid are omitted in the interests of space, since they are well covered elsewhere. (For the former, see the author's *Weather for Sailing* published by Adlard Coles Nautical.)

In order to avoid frequent repetition, the masculine gender has been used to describe the crew and their work. It should, of course, be considered representative of both sexes. On the other hand, despite the genderless nature of much of the English language, boats, particularly yachts, should always be feminine.

Ray Sanderson
1992

AN INTRODUCTION TO THE FIRST · CRUISE ·

HOW TO BEGIN CRUISING

As you leave harbour, and as the sails are trimmed to the wind, a yacht heels and accelerates. The effect is exhilarating, with the sound of wind and waves providing an appropriate background as the crew match their skills against the elements. The exhilaration is disproportionally large, since the yacht speed may only be 6 knots or so (less than 10 mph). Yet for the helmsman especially, who can directly feel from the rudder the thrust of the hull through the water, the effect may be blood-tingling. If this scene is appealing then it is probable that offshore sailing will become for you an enjoyable activity, perhaps a lifelong one. But how does one begin?

The best way is by joining a course for novices run by a sailing school recognised by the Royal Yachting Association (RYA House, Romsey Road, Eastleigh, Hants SO5 4YA) who will send their list of schools on application. If possible, choose one from personal recommendation. These beginners' courses, of usually five days' duration, are run 'afloat', though most nights are spent in harbour.

Some people may choose to sail first on a friend's yacht. In some ways this can be a good first introduction though the information and instruction will normally fall short of that given at an RYA approved school.

WHAT GEAR TO TAKE

Having booked a course, the next decision is what to take with you. Stowage space on most yachts is very limited, so you should ruthlessly restrict what you pack to those items you will definitely need. These will be good oilskins (check whether the sailing school provides these) and yachting boots (land substitutes just will not do because they offer little grip). At this stage try to borrow these items from a friend if possible. If not, try the yachting press for hiring. As a rule, delay buying these expensive items until you are sure that you will take to sailing and until you have sought advice during the course about what type to buy. Soft inexpensive deck shoes with a 'yachting' sole for grip should be purchased straightaway. Trainers are generally discouraged for they are potentially dangerous on a wet deck.

The remainder of the gear will be your non-specialist personal effects. Irrespective of the time of year, take two warm woollen sweaters (natural wool is better) and two pairs of warm trousers as well as jeans and lighter sweaters, for it is always much colder at sea than on land. You will need two of each in case of a real wetting. Remember, too, that several layers are warmer than one thick heavy garment. Skirts, of course, are just not practical on a yacht – even for going ashore. In warmer weather include some summery items such as swimming gear and shorts. Take enough underwear, etc to last the five days, for it is unlikely that there will be a chance to visit a laundry. It is a good idea to pack all the different types of clothing such as underwear, socks, etc, in small plastic 'freezer' bags, since there is no guarantee that your locker will remain completely dry throughout the course. Personal toilet gear and a large and small towel (the smaller one may be usefully worn around the neck when the going is wet) should also be packed.

By all means take your camera, more especially for the lighter moments, but cine and video cameras and radios will normally not be welcome. It should be assumed that sleeping bags are not provided so take your own. Two 'luxury' items I have always found invaluable are a pillow and a pair of slippers. A book on sailing, yes, for any quiet moment during the day, but one for bedtime is not on as other crew members will want to sleep.

If, for health reasons, you must have certain foods only, then declare this before the booking is confirmed, since most schools will provide little or no choice at mealtimes. Again, if you suffer from a recurring illness such as diabetes, asthma, migraine or the like, tell the principal at the outset. Most such illnesses will not affect your selection to join a course, but it is only common sense to tell the school about it.

A word on seasickness; despite claims to the contrary, very few people are totally immune. At the same time very few people are so totally incapacitated each time they go to sea as to prevent their taking up sailing. In deteriorating weather, a good preventative is to don plenty of warm and protective clothing in good time. Any delay here may well induce the first symptom, apathy; coldness following as a consequence will soon produce more drastic results. Certain medicinal remedies seem to work for some people, but beware those which produce drowsiness as a side effect. If in any doubt, seek professional advice. It is common experience that those sea conditions which may produce seasickness in the novice, may well fail to affect him when he becomes more competent and more involved in the running of the yacht. For this reason mainly it is unlikely that the school yacht will venture into even moderately rough seas in the first day or two. So, having selected the gear, how should it be packed?

TRANSPORTING GEAR

Sausage-shaped zipped holdalls are by far the best containers; one for the sleeping bag and pillow and one for the remainder of your gear;

nothing should be carried loose. Suitcases and rigid bags are totally unacceptable because they cannot be stowed away in the average yacht. Large plastics bags, such as dustbin liners, are also unacceptable; they just do not travel well. In case it is wet on arrival, stow oilskins and boots at the top; if dry, deck shoes should be to hand, if not already worn. Leather soled shoes play havoc with the woodwork and must not be worn on board.

ARRIVING AT THE YACHT

Before departure be certain that the joining instructions are absolutely clear. Make sure you know the name of the yacht and, if berthed in a marina, which marina and which berth (places like the Hamble river have several marinas). It may be that the berth number is unknown so on arrival find the marina office and ask where the yacht is berthed. In a large marina – and some harbours have many hundreds of yachts – it will take a very long time to identify a yacht by name alone.

On arrival at the yacht, a confident call of 'anyone aboard?' or better still 'ahoy . . . [yacht name]!' will soon bring the skipper on deck to welcome you and invite you on board. It is a nice courtesy to wait for this invitation. Ready hands will take your gear, especially if well stowed, then you should proceed along the pontoon to the area of the mast and, grasping the shrouds which support it, climb quietly aboard, ensuring that the shroud is gently released and not 'twanged' to the annoyance of everyone below. Common courtesy is highly important when several people have to live together in the close confines of a yacht; the correct courtesy from the start will make an excellent impression.

At the earliest opportunity go below and ask which is your bunk and where to stow your gear; stow it immediately, ensuring that warm and wet weather gear is easily to hand. Do not 'expand' beyond your fair share of stowage space, especially in the toilet area (the heads) where space is generally even more limited.

A word on the use of the heads, for there are rules here which must be adhered to for the wellbeing of all. Yachts are not fitted with normally flushing toilets. Instead, the flushing process is achieved by the operation of a pump fitted to the bowl. There are several different types of yacht toilets, and it is important that the flushing system is clearly understood before operating the pump. You will normally be briefed on the use of the heads. Since this pump is small it is vitally important that the bowl is not used for the disposal of *anything* which has not passed through the human system, other than toilet paper. Failure to observe this rule will soon make the heads inoperative, a state much less acceptable than the strict observation of this rule. As a general point, aim to leave the heads in an even cleaner condition than you found them.

Another area which should remain taboo until explained is the galley (kitchen). Most yachts are fitted with bottled gas for cooking and for heating water. Gas is perfectly safe to use on boats providing certain precautions are *always* observed. Escaping bottled gas, being heavier than air, will sink to the bottom of the yacht (the bilges) to build up a reservoir of a potentially lethal mixture of gas and air which, if undetected, will increase insidiously to fill much of the saloon space. It will explode violently if ignited, perhaps destroying the yacht instantly.

The dangers of escaping bottled gas on a yacht cannot be overstated. When using the gas cooker, check continuously that all taps except those in use are turned off; when finished with the cooker turn off the gas at the bottle. The whole crew should develop the habit of visually checking gas taps each time they are in view, whether the cooker is being used or not. Gas detectors and other devices notwithstanding, there is no substitute for sight and smell.

If gas is smelt, no matter how faintly, all naked lights should be extinguished immediately and the gas bottle turned off. Then check for the smell of gas at floor level. Even if it is not worse there and there is no real threat, it is as well to pump the bilges to resupply the very bottom of the hull with clean air. In fact, as a precaution, this process should be carried out daily whether a gas leak is suspected or not. If gas has escaped into the bilges then they will have to be pumped out immediately, if necessary with the help of a bucket lowered into the bottom and then 'emptied' clear overboard. Dockside comments will have to be ignored!

Last, in this cautionary sequence, if you must smoke then do so only on deck and never down below. When sailing, stand downwind from the rest of the crew and ensure that the cigarette end comes nowhere near the sails. When finished, ensure that it goes safely into the sea. Never smoke when handling the sails.

So, having stowed your gear and having been briefed on the gas precautions, by all means offer to brew up rather than sit down and twiddle your thumbs or just remain standing in the way. When moving about down below, you will soon realise that a move towards someone in the way or a gentle hand on the shoulder is normally sufficient for them to move.

If time permits, look into each locker to discover what it contains. Most will contain food but some are dedicated to bosunry, tools, batteries and first aid, etc. Then go on deck, again if time permits, and try to discover for yourself the purpose of at least some of the equipment even if only the steering system. An early familiarity, no matter how limited, will always help, though all equipment both on deck and down below will soon be explained in a general briefing when the whole crew has arrived on board.

A GUIDED TOUR OF · THE YACHT ·

Even before a 'guided tour' has begun, the beginner will already have discovered that a different vocabulary is used on boats, sometimes with strange pronunciations. You may well wonder whether this nautical vocabulary is necessary, especially in view of all the other things which have to be learnt, but the vocabulary, common to all vessels, has stood the test of time over many centuries because each word or phrase is, almost without exception, unambiguous. Where identical words have different meanings the context will always eliminate any ambiguity. Safety of life at sea depends on clear, concise, unambiguous communication, and the nautical vocabulary has evolved to meet this requirement. So you will need to learn these new words, and in so doing you may as well learn the few strange pronunciations.

AROUND THE YACHT

There are many different yacht designs and types. Our guided tour will take place on the most common type, a **sloop** (which has one mast, and it will begin in the **cockpit** where much of the business of sailing a yacht takes place. In our yacht the cockpit is aft with little or no **afterdeck**), and the stern is squared off to form a **transom**. The cockpit contains the means of steering, either wheel or tiller, and is itself contained within the **cockpit coaming**. There is a small **bridgedeck** at its forward end immediately under the **companionway** which leads via the **mainhatch** to the accommodation below. The tops of the side benches are hinged to give access to large lockers for stowing warps, fenders, etc. The cockpit floor, or **sole**, has self-draining holes in the corners, and the sole is normally covered by a wooden **grating**. Yacht instrument dials are often located over the companionway and, except on older yachts, the ropes (**halyards**) for hoisting the sails are led aft from the foot of the mast into this region on the after end of the coachroof. Winches are mounted there for handling the halyards, while more substantial winches for controlling the sails are on the coaming on both sides of the cockpit.

Stepping over the cockpit coaming and moving forward, the side decks are separated to port and starboard (left and right respectively when facing the bow) by the **coachroof**, the after end of which is sometimes raised to form a **doghouse**. A **grabrail** is usually fitted along each side of the coachroof top for the safety of those going forward to the bow when at sea. The side decks lead forward to the mast area and beyond that to the **foredeck**. A low **toerail** surrounds the deck, and the whole deckspace is fenced in by **lifelines** and **staunchions** (pronounced 'stanshons'). The lifelines meet near the bow at a more robust structure called the **pulpit**, and at the stern, at the **after pulpit**, sometimes called the 'pushpit'.

The mast is either stepped (mounted) on a **tabernacle** on the coachroof or is stepped directly, through a hole in the coachroof, on to the keel. It is supported by fore and aft wire ropes called **stays** (forestay, backstay, etc) and **shrouds** which are rigged across the yacht. These wire ropes are collectively called the **standing rigging**, meaning 'permanent' rigging, and are labelled in Fig 1a and 1b.

The **main boom** runs aft from the mast and is supported at its after end by the **topping lift**, a rope which runs to the masthead. The **halyards** for hoisting the sails are also located in this region, though the 'hauling' ends of the halyards are led aft to the cockpit for easy

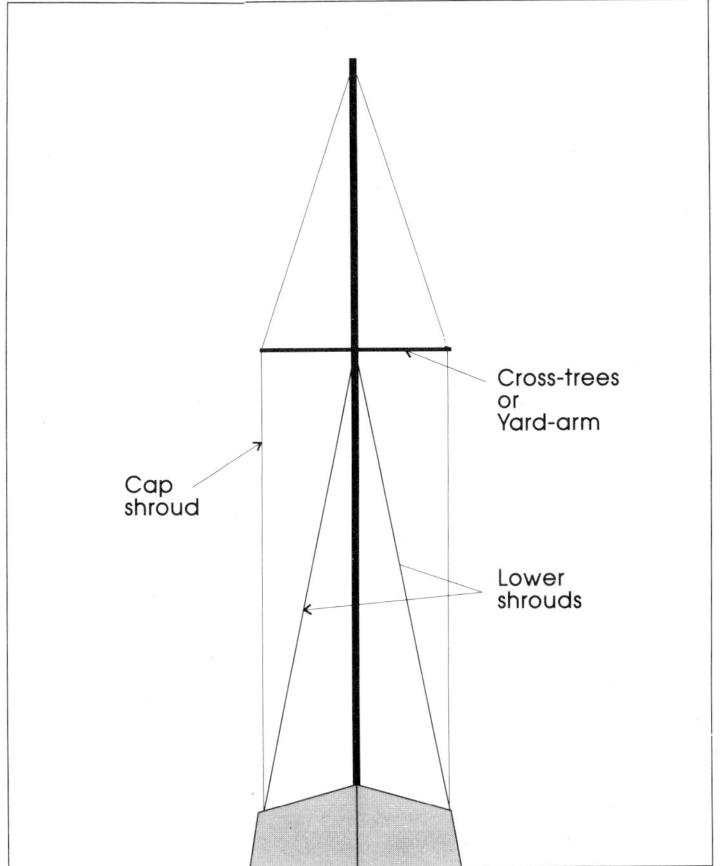

Fig 1a. Rigging from ahead.

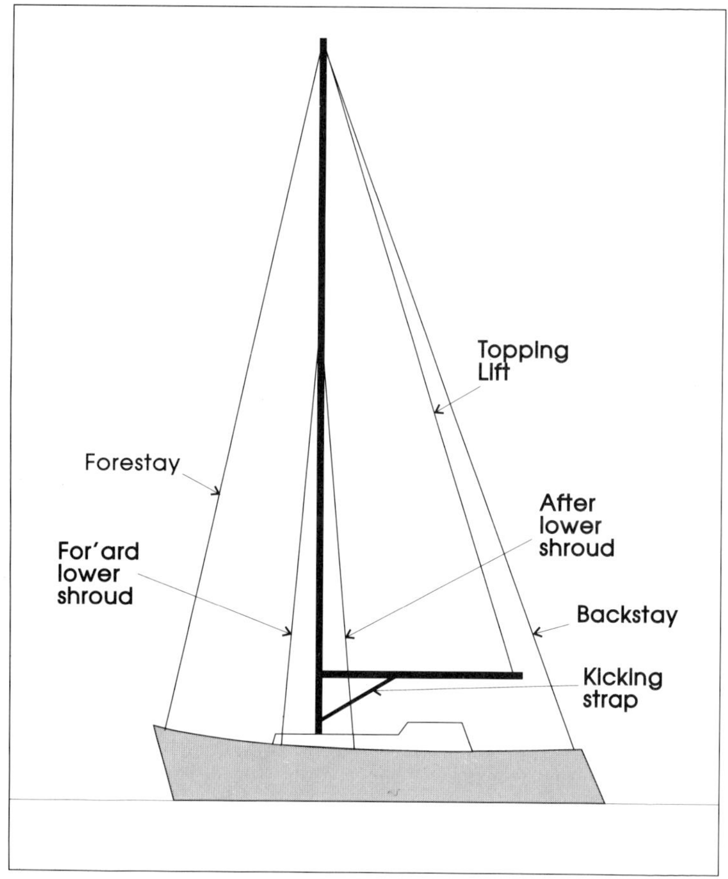

Fig 1b. Rigging from abeam.

handling. The halyards are known as the **running rigging**.

The sides of the hull above the waterline are known as the **top-sides**; these meet forward at the **stem** and the stem meets the water at the **forefoot**. The stem and deck meet at the **stemhead** or **bow**.

The foredeck is worth a closer inspection for there are numerous fittings in this area. As the yacht is moored alongside to a pontoon, the mooring lines, known as **warps**, are led through **fairleads** (to reduce wear) located on or within the toerail, to be secured to **cleats** on either side of the foredeck, or to a short stout post with a horizontal bar; the whole post is called the **bits**. Fairleads and cleats are also fitted on the afterdeck to secure the stern of the yacht.The anchor and chain are normally stowed away in an **anchor locker** set into the foredeck. The anchor chain, when in use, is led over the bow through the **stemhead fitting**. Some yachts are fitted with an anchor winch located in the centre of the foredeck. The **forehatch** is located on the foredeck, sometimes on the forward end of the coachroof, and gives access to the **forecabin**.

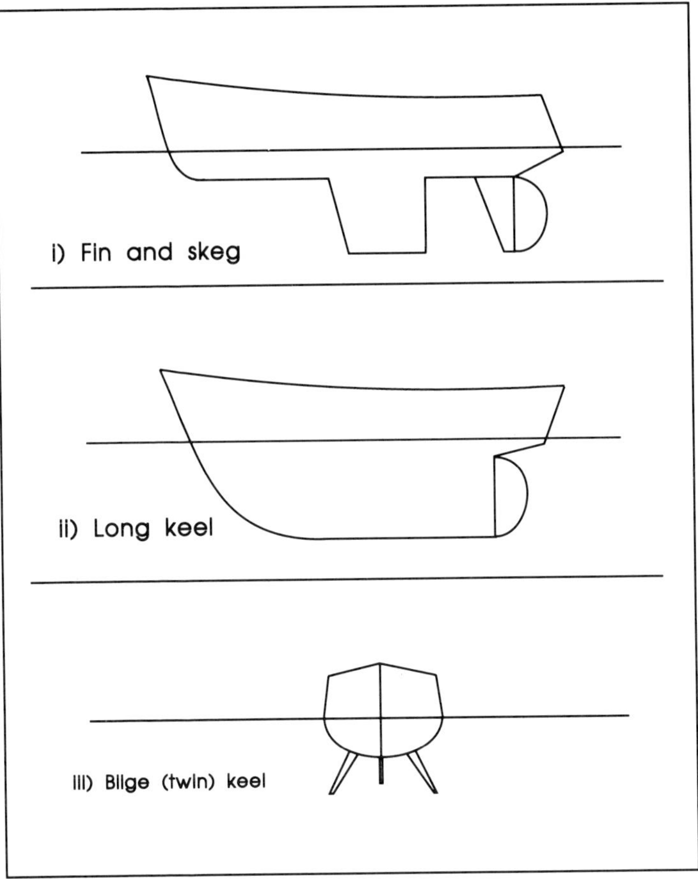

Fig 1c. Underwater keel shapes.

The nautical vocabulary continues to apply down below. Here, the floor is the **cabinsole**, the ceiling is the **deckhead**, and the interior walls are **bulkheads**. The rooms are called **cabins** and the kitchen, the **galley**. The toilet is known as the **heads**, the wardrobes, **hanging lockers** and the beds are called **bunks**.

Keel shapes

To complete the picture, though this will not be seen in such a briefing, below the waterline there is a deep keel which prevents the yacht being blown sideways through the water by the wind. The configuration of the keel can be **fin** shaped with a **skeg** further aft to support and protect the rudder. (In some smaller yacht designs the rudder post is unsupported by a skeg.) Other underwater configurations are a **long** keel which begins as an extension of the stem and sweeps all the way aft, finally to support the rudder-post, and **bilge** (twin) keels (Fig 1c).

SAFETY ABOARD

The last and very important part of this tour is a briefing on safety and emergencies. You will probably notice fire extinguishers placed strategically around the cabins, especially near the galley and the engine compartment. Your briefing will explain how and when to use them. Then flares, both distress and other types, will also be explained in detail. You should ensure that you are familiar with the written instructions on both flares and fire extinguishers; your life and that of others may depend on it. In case anyone falls overboard, the appropriate gear – usually a **sparbuoy** (or **danbuoy**) to assist in locating him, lifebuoys and a throwing-line – will also be explained. The sailing method of recovery will come later.

You will also be taught how to put on and use a lifejacket and safety harness. Both will be worn in moderate or rough sea conditions, at night and in fog, in the dinghy and at any other time you may wish to do so. Non-swimmers should wear a lifejacket at sea at all times when on deck. Next will be a briefing on the operation of the emergency life-raft. The dangers of gas will also be discussed, as explained earlier. And lastly the **bilge pump**, which removes any water or gas which has gathered in the bottom of the yacht. Few yachts are completely 'dry'; most will make a little water from the engine and where the propeller shaft passes through the hull at the **sterngland**.

Since all this equipment, maintained in good order and reaching safe standards, is a requirement for RYA sea school approval, this alone is a good reason for beginning your sailing 'career' at an RYA recognised establishment.

PREPARING · FOR SEA ·

First, to the engine compartment – for an explanation of the daily checks, simple maintenance, and how to start and stop the engine. This is very important, for you may be asked to start the engine when more experienced crew are involved in a crisis on deck. The location and operation of the engine **seacocks**, which control the intake and outlet of seawater for engine cooling, will be carefully explained. It is also likely that the position of the other seacocks for the galley, heads, etc will be shown to you though this is often left to a later stage. There are a surprising number of holes in a yacht below the waterline; my own Nicholson 38 had 17! – and all of them necessary. These 'holes' are called **skin fittings**. Next, you will go on deck to see to flags, the preparation of the sails, and how the warps securing the yacht to the pontoon will be cast off.

The **burgee** is a small triangular flag flown at the masthead. Its chief purpose is to indicate the wind direction, but nowadays with electronic wind instrumentation and other gear at the masthead it is more commonly hoist at the yardarm in its secondary role, which is to indicate that the owner is aboard. The burgee's design also indicates to which club the owner belongs. When hoist at the masthead, the burgee is fixed to a staff, which itself is secured to the burgee halyard by two clove hitches (see page 20). The staff ensures, on hoisting, that the burgee remains reasonably parallel to its halyard. It can be difficult to hoist since both the flag and staff have to clear a converging pattern of standing rigging at the masthead. There is no substitute here for being shown by an experienced hand.

A red ensign (the maritime national flag for the UK) will also be flown, rigged to a staff and set into a socket on the stern. Ensure that its line or **lanyard** secures the ensign and staff to the after pulpit or the lifelines. The ensign remains hoist at sea, but is lowered in harbour between sunset and sunrise. As a courtesy, the ensign is normally 'dipped' (partially lowered) when passing naval vessels belonging to any nation except in the close vicinity of any busy naval port.

THE SAILS

Now for the sails and in this exercise we shall assume that all the sails have been stowed in the sail locker, though more commonly during the season the lowered mainsail is left attached to the boom and protected by a cover. (Sails are usually made from terylene which slowly deteriorates in prolonged sunlight.) The parts of the sails are shown in Fig 2.

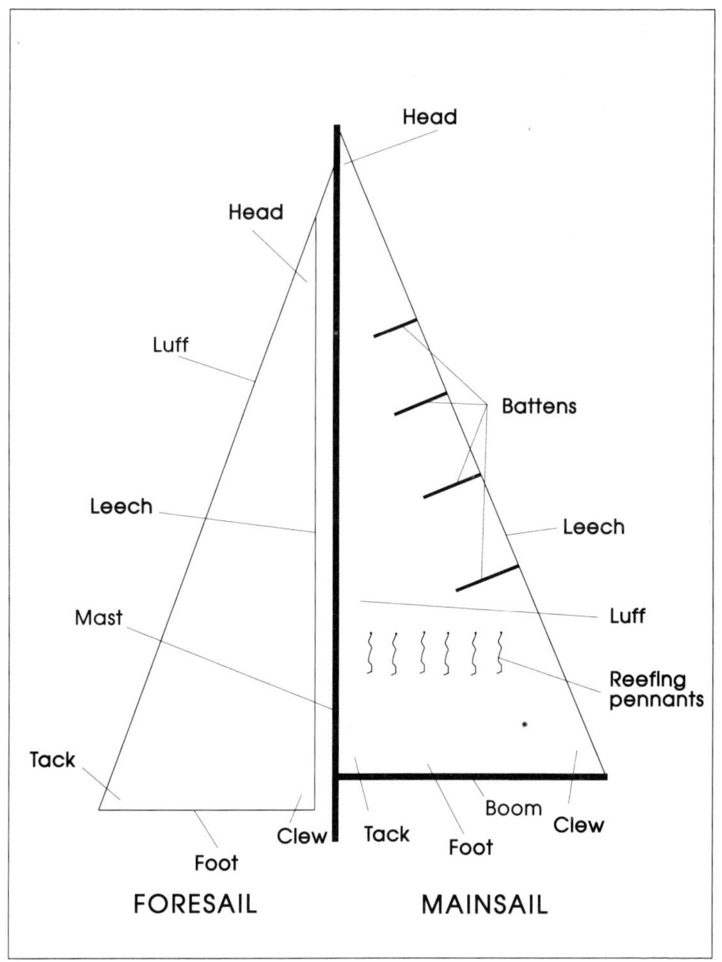

Fig 2. Parts of sails.

It is common practice to prepare the sails ready for sea whilst still alongside, though they should not be hoist until the yacht is clear of the harbour. This process is called **bending on the sails**. The mainsail is emptied out of its bag and the **clew** identified. If the corners of the sail are not labelled you will recognise the **head** because it has a solid **headboard** (a triangular stiffener about 15–25 cm long). The **tack** is a right-angle (on the mainsail), so the other corner with a wider angle than the head is the clew. The holes in the corners of all sails are reinforced with brass rings called **cringles**. You will probably have noted that **boltrope** is sewn into the **foot** and the **luff** of the sail, since these two edges of the sail will eventually locate in grooves on the top of the **boom** and on the rear of the mast, respectively.

The clew is taken to the forward end of the boom so that the foot of the sail can be fed into its groove on the top of the boom at this point.

The foot is then worked aft by pulling on the clew until the tack is in line with its fitting. This may be a shackle or more commonly a **staghorn** on the forward end of the boom. The foot of the sail is then tensioned by pulling aft on the clew, under the direction of the skipper, then securing the clew by its **lanyard** or sometimes by a threaded, steel **outhaul** which is operated by a detachable handle. The **battens**, which stiffen the leach and which decrease a little in size with increasing distance from the clew, are now matched for size and gently placed in the **batten pockets**.

The main is then carefully **flaked out** on the top of the boom in slabs, 60–90 cm wide and the whole is then secured to the boom by a series of **ties**. When the halyard is attached and the sail hoist, its setting is controlled by a rope known as the **mainsheet**, a rope and block leading from the outer end of the boom to the cockpit.

There is no such arrangement for controlling the set of the foresail when it is hoist. Instead, two separate ropes (**foresail sheets**) are led from the foredeck, outside of the shrouds on each side, then in through the lifelines and through a **fairlead block** to the sheet winches on each side of the cockpit. A **stopper knot** (see page 18) is then applied to the winch end of these sheets to prevent them running away through the fairlead blocks. The foresail is then removed from its bag and the tack secured to its fitting near the stemhead. After working aft along the foot of the sail from the tack to the clew to remove any twists, the foredeck end of both sheets is then attached to the clew, usually by a **bowline** (see pages 21–2). The foresail (also referred to as the headsail, genoa or jib – all meaning, in most contexts, the sail which is set forward of the mast) is now stretched out along the foredeck, on the opposite side from the mooring warps so as not to be in the way. It is then secured to the lower lifeline by ties so as not to obstruct forward vision when the yacht is being manoeuvred away from the pontoon.

The halyards for both sails are left secured in their 'harbour' positions and are not attached to the head of each sail until ready for hoisting, well clear of the harbour. This is because the otherwise partially slack halyards would inevitably snag up on some part of the mast's rigging. Now that the sails are bent on, the briefing switches to the mooring warps and how these will be let go.

MOORING WARPS

Fig 3 (page 24) shows the most common pattern of **warps** for securing a vessel. In rough conditions these may be backed up using spare warps while larger vessels will sometimes add **breast-ropes** which run perpendicularly from bow and stern directly to the pontoon or wharf. We shall assume that tide and wind conditions are 'quiet' and that our departure will be straightforward. In order that no one will be on the pontoon as the yacht leaves, the bow and stern warps are 'doubled-back'. This means that each warp is led out around a cleat (or through a ring if that is the pontoon fitting) and then taken back onboard to its own end of the boat, maintaining the strain all the while, and secured. The springs are then let go. When the order is given to 'let go forward', the shortest end of the doubled-back warp is let go and the warp is hauled aboard from its other end. It is important to check at the outset that there are no kinks or knots in the warp which will snag as it runs through the pontoon fitting. The process is repeated for the stern warp when that is let go.

The initial briefing having been completed, the yacht is now in many respects ready for sea. However, since we are a crew of novices we must pause here before casting off to learn something, in the next four chapters, about ropes and knots, sails and the theory of sailing, as well as steering, so as better to enjoy the day's cruise which will soon follow.

· ROPEWORK ·

Nowadays, rope is almost entirely made from man-made fibre such as terylene, nylon and polyester, since they last longer than natural fibres like manila and sisal, which will rot when stowed wet. Whatever the fibre, most people will be aware of rope's frustrating tendency to twist, kink and snag. Loose rope can be relied upon to do so and has no place on a yacht, for it may trip a crew member causing him to fall overboard. Further, a rope trailing in the water will almost certainly foul the propeller.

A rope's tendency to twist is due entirely to the way that it is made. Fibres are twisted to form yarns, these are twisted together in the opposite direction from the fibres to form strands; and finally the strands (usually three) are twisted in the opposite direction to the yarns to form rope (Photo 1). Rope is usually 'laid-up' right-handed, as shown. The twisting process prevents rope from unravelling (except at unbound ends) though it does encourage loose rope to finish up in a tangled mess. This mess is unseamanlike; not only is it untidy, but it prevents the immediate use of this rope when required in a hurry.

The only way to prevent such 'knitting' is to keep slack or loose rope coiled in a tidy fashion. This is particularly true on sailing yachts which carry a great deal of rope by way of sheets, halyards, mooring and anchoring warps. It has been estimated that an 11 metre yacht will carry almost half a kilometre of rope!

If you find a jumbled mess of rope on deck, it is best to 'end-for-end' it before coiling. Start at one end and pull the rope steadily through your almost-closed other fist, to remove twists, gently laying the 'pulled-through' rope in fairly tidy coils on deck. In the worst cases, this process may have to be repeated before the rope is ready to be coiled. When handling rope of average size (about 12 mm diameter on a yacht) hold the rope between the ends of your forefinger and thumb, and curl the ends of your remaining fingers loosely over the

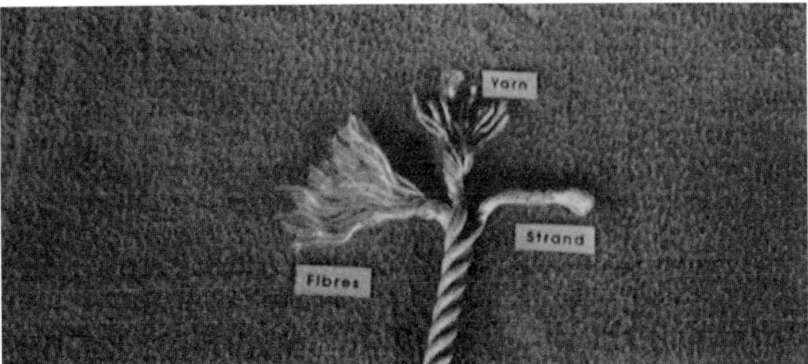

Photo 1. How rope is laid up.

rope as it crosses the 'top' of the palm. In this way, you achieve maximum manipulation for coiling or tying knots. Unless the rope size is very large, do not hold it in the 'hollow' of the palm for you will then lose finger control.

Even after end-for-ending, a rope will still retain a tendency to twist. Right-handed rope will tend to twist less if it is coiled in a clockwise direction. The size of each coil is best determined by extending your arms on both sides until comfortably short of a full stretch. The right hand then comes in to form the first clockwise coil. As it does so, the individual coil invariably tends to twist into a figure of eight. This tendency can be overcome by rolling the right wrist away from you (naturally) as it comes in, thus putting a half twist into the rope by the time the coil is complete. Repeat this 'twist of the wrist' for each coil.

To complete the task several turns of the end of the rope are required around the middle of the coils to keep them neat and together. Allow about the original arm span of rope to do this. Holding the top of the coiled rope in the left fist, wind about six horizontal turns around the middle of the coiled rope, working upwards, pulling each turn fairly tight. Move the left hand to hold these turns tight. There should still be enough tail to form a **bight** which is passed through the coils, above the turns (Photo 2), though still leaving about half a metre of tail on the original side. Let go with the right hand and move it round to grasp the bight; then pull the bight right over the top of the coils to lie next to the turns. Pull the tail tight and the coiled rope is tidy and secure for stowing away.

On a well-found yacht the warps will be hung in their own locker, with each hook labelled. To hang a coiled rope, place the uppermost, horizontal turn (not the bent-over bight) on the hook. If a coil is used it will pull through to leave an untidy mess. Some ropes, such as spinnaker sheets, have a shackle spliced to one end. Start coiling these ropes from the other end so that the shackles are at the finishing-off tail, and then use them to hang the sheets. With spinnaker sheets

Photo 2. Finishing off a coiled rope.

especially, the turns are often slid up the coils to trap the tail once the bight has been doubled back.

When the rope is next required, hold the securing turns in the left hand and take the 'bight' over and to the back of the coils, then pull the tail to remove the bight. Transfer your left hand to the top of the coils and remove the securing turns with your right hand. With spinnaker sheets, slide the turns back down to the middle and carry on as before. If the coiled rope then has to be put down temporarily, place it over a ventilator or some other protruding deck fitting which will keep the coils reasonably tidy.

Throughout this whole operation, it is vital that you hold the top of coils continuously in your hand until the securing turns have been made. If the rope is very long and becomes too big to hold in the hand, place the coils on the deck, open them to a nearly circular shape and then continue the coiling, still with a half twist, to finish as before. Again, if it is a large size rope, say 25 mm diameter or more, then start the coiling process on deck or, better still, on the pontoon where there is more room.

Rope is put to several different and often dedicated uses on a yacht. For example, sail halyards remain rove through sheaves (passed through a block) at the masthead and are only removed for repair or replacement. They are commonly made of pre-stretched terylene, though the foresail halyard sometimes has a wire tail at the sail end. Sheets, for setting the sails, are used for this purpose only. Those which control the foresail and spinnaker are removed and stowed after each cruise, whereas the mainsail sheet tackle is usually left set up to control the bare boom. Sheets are also made of pre-stretched terylene but they commonly have a soft, plaited covering which is kinder to the hands; at sea, sheets are constantly being adjusted. Mooring warps are usually the largest size of rope on a yacht. They are commonly used only for this task and are usually made from unstretched terylene. Anchor warps are usually made of nylon, which has even more 'give' under strain.

In order to identify ropes easily when stowed, and quickly when in use, they are often colour coded, either by coloured strands running along white rope or the whole rope may be in a distinguishing colour.

KNOTS

When a rope is tied to another rope, the knot is called a **bend**; if to a rail or the like it is called a **hitch** and if on itself – just a **knot**. These are generalities and there are exceptions, but these definitions go some way to account for 'knots, bends and hitches' which, generically, are all 'knots'.

Originally, each knot was designed for a specific task. These uses still apply today and will be explained in context. However, novice crew will be shown which knot to use when, and how to tie it. With experience, having been given a task, you will come to know which knot to use.

The various parts of a rope are labelled in Photo 9. A loop made in a rope is called a **bight**; the end of the rope is called the **tail**. The last part is the **standing part** to which the knot is applied and which normally carries the strain.

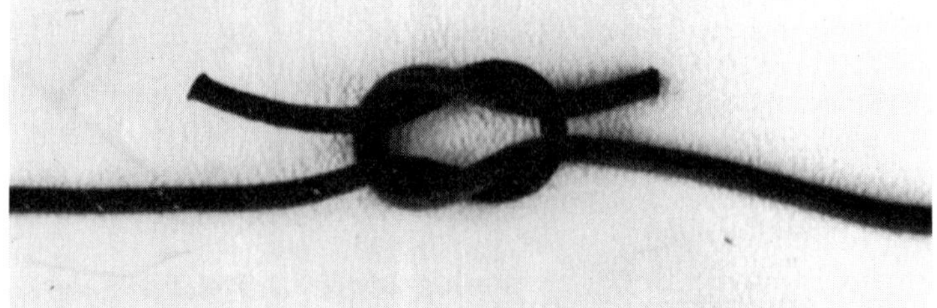

Photo 3. Reef knot

Reef knot.

Though the simplest and best known, this knot is not the most frequent one used on a sailing vessel. It is tied by taking two rope ends, passing one end over then back under the other, and then passing the same end over and under again in the opposite direction (Photo 3) and pulled tight. Or:

> '**left** over **right** and under, then **right** over **left** and under' and vice versa.

A reef knot is used to join ropes of the same size such as reefing pennants (Fig 2, page 12). These emerge from both sides of the sail and are tied around the boom when shortening sail. However, there are few other uses for a reef knot on a boat or a yacht. To undo, hold the four 'ends' in your hands, close to the knot, and work your hands together until it opens up.

Stopper knot or **figure of eight knot**

This is tied by forming a bight(loop) in a rope's end, then passing the tail (end) over and round the back before bringing it down through the loop (Photo 4) and pulling it tight. Its use is to prevent or 'stop' the end of a rope from unreeving through a block. On a yacht it is tied on the end of all sheets and halyards.

Photo 4. Stopper or figure of eight knot.

Sheet bend
When joining two ropes of different sizes (diameter) use this knot. A bight is formed in the larger rope and the end of the smaller one is fed up through the bight, round the back, and then passed underneath itself as it recrosses the bight (Photo 5).

Double sheet bend
This is tied as the sheet bend above, but the tail is passed round the back and 'under' once more (Photo 5) for greater security. It is often used to join two mooring lines together to 'warp', or pull, the yacht across a wide space.

Photo 5. Single and double sheet bend.

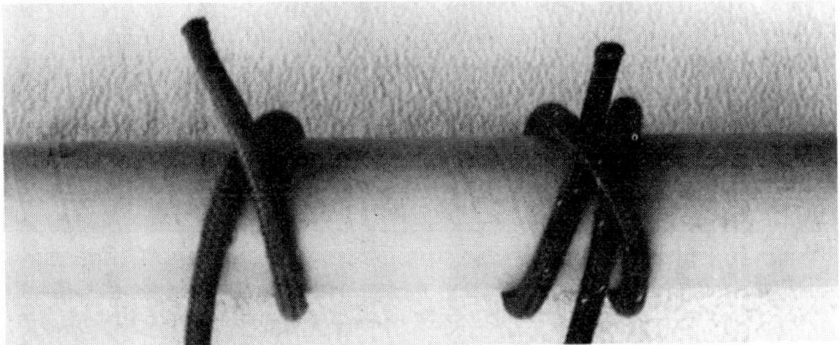

Photo 6. Clove hitch on a rail.

Clove hitch
This is one of the most common knots on a boat. It is used for tying a rope to a spar when the strain is perpendicular. Pass the tail slightly obliquely over the rail and complete the turn so that the tail crosses over itself. Turn the tail over the rail once more and bring it up under this second turn so that it emerges parallel but opposite to the standing part (Photo 6).

This method of tying is used when the rail is 'endless', and is ideal for securing fender lanyards to the lifelines or to the grabrails on the coachroof. However, they should always be finished off with a half hitch (see Photo 8).

When the knot is to be tied to an open-ended post, it is easier and quicker to tie by forming two identical loops side by side and then

Photo 7. Clove hitch on a post.

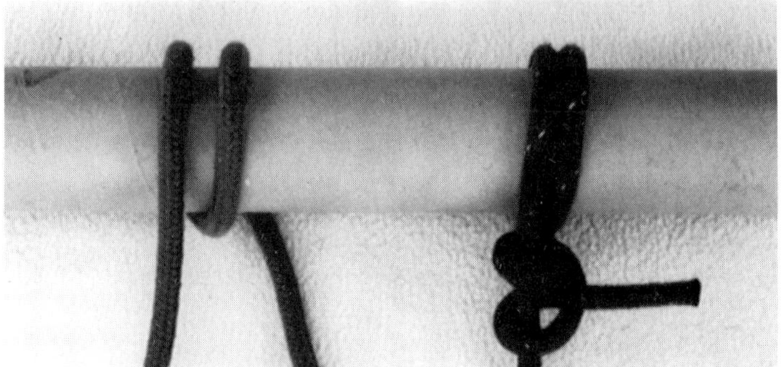

Photo 8. Round turn and two half hitches.

placing the second loop behind the first. The loops are then placed over the post and pulled tight (Photo 7). When the knot is viewed 'vertically' it should look the same as Photo 6.

With both methods a decent tail (30-40 cm) should be left once the knot is pulled tight, for a 'snatching' strain on the rope will tend to 'work the knot' through the tail and undo it. To overcome this a half hitch (see Photo 8) should be tied on the standing part of the rope if the clove hitch is required for longer than about half an hour.

A particular application of a clove hitch arises when securing a burgee on a staff to its halyard (usually 5 mm or less in diameter) for hoisting to the masthead. Form two loops as above, placing one behind the other to form a clove hitch and slide the knot approximately half way up to the base of the burgee before pulling it tight. Since we need to have two clove hitches on the staff (one a little over half-way to the burgee and the other near the foot of the staff) the second knot will need to be started on the halyard near the foot of the staff. Slide the first knot back to a little less than half-way from the base to allow some slack then tie the second clove hitch and place it 2–3 cm from the foot of the staff and pull it tight. The first knot is then slid back up the staff, hopefully about two-thirds towards the burgee, until the joining string between the two knots is taut. This arrangement should ensure that the burgee and staff will balance correctly as they are hoist.

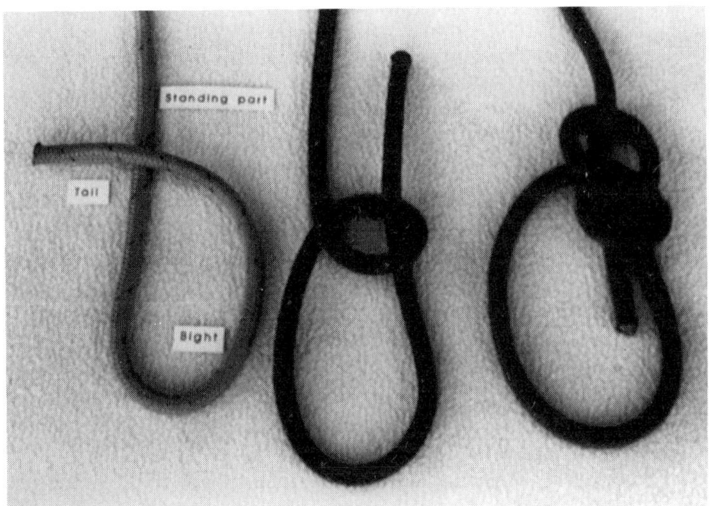

Photo 9. Bowline.

An identical arrangement is used on ketches and yawls (two-masted yachts) where the ensign is hoist to the mizzen masthead (the 'after', smaller mast).

Round turn and two half hitches

This knot is used for tying a rope to almost anything, apart from another rope. Pass the tail over a rail and follow round once more until the tail comes back parallel to the standing part but in the opposite direction (Photo 8). Though this is strictly a turn and a half, it is called a 'round turn' in nautical use. Two half hitches, each identical, are then tied to the standing part and the whole pulled up tight. It is most commonly used for tying a warp to a ring on a pontoon.

Bowline

A bowline (pronounced 'bowlin') is tied whenever a 'permanent' bight is required in a rope's end. It is one of the most important knots in boating. It can be used for tying sheets to foresail clews, for securing mooring warps to bollards on the quay or to cleats on the yacht and is the most secure way of joining two warps together. In man overboard situations it is tied to the end of a warp to secure the recovered man to the boat before hoisting him aboard.

There are several ways of tying a bowline. What follows is the Admiralty method which, once mastered, is never forgotten. The tail is crossed over the standing part to form a bight (Photo 9 left). This crossing is held by the right hand, thumb upwards. The left part of the bight, held in the left hand, is then moved towards this crossing point and a loop is formed which contains the tail (Photo 9 centre). (It may help to point the right thumb upwards and then wind the loop anti-clockwise around the right thumb.) The tail is then passed behind the standing part and then down through the loop (Photo 9 right). Pull tight on all three parts (the bight, the tail and the standing part) to complete the knot. Once properly tightened, a bowline will not slip and neither will it jam. The method 'flows' from beginning to end so that, with only a little practice, even a novice will be able to tie it in the dark – potentially a life-saving ability in an emergency. To undo, grasp the rounded parts of the actual knot in both hands and work the wrists until the knot loosens.

The knot may also be tied by forming a loop in the rope and passing the tail through as at the second stage in Photo 9, and then carrying on as before.

If the bight is too small then loosen the knot and work enough slack from the standing part down through the knot to enlarge the bight. If too large, so that it may easily slip off a cleat for example, feed the surplus from the bight through the knot into the standing part; and if the tail is too short then 'steal' a little from both the bight and the standing part.

With this knot particularly, especially when used on sheets, leave plenty of tail (at least 50 cm) even when pulled up tight by hand, for the 'snatch' as the strain is taken up may work the knot down through the tail.

Rolling hitch

This is the last of the knots required in the RYA syllabus for competent crew. It is used for tying to a spar (or rail) or another rope, when the strain on the standing part is to be parallel to the spar. The knot is tied according to the direction of the parallel strain. It will slip if the strain veers away from this direction. A rolling hitch is often used to take the strain temporarily on a warp so that the warp's inboard end may be adjusted, or even moved to a better cleat, with some ease. (This exercise is called 'passing a stopper'.)

First establish the direction of the strain on the standing part, because this determines how the knot will be tied. The rolling hitch is perhaps best learnt as left-handed or right-handed according to the strain and therefore requires a little ambidexterity.

If the strain is towards the *right* hold the tail in the *right* hand and place the left hand and the standing part on the rail. Now pass two 'jamming' turns over the standing part with the right hand (Photo 10

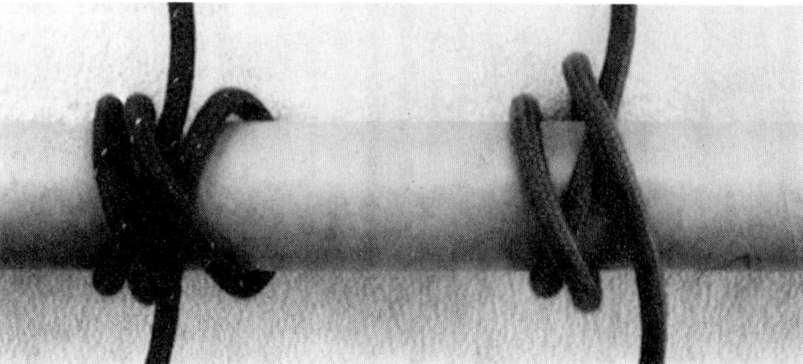

Photo 10. Rolling hitch.

left). Then make a third turn over the standing part, but this time the tail comes up to pass under the third turn (Photo 10 right). Pull the knot tight and take the standing part over to the right until parallel with the spar for this is to be the direction of the strain (Photo 11 right). The jamming turns prevent any slip towards the right only. If the strain is likely to veer away from this direction, even if only a little, then a 'locking' half hitch should be tied on to the standing part.

When the strain is to be towards the *left*, take the tail in the *left* hand and place the standing part, within the right hand, along the spar. Then, using the left hand, take two jamming turns around the standing part. The final turn is applied as before, and the standing part carried away to the left to take the strain (Photo 11 left).

In both cases, if the strain is to be heavy, an extra 'jamming' turn

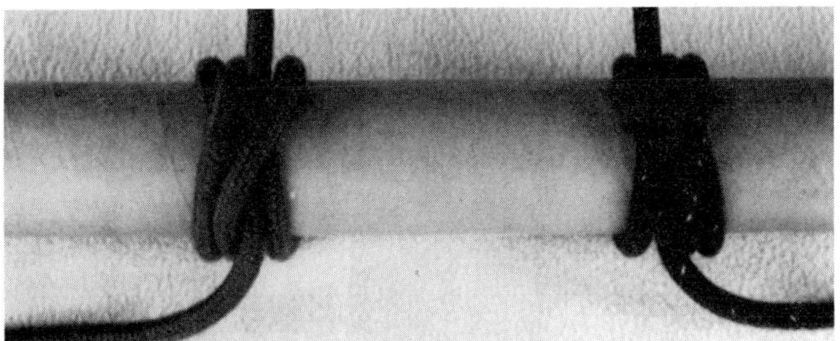

Photo 11. Rolling hitch, direction of strain.

should be taken before finishing off with the final turn. As with all other knots, allow plenty of tail after the knot has been pulled up tight. With this knot in particular, allow plenty of tail before beginning to tie the knot. The tail shown in the photographs is necessarily (for clarity) much too short.

SECURING WARPS

One final section on ropes concerns the securing of warps for mooring a yacht to a pontoon. Though specific occasions are described in the narrative account of a training cruise which soon follows, there are some general points which are best covered here.

From the crewing point of view, leaving the mooring is simply a question of letting go the mooring warps in the given order, and then coiling and stowing them, and the **fenders**, (protection for the boat's side) in their lockers. Arriving at a harbour or marina is different because the skipper may not know in advance which berth he is to take and, if the marina is strange, he may not know what fittings there are on the pontoons. Whereas harbour quays are normally fitted with bollards, to take a bowline, marina pontoons are commonly fitted with either cleats or rings, and much less commonly with bollards.

Having been allocated a berth, the skipper will brief the crew on the preparation of mooring lines and fenders and, since by then he will have observed the type of pontoon fitting, the briefing will include securing the warps to the pontoon.

Two hands will jump ashore just before the yacht is stopped by astern power, one **forward** (pronounced 'for'ard') with the bow warp and the other aft. At this stage control of the boat is virtually handed over to the crew ashore, for there is normally little or nothing that can be done to manoeuvre the yacht with rudder and engine power (at least with any dignity) in this final part of the approach.

The crew member forward should walk briskly along the pontoon to the mooring fitting *beyond* the bow, taking care not to slip if the pontoon is wet, paying out on the warp but keeping it reasonably taut. If the fitting is a cleat, he should make a 'round turn' on the cleat with the warp now taut (most important) and also allow no slack in the tail between the cleat and his hands. The order given is 'take a turn', meaning a round turn. This is quite sufficient to hold the yacht except in extreme conditions of wind and tide.

If the fitting is a ring, then take a turn round the ring and hold the warp taut. Should there still be a large amount of spare warp on reaching the ring, say several metres, then make a bight in the warp and make the turn with the 'doubled' bight. At this stage, time is of the essence and taking a turn with a lengthy tail may take too long. The secret here is to make a big enough bight to take the turn so that the tail of the bight is long enough to hold taut in your hand. The operation is very similar for the crew member with the stern warp

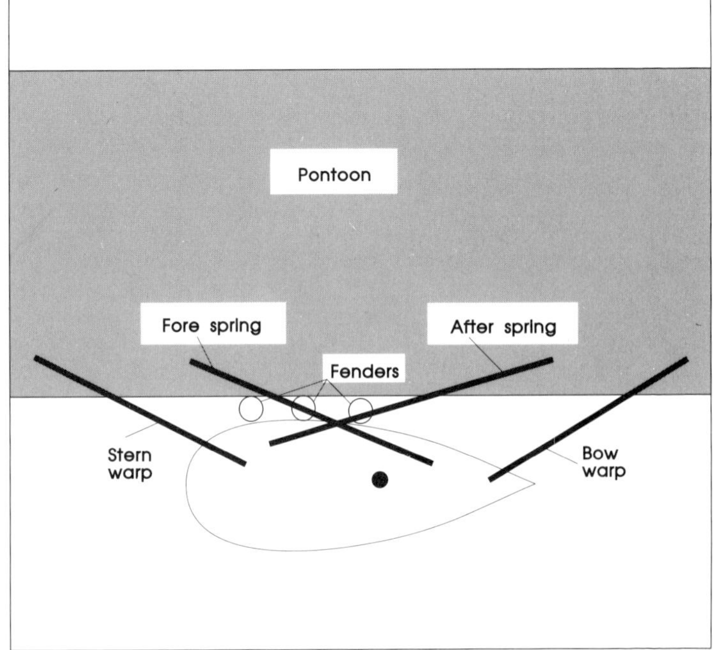

Fig 3. Mooring warps.

who should go to the next pontoon fitting *beyond* the stern of the yacht.

Once a turn has been taken, fore and aft, the yacht is then under control of the warps. Final adjustments will be made to centre-up the boat, under the skipper's direction, and the order given to 'make-up the warps'. If the fitting is a cleat, then leave the round turn on the cleat, make two figure of eights over the cleat with the tail, leaving enough room to make a half hitch on each horn. Should there still be a long tail, then coil this up tidily to lie by the cleat. If the round turn is on a ring then finish this off with two half hitches on the standing part as in Photo 8, page 20. The half hitches may be made using the bight if one has already been necessary. Springs (Fig 3) are then made up to the pontoon in a similar manner. These prevent the yacht from

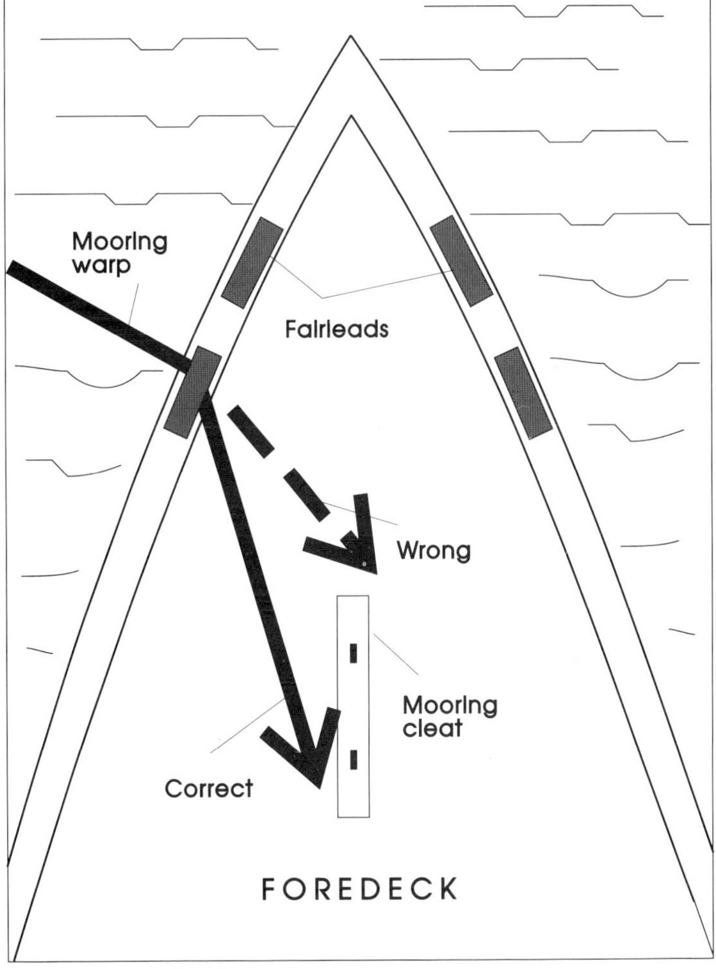

Fig 4. Correct lead to cleat.

'ranging' to and fro along the pontoon under the influence of wind and waves.

The procedure is different if alongside a quay, where the round turn will have been made on a bollard. The only knot which should be left on a bollard is a bowline; this is so that others may use the same bollard without hindrance. The form is that each successive bowline is passed through the bights, from underneath, of all the others already on the bollard. This allows earlier arrivals to remove their warps easily without the hindrance of sorting out everyone else's. In quiet conditions, take off the round turn and tie the bowline reasonably quickly (15 seconds or so) allowing ample bight and tail. If tide and wind conditions are not favourable (and it may not be possible to achieve a bowline in sufficient time even with the assistance of another hand to keep the strain on the warp) tie the bowline in a spare warp and throw the coiled end back on board (after placing the bowline over the bollard). Then remove the original warp completely. The inboard end of this new warp is led through the appropriate fairlead to be made up on the nearest cleat. Here, as in all such cases, it is important to see that the warp arrives at the cleat with the correct angle of attack before making the round turn (Fig 4).

Lead the warp to the far end of the cleat first; if taken round the near end first it may jam under the next turn when the strain is taken. Make a round turn, then one or two figure of eights, before tying a half hitch on the horn nearest to the fairlead.

THEORY · OF SAILING ·

Unlike a motor cruiser which can set a course in any direction, safe navigation permitting, the handling of a sailing yacht is almost entirely dependent on the wind direction and strength. A yacht cannot sail directly into the wind because she will lose the drive in her sails. For this reason, a yacht can be stopped, in an emergency, by turning the bow directly into the wind. An alteration of the yacht's course will produce a new wind direction relative to the sails so they will have to be trimmed to accommodate this new wind direction. It is fundamentally important that novice crew soon develop the ability to recognise the wind direction, especially relative to the yacht. (Note that when dealing with the wind, it is always labelled with the direction from which it is blowing, and not to.) But how do you tell which way the wind is blowing?

On a yacht there are several ways of determining the wind direction. The burgee at the masthead, or a Windex instrument (Photo 12) if fitted, are excellent indicators since they are clear of all obstructions, but this means craning the neck upwards to see them. Many yachts are fitted with wind dials which give the direction relative to the yacht's heading, often diagrammatically. **Telltales**, small ribbons of light material tied to the shrouds, are also good indicators when exposed to the wind and not blanketed by the sails. Another way to tell the wind direction is by observing the wave pattern and

Photo 12. Windex.

Photo 13. Wind direction dials.

movement. The wind generates waves whose crests, parallel to each other, are perpendicular to the wind and move steadily downwind. Then there is the 'feel of the wind on the cheek'; a very real indicator which almost everyone develops, but it is not as precise.

From this list you will develop your own system for determining the wind direction, but develop it you must. Perhaps the easiest method is the wind direction dial which shows a wind arrow pointing towards a plan view of the yacht (Photo 13). However, the yacht's own movement affects the wind direction (and speed) so what exactly is this wind direction which we must be able to determine?

APPARENT WIND

In the same way that a cyclist will feel an apparently different wind from a pedestrian due to his faster movement through the air, so the wind blowing across a moving yacht is apparently different from the true wind on a yacht at anchor in the same area. This **apparent wind** is accounted for in Fig 5. The effect of the yacht's own movement is to 'draw' the apparent wind forward of the true wind.

If the true wind is on or forward of the beam, the apparent wind speed is greater than the true wind speed, and if it is aft of the beam then the apparent wind speed is less. This effect is most marked when, after sailing downwind, the yacht is turned round to sail at an angle of only 45 degrees from the wind direction: the apparent increase in wind speed is dramatic. For example, if sailing downwind at 6 knots before a wind of 14 knots, the apparent wind speed is 8 knots. On rounding up to sail more towards the wind, say at 45 degrees, now at 7 knots, the apparent wind speed will rise to 20 knots – an apparent rise from Beaufort force 3 to force 5, almost force 6! This effect is sometimes misread as an increase in true wind speed.

The example illustrates that the wind felt blowing across a yacht, and to which the sails are trimmed, is the apparent wind. Throughout the remainder of this chapter, 'wind' means 'apparent wind' unless it is qualified as 'true'. So how does this wind drive a yacht?

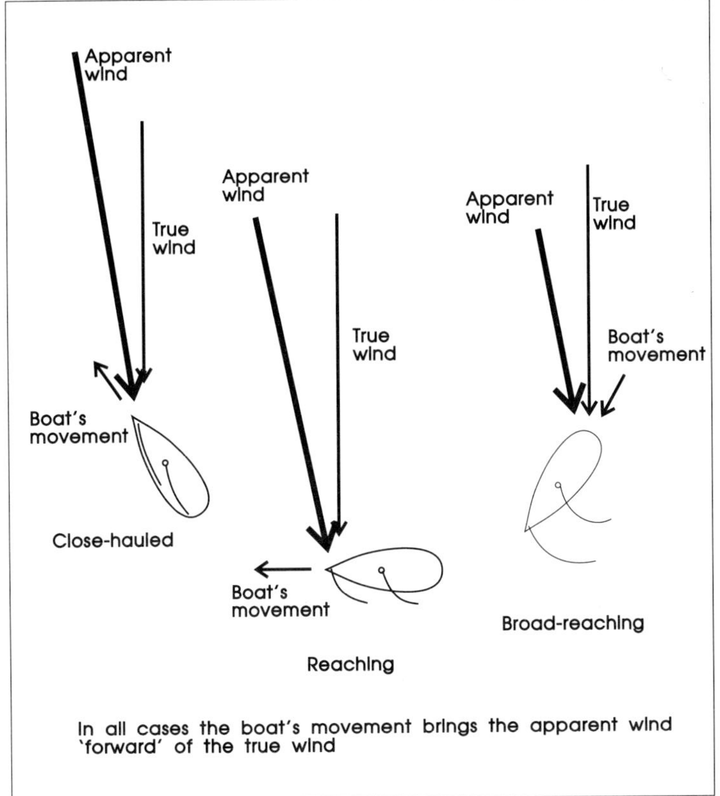

Fig 5. The apparent wind.

The easiest case to understand is with the wind blowing from dead astern – the 'barn-door' effect – with the sails set more or less at right angles to the wind (Fig 6). This is a slightly simplified explanation since the curvature of the sails also plays a part.

Sail curvature becomes more important as the yacht is steered away from a downwind course. The curved sail has many of the attributes of an aircraft wing. In the same way that the aerofoil section of a wing provides lift, so the 'aerofoil' shape of a sail drives a yacht along its course. The effect is most striking when the yacht is sailing close-hauled (see Points of sailing below) for then the yacht is sailing at 45 degrees *against* the true wind. This almost unbelievable ability is explained in Figs 7 and 8.

The same forces act on the foresail, the yacht's forward speed being due to the combined drive from both mainsail and foresail.

POINTS OF SAILING

Instead of describing the yacht's course in compass terms, it is often given in terms of the wind relative to the boat's heading. The main

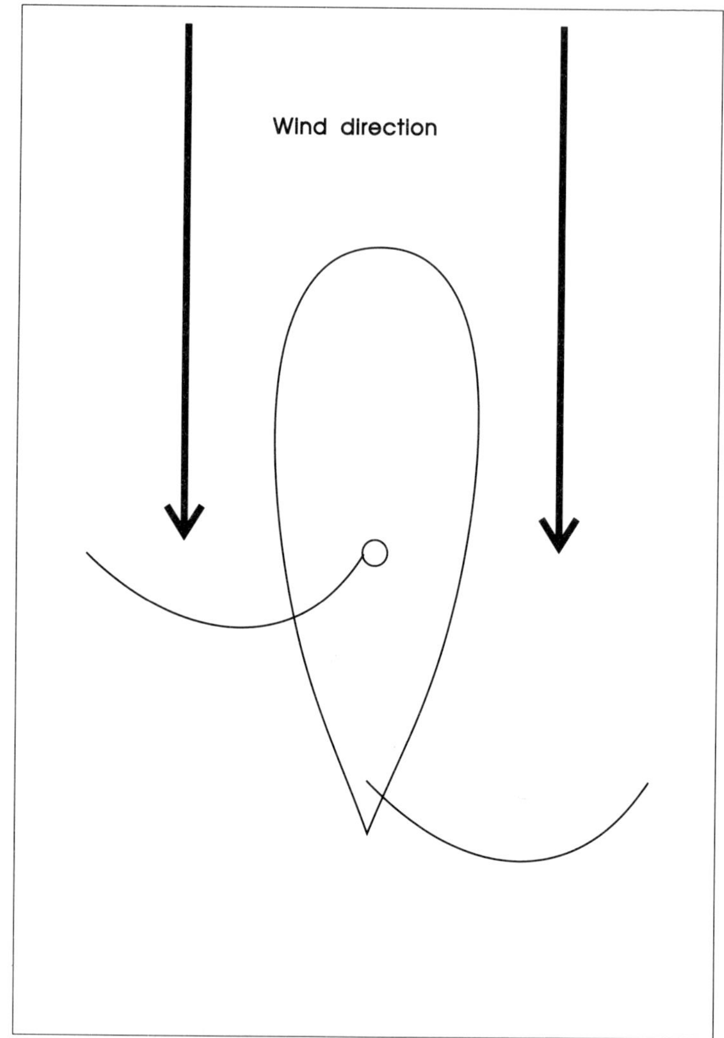

Fig 6. Running downwind.

'relative courses' or **points of sailing** are shown in Fig 9 (page 33).

A yacht cannot sail directly into the wind because the sails will then flog and will not take on an aerofoil shape to produce drive. There is therefore a 'no go' sector of roughly 90 degrees, composed of two 45 degree sectors on either side of the true wind direction.

The closest a yacht may sail to the true wind is about 45 degrees though this angle will vary from boat to boat. To sail this close to the wind, the sheets on both the headsail and the mainsail have to be hauled in as far as they can go. This point of sailing is, unsurprisingly, called **close-hauled** and is shown at the 0130 and 1030 clock

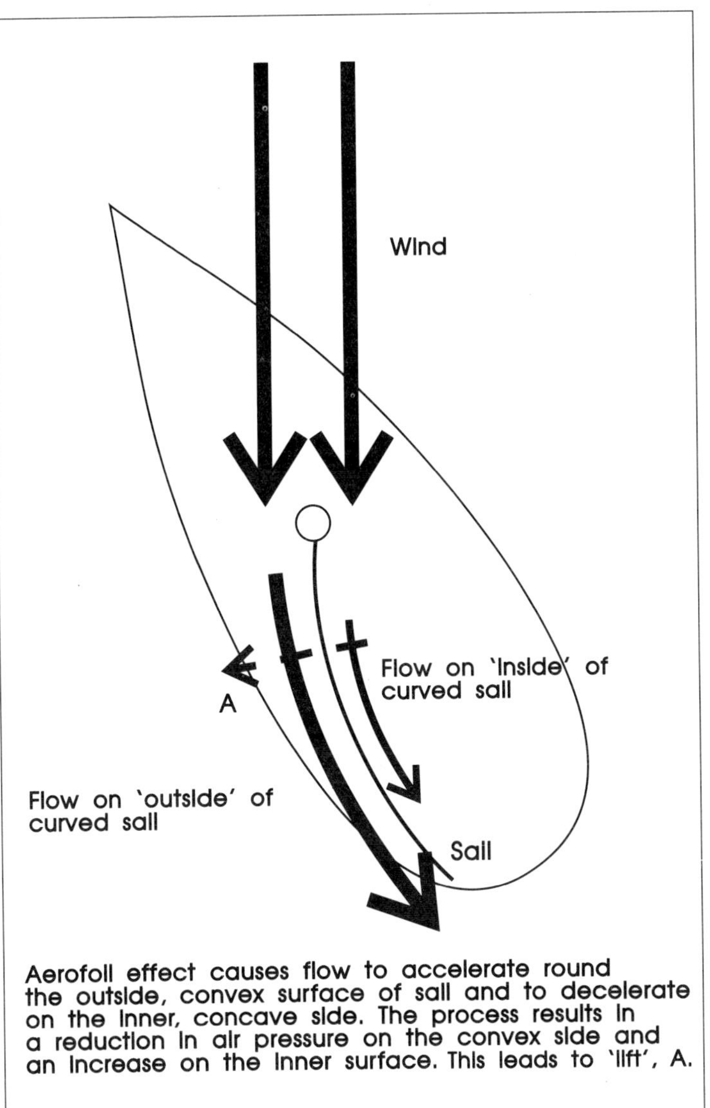

Wind
Flow on 'inside' of curved sail
A
Flow on 'outside' of curved sail
Sail
Aerofoil effect causes flow to accelerate round the outside, convex surface of sail and to decelerate on the inner, concave side. The process results in a reduction in air pressure on the convex side and an increase on the inner surface. This leads to 'lift', A.

Fig 7. Windflow around aerofoil-shaped sail.

positions in Fig 9. It is also referred to as **beating**. Turning further off the wind we arrive at the **reaching** position when the wind is abeam (sometimes called a **beam** reach). By turning further off the wind we come to the **broad-reach** point of sailing; the 0430 and 0730 positions on Fig 9. Finally by turning to bring the wind dead astern we are **running downwind**. The position between close-hauled and reaching is sometimes labelled as **fine-reaching** or **close-reaching**.

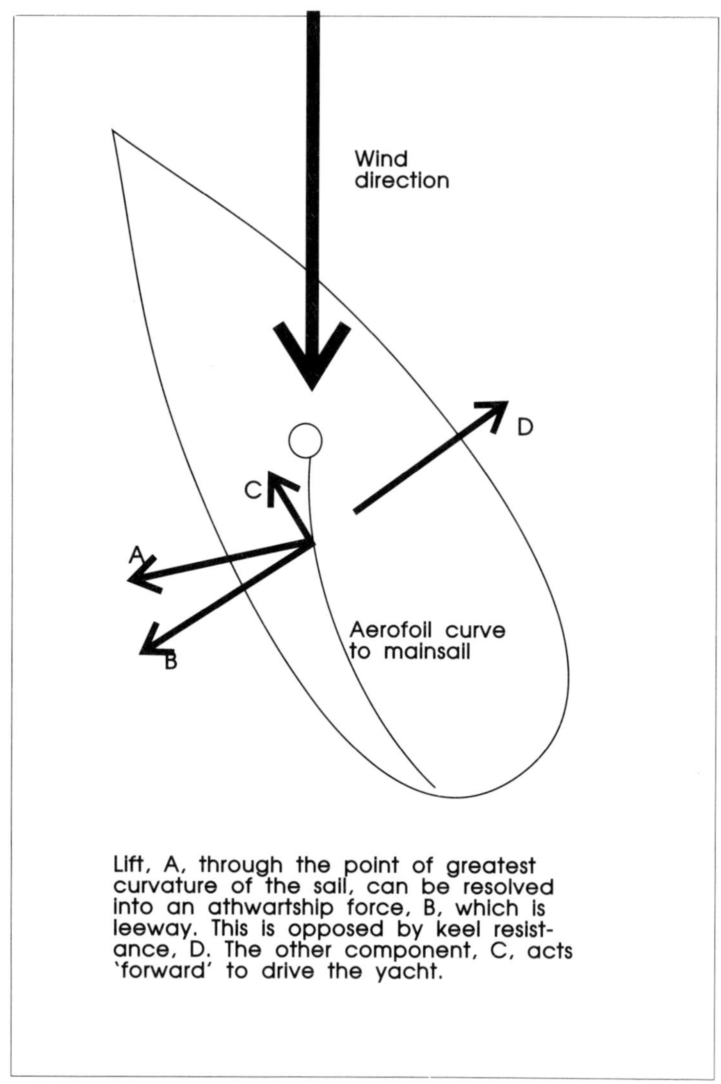

Wind
direction
D
C
A
B
Aerofoil curve
to mainsail
Lift, A, through the point of greatest curvature of the sail, can be resolved into an athwartship force, B, which is leeway. This is opposed by keel resistance, D. The other component, C, acts 'forward' to drive the yacht.

Fig 8. 'Lift' converted to 'drive'.

PORT AND STARBOARD TACKS

The left side of Fig 9 is a mirror image of the right. Consequently, the sails are set on the opposite side of the boat in each side of the diagram. These differences are very important, for they determine a yacht's right of way over another sailing vessel. If the sails are set out on the port side, or more particularly, if the main boom is set out to port, the yacht is on **starboard tack**; and if the main boom is set out on the starboard side, the yacht is on **port tack**. In both cases, the tack is labelled according to *the side of the yacht over which the wind is*

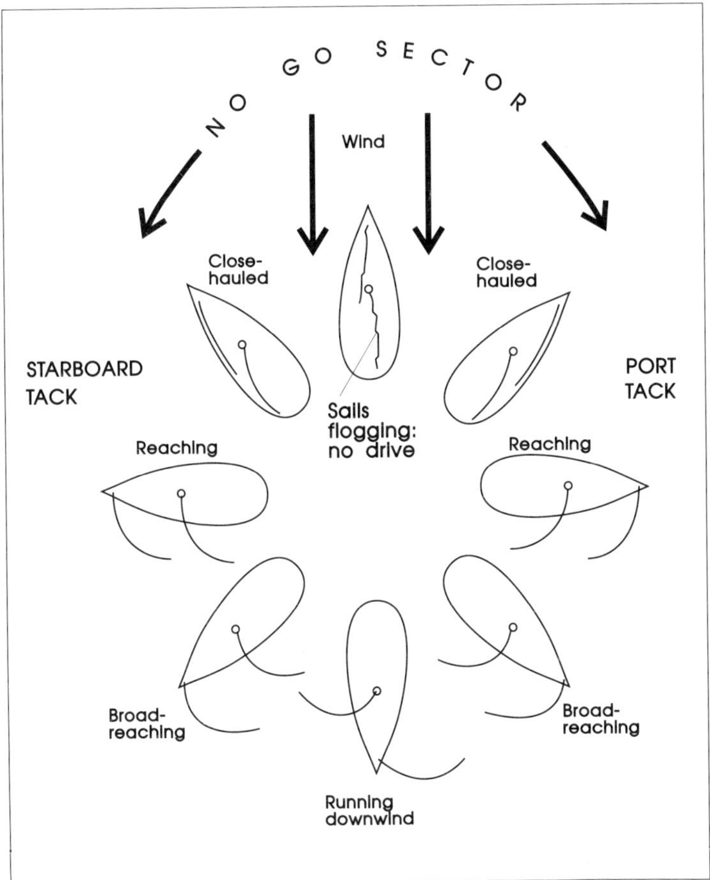

Fig 9. The points of sailing.

blowing, but the determining factor is the position of the main boom.

For example, when running dead downwind, so that the wind is neither blowing over the port nor the starboard side of the yacht, the main boom will be set out on one side or the other. In Fig 9, the boom is out to starboard in the running downwind point of sailing, so, for right of way purposes, the yacht is on port tack. (You will note that the foresail is set out on the other side so that it is not blanketed by the mainsail.) The foresail has no bearing on which tack the yacht is on, unless it is the only sail hoisted. The 'rules of the road' will be discussed later, so you can simply note here that a yacht on starboard tack has right of way over one on port tack.

BEATING AND TACKING

We have seen that a yacht may sail on any course outside of the 'no go sector', but what if the destination lies within this arc? The yacht can

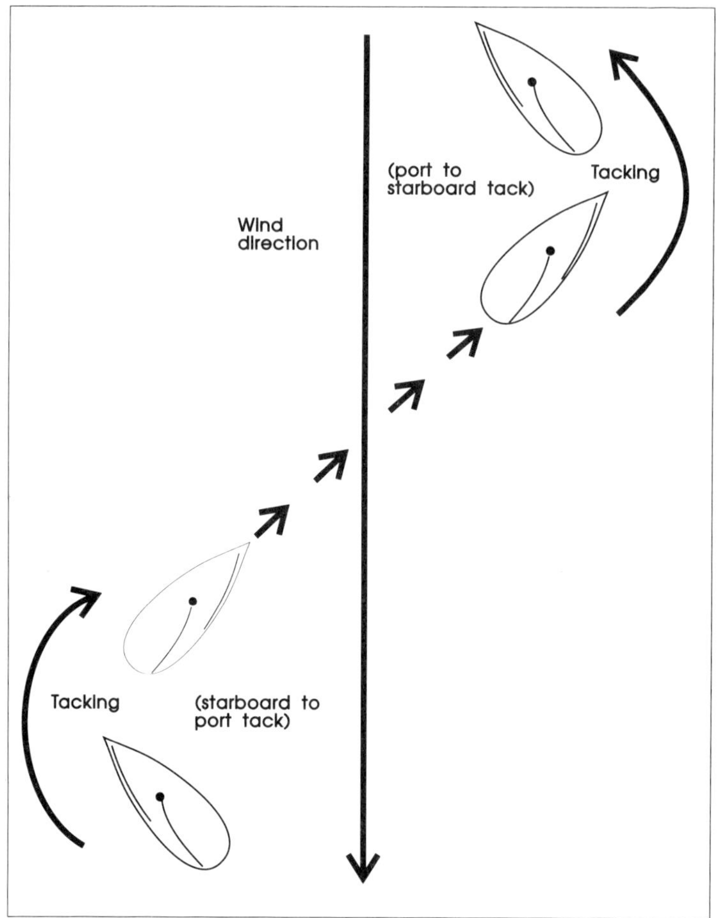

Fig 10. Beating.

still sail to this destination, but not directly. It will have to adopt a zig-zag course, close-hauled, first on one tack and then on the other (Fig 10), with the skipper determining the lengths of these tacks or **boards** according to both the tide and the bearing of the destination relative to the wind direction. The procedure is known as **beating**.

The process of changing course from the one tack to the other is called **tacking**. When tacking, the bow is turned *towards* then *through* the wind. The helmsman's involvement in tacking is described on pages 68–77, while crew action is discussed in the cruise which follows it.

When changing course *away* from the wind, by contrast, the sheets are eased out to trim the sails to the new wind direction. As the changing course approaches the downwind direction, the foresail becomes increasingly blanketed by the mainsail. It is common practice then to set the headsail on the other side of the yacht (Fig 9 – running downwind) often using the spinnaker pole to keep it set.

Running downwind is potentially dangerous since, should the apparent wind direction change either through a change in the true wind or a change in course, the wind may blow into the 'back' of the mainsail (Fig 11). If this happens, the main boom will 'scythe' across the boat in a second or so, and will severely injure anyone who is

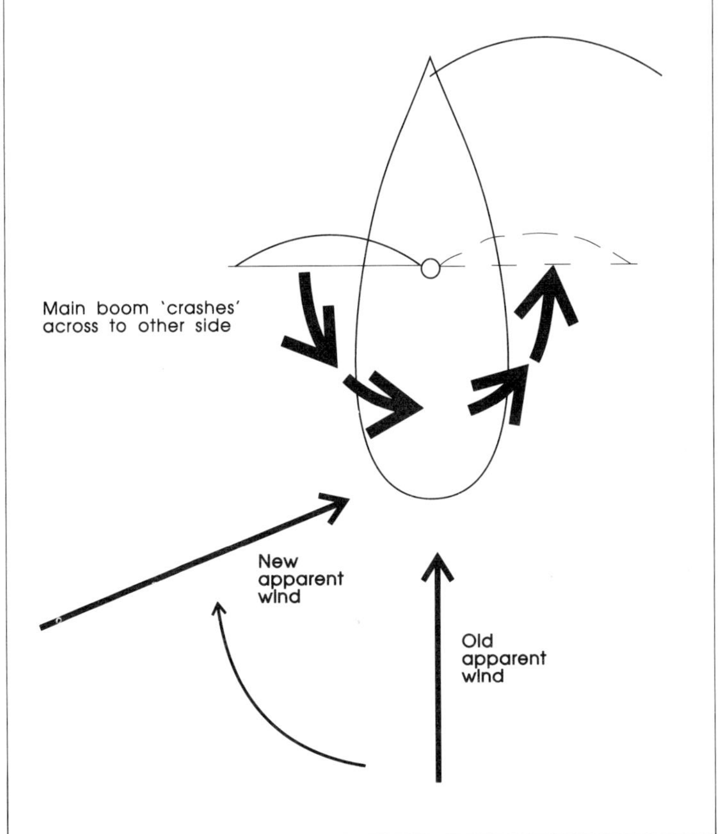

Fig 11. Accidental gybe.

in its path. (Just how easily this happens is shown in Fig 19, page 47.)

When running downwind, a rope **preventer** is usually rigged from the outer end of the main boom forward to a block in the bows and then led aft to the cockpit (Fig 12). Should the mainsail become 'back-winded', as described, this rope will prevent the boom from crashing across in an **accidental gybe**.

Because of an adverse shift in the true wind direction or for navigation reasons, it may become necessary to alter course so as to turn the stern through the wind and thus deliberately back-wind the mainsail. This deliberate **gybe** is carried out retaining full control of the main

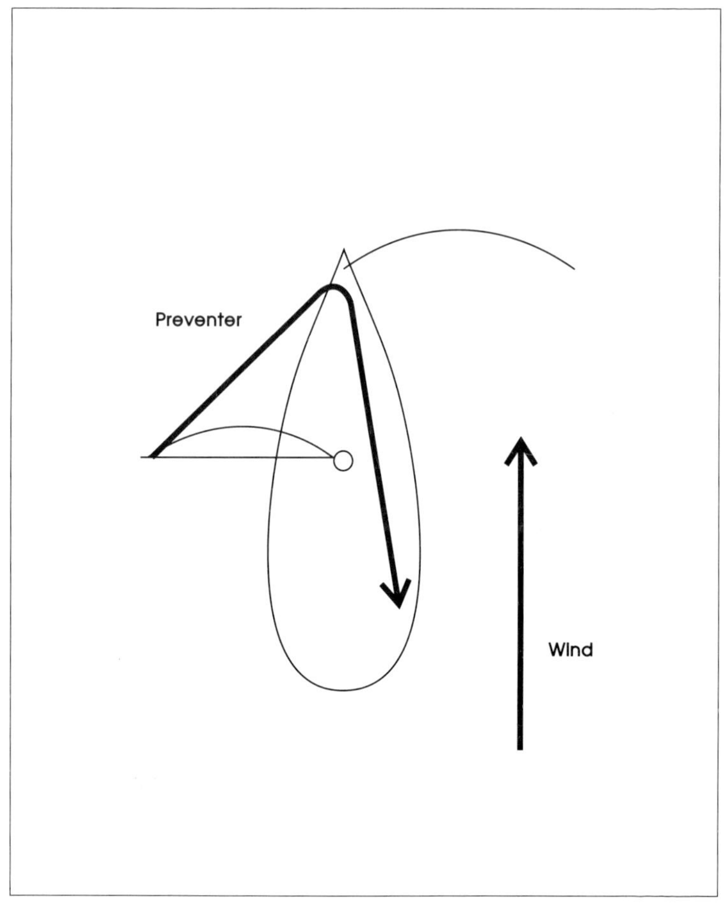

Fig 12. A preventer rigged to avoid an accidental gybe.

boom as it is slowly brought across the boat from one side to the other. It is a very proper manoeuvre. The process of **gybing** is described from the helmsman's point of view on pages 116–117 and 119–120, and several times for crew involvement in the cruise narrative.

There is one further danger when sailing before the wind (downwind) and this is **broaching**. In rough seas, a larger wave overtaking the yacht from astern may, if allowed, push the stern so far off course as to bring her beam on to wind and wave, which will roll the yacht over towards the horizontal. Broaching, since it chiefly concerns the helmsman, is more fully described in the following chapter.

· STEERING ·

Steering is the most important part of crewing a yacht. Bad helmsmanship, allowed to go unnoticed for too long, will certainly endanger the yacht for she will then be a considerable distance off a safe course. Steering a yacht is no more difficult than steering a car. In some ways it is easier because there are no distracting pedal movements or frequent gear changes. On the other hand, a boat will wander off course only too readily and so has to be held constantly to the required heading. This wandering or swinging off course is due to wave and wind action, both of which constantly vary. As with driving a car, some people acquire the ability to steer more quickly than others; few fail to learn eventually.

The art of steering lies in the early recognition of the boat's head swinging off course and then promptly applying the correct amount of opposite swing to bring her back to the required heading. The rate of swing, both off and then back on course, will vary depending on wave, wind and rudder angle (as well as the propeller when under power). It will often suddenly increase as the boat's heading wanders further off course and it will also tend to increase suddenly as the bow finally returns towards the required heading. Novice helmsmen soon become aware of this swing and on bringing the boat back on course, will commonly allow the bow to swing beyond the correct heading, with a resultant zigzag course, often with increasing amplitude!

DUTIES OF THE HELMSMAN

The helmsman's main duty is to steer the course which is required, under the direction of the skipper or watch leader. The helmsman is part of the crew and *not* in charge of the boat. He should also ensure that a good lookout is maintained, reporting to the skipper or watch leader if a possible collision situation is developing or if there is a large wind shift requiring sail adjustment.

DIFFERENT STEERING SYSTEMS

There are two quite different steering systems. Smaller yachts, say under 9 metres or so, are commonly steered by a **tiller** – a long wooden arm directly attached to the rudder post and extending forward into the cockpit. Fig 13 shows how the boat is steered by pushing the tiller one way or the other.

The second method of steering is by wheel. The helmsman normally stands behind the wheel with his hands in the '10 to 2' position. As with car driving, turning the wheel to the left will turn the boat's head to the left (port) and turning to the right will turn the bow to the right (starboard). Note that with steering orders, 'left' and 'right' are

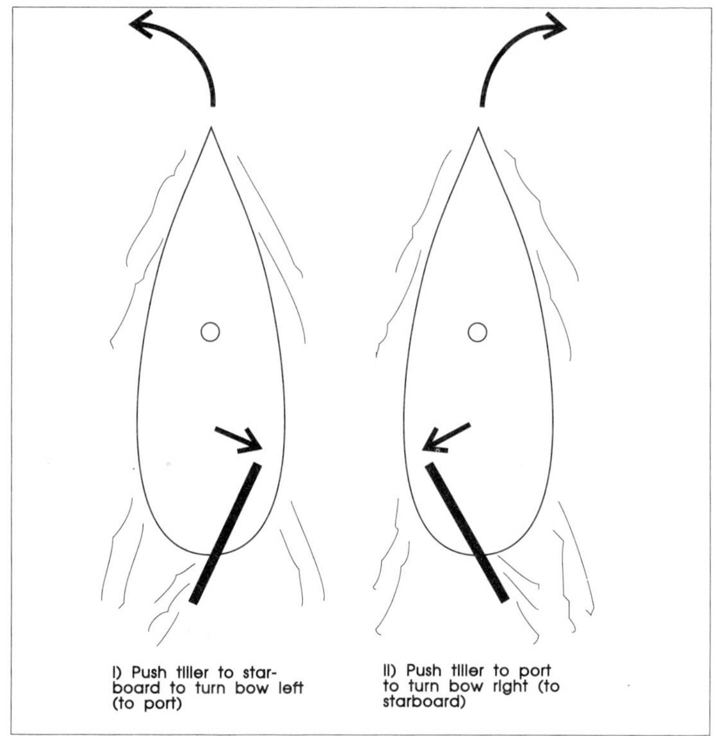

I) Push tiller to starboard to turn bow left (to port)
II) Push tiller to port to turn bow right (to starboard)

Fig 13. Tiller steering.

commonly used and are preferred throughout this book because they are more familiar to all, novice and experienced alike, than port and starboard. Since the helmsman faces forward there is no ambiguity. The use of left and right for steering is not unseamanlike; these terms are used by the Royal Navy – but these directions apply only to steering. Port and starboard should otherwise always be used to avoid ambiguity from crew members facing in different directions.

HELMSMAN'S POSITION

Whether novice or experienced hand, the steering position in the cockpit is almost sacrosanct. No one, not even the skipper, should impede the helmsman's movements or view, or stand between him and the instruments – especially the compass and, if inshore, the echo sounder. He should be allowed to adopt as comfortable a position as possible, whether standing or sitting, with plenty of room for his feet. Here, any intruder should simply be trampled on: the offending feet will soon move. Similarly a tap on the shoulder should remove anyone obscuring the instruments. These gestures are effective and sufficient; a courteous spoken request may not produce an acceptably prompt response. Each crew member – and that means everyone – must learn to give the helmsman room to see and to move.

Steering 'small'

As a general point, with both steering systems, rudder movements should be kept as slight or 'small' as possible. Large rudder angles produce considerable drag as the rudder loses its turning effect and acts more as a brake. For a 'hard' turn, the maximum rudder angle should be 45 degrees; beyond this angle there is no further turning effect.

STEERING TERMS

To complicate matters, many new words or expressions are used when steering. While most beginners will be familiar with 'a trick at the wheel', few will understand such terms as 'up helm' or 'down helm', or will ever have heard of 'weather helm' and 'lee helm', 'falling off', 'pointing', 'keep her up' or the like. These and other terms will be introduced as appropriate in the course of this chapter on steering.

The steering technique differs on a sailing yacht according to whether the wind is 'free' (ie coming from across the yacht or from astern) so that the desired course may easily be steered (see pages 29–36), or whether the wind 'heads' the yacht so that she has to beat to reach her destination.

Beating, which is quite different for the helmsman than for any other point of sailing, is treated separately in the next chapter.

TILLER YACHT: 'UP HELM'/'DOWN HELM'

When the wind is free the helmsman will be told where to point the boat, ie the course to steer. Initially, the beginner will be told to point the boat at an easily identified fixed object, such as a bold mark on land. After a little experience he will be expected to steer by compass.

Imagine being on a tiller-steered yacht with a steady force 3 wind blowing across the yacht from the starboard side – we are reaching on starboard tack. Since the yacht will be heeled over by ten degrees or so away from the wind, the best place for the helmsman to stand (or sit providing he has a clear view) is on the 'uphill' (windward) side of the tiller (Fig 14).

By pulling the tiller (helm) 'up' towards him, the yacht will turn away from the wind, ie to port, and by pushing the tiller 'down' the bow will turn towards the wind, ie to starboard. Hence the orders 'up helm' and 'down helm' to turn the yacht away from or towards the wind, respectively.

These terms are commonly replaced by 'turn left' or 'turn right' on wheel-steered yachts.

Offset steering effects

When steering from the side of the tiller, the helmsman is offset from the yacht's centreline. In steering for a fixed, distant mark he should not point the bow at that mark but should allow for this offset effect by choosing a point on the foredeck or pulpit which is offset from the

Helmsman's position on the 'uphill' side of tiller.
Pulling tiller 'up' turns bow to port; pushing tiller 'down' turns bow to starboard

Fig 14. Helmsman's position – tiller steering.

yacht's centreline by a similar amount. This point, instead of the bow, is then kept in line with the distant mark (Fig 15). Failure to allow for this will result in the yacht's course describing a slowly tightening arc which may take her over shallow water.

Even in quiet conditions of light wind across the starboard beam and consequently nearly flat seas, the boat's head will easily wander off course. If the mark steered towards apparently moves to the left of the foredeck reference point, pull the helm 'up' (towards you) to bring the reference point and the distant mark back in line. Conversely, should the mark wander to the right, then push the helm 'down' to bring the bow round to the right. There is no substitute here for hands-on experience.

It is only too easy to over correct to bring the boat back on course so that the boat's head quickly swings past the target, to lie on its other side. The opposite, tiller movement is then required to bring her back. In the early stages, overcorrection will follow overcorrection with a resultant zigzag course. The secret is to move the tiller back gradually to 'midships' just before the foredeck reference point comes back in line with the distant mark. The remaining momentum in the swing will bring her exactly on course. This ability will soon be acquired in quiet conditions.

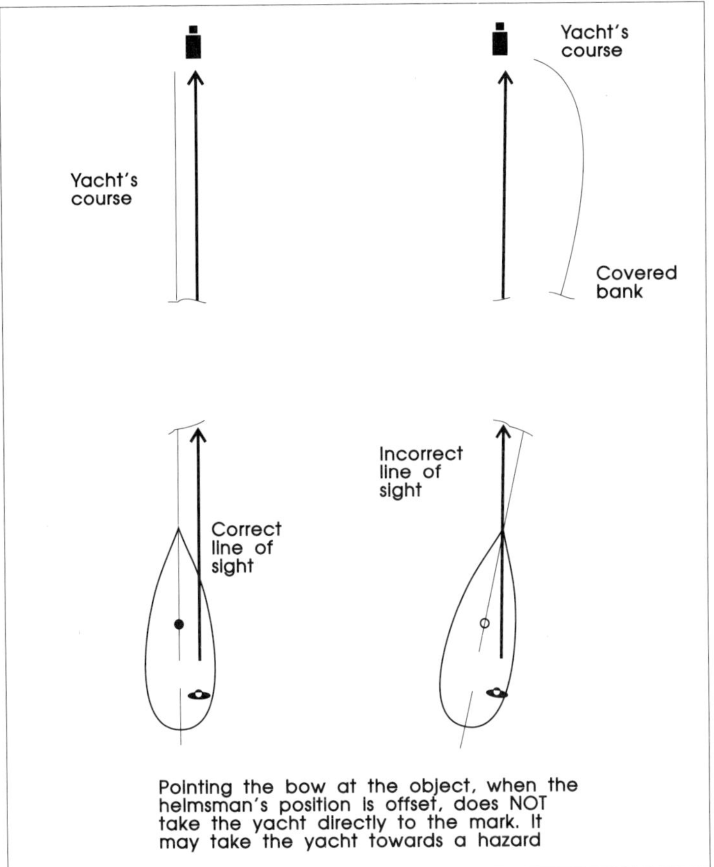
Yacht's
course
Yacht's
course
Covered
bank
Incorrect
line of
sight
Correct
line of
sight
Pointing the bow at the object, when the helmsman's position is offset, does NOT take the yacht directly to the mark. It may take the yacht towards a hazard

Fig 15. Offset steering position.

WHEEL STEERING

Wheel steering is usually slightly less sensitive than tiller steering due to the linkage between the wheel and the rudder post. To a greater or lesser extent there will be a little slack in the system dependent on the type of linkage and the age of the boat. This slack has to be 'taken up' before the rudder actually turns. Steering wheel systems have stops fitted near the rudder post which limit the maximum rudder angle to about 45 degrees. The amount of wheel turn to reach this limit varies a little from boat to boat; the average is one complete rotation. The midships position is usually marked on the wheel, and some large yachts may be fitted with a rudder angle indicator dial.

Most wheels are mounted on a pedestal on the yacht's centreline, so the helmsman, standing behind the wheel, is also on the centreline. When steering for a distant fixed mark, the mark should be kept on the bow or behind the mast.

In some ways, initially, steering by wheel is easier than by tiller, since the wheel is turned in the same direction as you want the boat to turn. As the boat's head drifts off course, small adjustments of the wheel will be needed to swing her back. With a wheel, more so than with a tiller, it is only too easy to overdo the return swing. The secret is to notice the drift off course as soon as it occurs and to correct this immediately. If the boat's head has gone to the left of the distant mark, then it will have to be swung back to the right by turning the wheel to the right. Apply enough wheel to make her respond immediately, and then steadily bring the wheel back until it is midships just before the bow comes back on line, letting the remaining momentum in the return swing carry her back exactly on course.

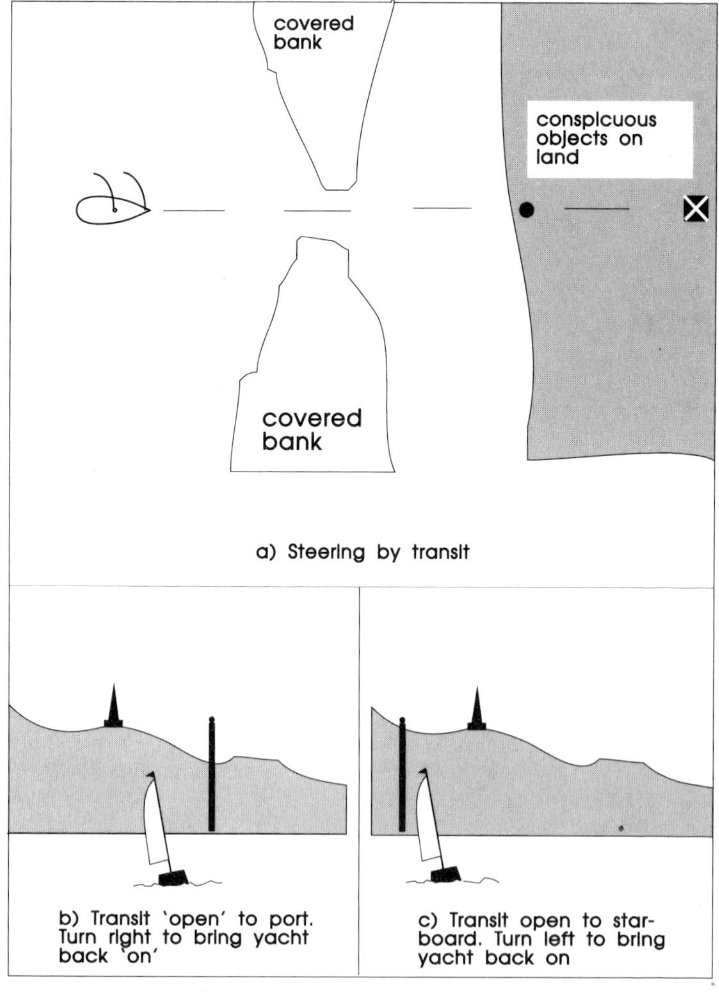

Fig 16. Transits.

Transits

A particular case of steering towards a fixed object arises when another fixed object is visible some distance directly behind it. This second object may be a detail on the skyline such as a small notch or isolated copse. By keeping both objects directly in line, you can follow a very accurate course, which automatically allows for any variations in the tidal stream. This is called 'steering by transit' (Fig 16).

When the more distant object lies to the left of the nearer one, the transit is said to be 'open to port'. Steer right to bring the boat back on course. As the gap decreases the transit is said to be 'closing' (in this case from the left).

If the distant mark lies to the right of the nearer one, the transit is 'open to starboard'. Steer left to 'close' the transit. If the distance between the objects is very small relative to the distance between the yacht and the nearer object, the transit is said to be insensitive, ie the yacht will have to wander some distance off the line to get the transit to open.

If the distance between the marks is greater than that between the yacht and the nearer mark then the transit will be too sensitive; it will open when the yacht is only just off the line. The ideal is when the distance between the marks is about half that between the nearer mark and the yacht.

WAVE EFFECTS

So far we have assumed quiet conditions, ie nearly flat sea and light winds. However, on most occasions there will be some 'sea'; waves running more or less downwind with their crests almost parallel to each other. These waves, all slightly different in size, will upset a regular steering pattern. Their effect on steering varies with their direction relative to the boat's head (Fig 17).

Waves on the bow

Waves coming from a direction on the bow (Fig 17i) will strike the bow first and throw it off downwind. As the wave passes the yacht's central (pivot) point, it will throw the stern downwind and therefore bring the yacht's heading back to the original course. The second effect is usually less than the first, so that some corrective action is required from the helmsman. Under these conditions (as with any other) the helmsman has to concentrate on keeping the bow in line with the object aimed at, correcting immediately when it is thrown off as the wave first hits the bow and then the stern. The ability to correct for this wave effect, and even to anticipate it to some extent, is soon acquired though it is usually not possible to set up a rhythmical correction pattern for long as few waves are the same.

With larger waves on the bow, say 2 metres or more in height, the technique is to turn the bow up (luff up) a little towards the wind as the yacht rises towards the crest and to bear away a little on the back of the wave. This not only gives a drier, more comfortable ride, but also reduces the boat's drift off to leeward to a minimum.

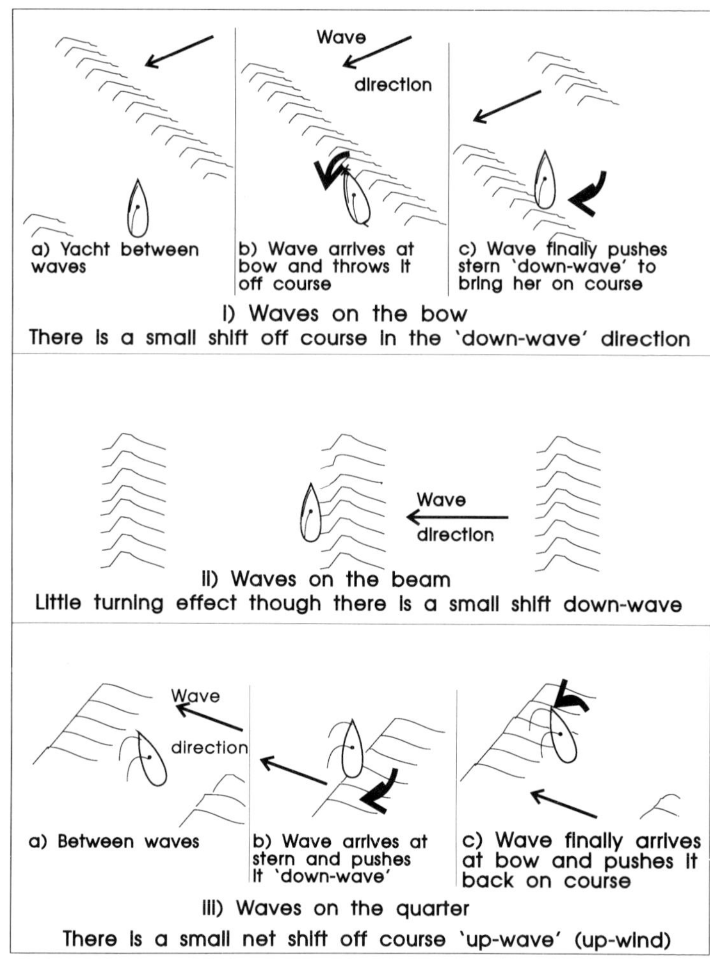

Fig 17. Wave effects.

Waves on the beam

It would appear that waves on the beam have little turning effect about the yacht's centre point (Fig 17ii). However, not all wave crests are exactly parallel so that some will throw off either the bow or the stern, which will have to be recognised and corrected as before.

Quartering seas

Waves arriving from a direction aft of the beam (Fig 17iii), quartering seas, are often more difficult to handle and are also potentially dangerous when large. In the first place, they arrive from behind the helmsman's normal area of vision. Secondly, when large, they may throw the stern so far off course as to bring the yacht beam on to the seas which may roll her over to a dangerous angle; this is 'broaching' (see page 36).

The general effect of quartering seas is to throw the stern off first, so that the bow swings some way towards the wind and wave direction and then, as the wave passes the pivot point, it throws the bow back towards the original course. This latter effect is usually less than the initial throwing off of the stern, so that the net effect is a slight shift of the boat's head towards the wind and waves.

In moderate or better conditions (say, waves of less than one metre in height) there are two schools of thought regarding steering in quartering seas. One suggests making no correction for each wave so that, with no rudder angle, drag is kept to a minimum, though a steering correction is made every four or five waves to compensate for the small net drift off course. This method submits at least part of the control of the boat to the waves and is against the axiom that the helmsman must always have complete control; he must never allow the yacht to take charge.

The other method, much preferred by me, requires steering corrections for each wave, first to compensate for the stern and then for the bow being thrown off course.

When a quartering sea arrives it lifts the stern as well as throwing it off course. This lifting is easily felt by the helmsman and is the best indication of the arrival of the next wave. By fixing attention on the bow and the object steered towards, the helmsman can apply correcting rudder to keep the boat on course. He should not attempt to steer by looking over his shoulder, except in rough conditions, and then only a glance to assess the size of the next wave.

Since no two waves are exactly similar and, more significantly, since an occasional wave will be much larger than its predecessor, it is wiser to compensate for each wave rather than to allow the stern to be thrown off towards a dangerous broach by a bigger wave, or to allow the bow to be thrown off towards an even more dangerous involuntary gybe (see pages 35–6).

Anticipation of wave effects

In all these conditions, regardless of their relative angle, the larger the wave the greater the throwing off effect, so more effort will be required to hold the yacht on course. In addition, the helmsman's response will have to be almost instantaneous. Since successive waves will usually arrive from nearly the same direction he can anticipate their effect to a large extent and compensate immediately with at least sufficient helm to retain control.

With tiller steering the helmsman's response is transferred immediately to the rudder, but with wheel steering there may be a little delay due to slack in the linkage between wheel and rudder post. In anticipating the wave effect, this slack should be taken up in the same direction as the wheel will soon be turned. In taking up the slack (ie wheel turning a little but rudder remaining stationary) the steering will be light, but when the slack has been taken up and the rudder begins to turn, the steering will become heavier immediately. There is no doubt about this take-up limit except at very slow boat speeds when the steering will always be light.

Figure 18 provides an example of this anticipation on both wheel- and tiller-steered yachts, broad-reaching on starboard tack in force 5 winds with 1.5 metre quartering seas. Waves from this direction call for more concentration than from almost any other direction.

As mentioned earlier, the net effect of quartering seas is to produce an overall shift in the yacht's course towards the wind. This is **griping**. It must be minimised by concentrating on the required course. Since, under the conditions given above, the double compensation for each wave will have to be repeated every five seconds or so, great concentration is required of the helmsman to keep the yacht on the required heading. A change of helmsman will be readily detected by those below, since it takes a little time to settle down to the pattern of waves, no matter how experienced the relief helmsman may be.

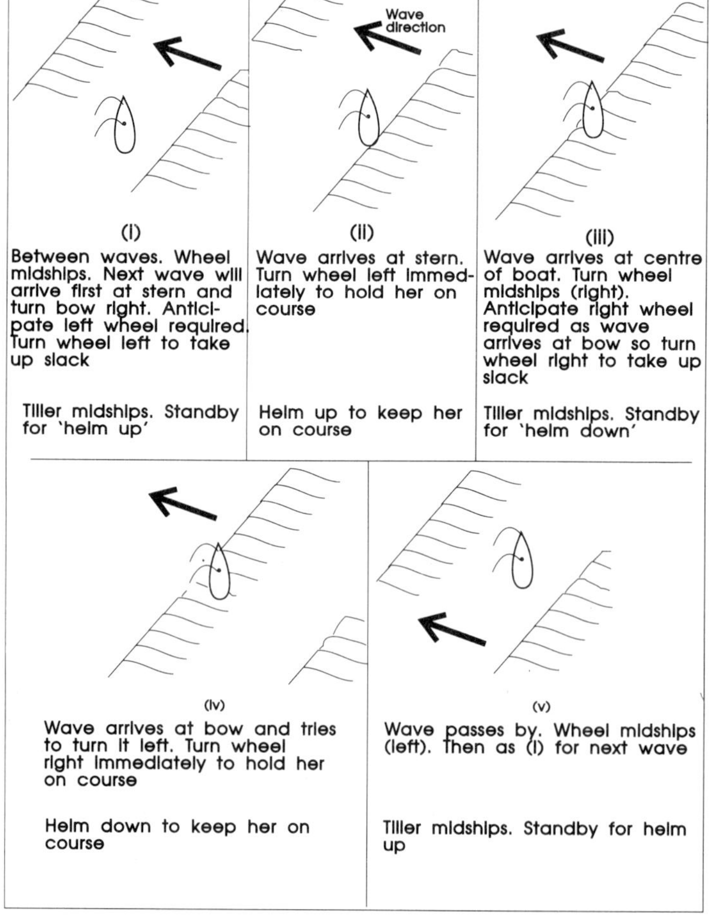

Fig 18. Anticipation of quartering wave effects.

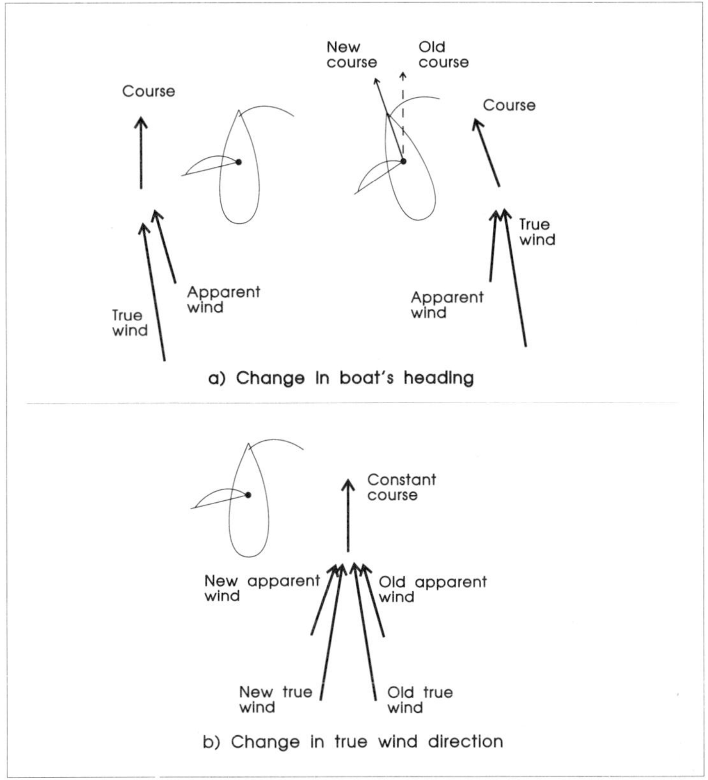

Fig 19. Apparent wind changes.

RUNNING DOWNWIND

Steering a yacht downwind, even in flat seas, is one of the two most difficult tasks the novice helmsman has to learn, because of the risk of an accidental gybe (see pages 35–6). (The other is sailing *into* the wind and is described on pages 60–82.) Figure 19 shows how quickly the apparent wind swings across the stern when the boat is allowed to wander off course by 20 degrees or so. If the wind itself also changes direction towards the stern, the accidental gybe will arrive even more quickly.

Whether steering for a distant mark or by compass when sailing downwind, the helmsman must glance frequently (ie every ten seconds or so) at the masthead burgee, Windex, or at the relative wind direction dial, in order to keep the apparent wind slightly on the opposite side of the yacht from the main boom (Fig 20i).

The wave effect on the stern will also have to be allowed for. As a precaution, irrespective of the experience of the helmsman, the skipper should always rig a preventer from the outer end of the boom, forward through a block on the foredeck and then led aft to the cockpit (see pages 35–6). This prevents the boom from rushing lethally

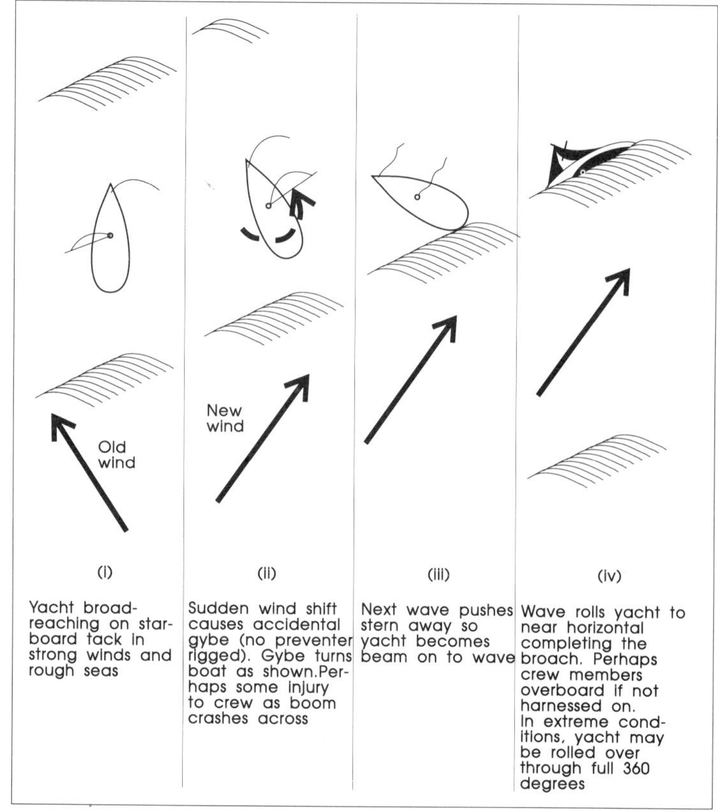

Old
wind
New
wind
(i)
(ii)
(iii)
(iv)
Yacht broad-reaching on starboard tack in strong winds and rough seas
Sudden wind shift causes accidental gybe (no preventer rigged). Gybe turns boat as shown.Perhaps some injury to crew as boom crashes across
Next wave pushes stern away so yacht becomes beam on to wave
Wave rolls yacht to near horizontal completing the broach. Perhaps crew members overboard if not harnessed on.
In extreme conditions, yacht may be rolled over through full 360 degrees

Fig 20. Accidental gybe leading to a broach.

across the cockpit as it crash-gybes. After all, a sudden shift in the wind direction may easily result in an accidental gybe just as much as a neglectful shift in the yacht's heading.

If an accidental gybe does occur, the next wave may throw the yacht's stern further off course towards a broach, which will almost certainly compound the hazards already facing the crew (Fig 20).

Again, any large wave striking the windward quarter may induce a direct broach (Fig 21) unless immediate correcting action is taken by the helmsman. With large waves it is essential that the stern is kept directly on (ie perpendicular) to the waves.

In spite of the foregoing, when running downwind, the helmsman must know the *safe* way to alter course to avoid an accidental gybe should he become disorientated. With the boom out on the port side (starboard tack) he must turn the bow to the right, and with the boom out to starboard he must turn the bow to the left, until he becomes orientated once again (Fig 22).

One further caution; because of these dangers, there is a tendency to steer a little to the windward side of the required course, away from the gybe. An awareness of this will help in maintaining the course.

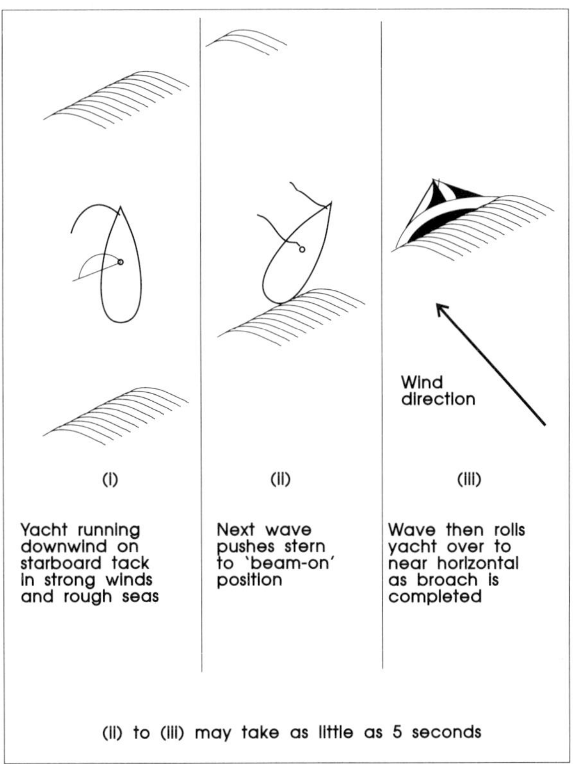

Fig 21. Direct broach.

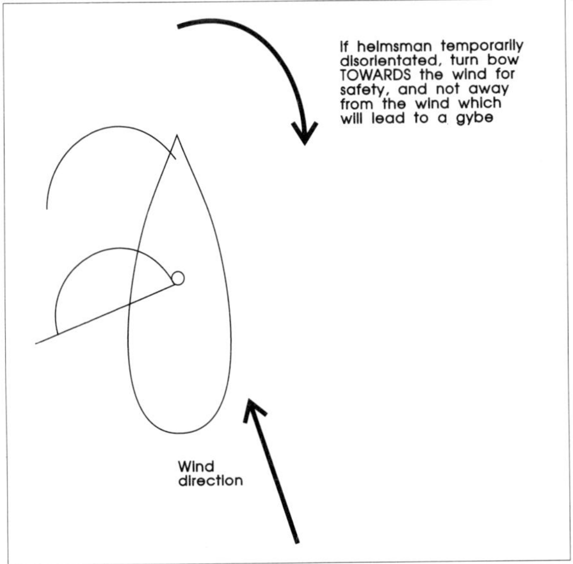

Fig 22. Safe way to turn if disorientated.

This point of sailing, especially, calls for maximum concentration from the helmsman; for this reason, tricks at the helm are normally restricted to 15 minutes or so.

STEERING UNDER POWER

A further complication arises when steering under engine power, due to the paddle wheel effect of the propeller. Most yachts are fitted with a right-handed propeller, ie when viewed from astern, it rotates clockwise when ahead gear is engaged (Fig 23). Since pressure within the water increases with increasing depth, it is greater at the bottom of the rotation than it is at the top. Thus the blades have more 'bite' at the bottom of their rotation with the result that the propeller attempts to 'walk' the stern to starboard (apparently turning the bow to port) as in Fig 24. If left uncorrected the boat will describe a slow but continuous circle to port. To compensate, the helmsman has to hold a small amount of right wheel, or move the end of the tiller a little to the left, in order to keep to the required course.

COMPASS STEERING

The foregoing has dealt with steering techniques in sight of land when the yacht is being steered towards a fixed object. Even then the helmsman should glance at the compass from time to time because

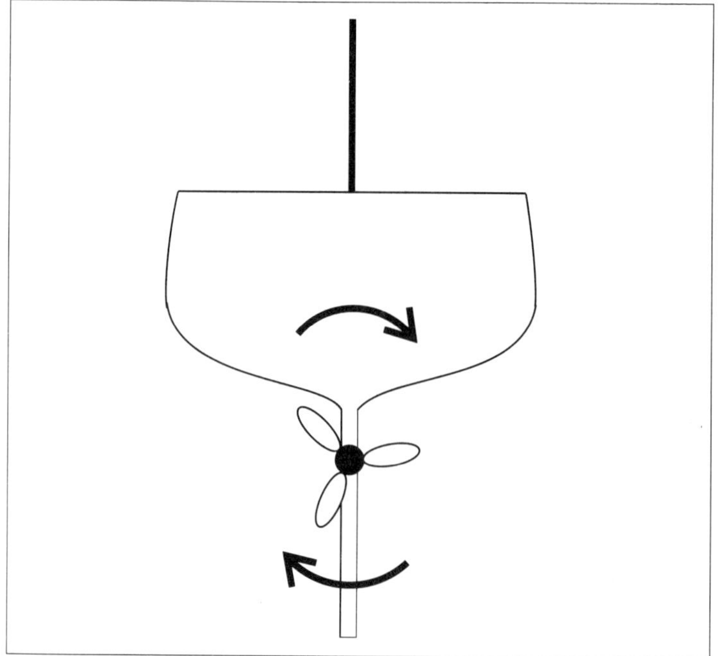

Fig 23. 'Right-handed' propeller.

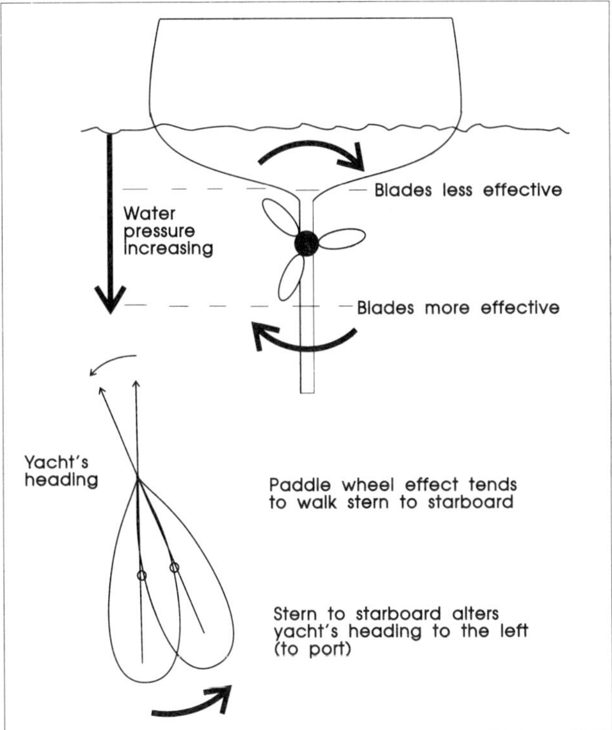

Fig 24. Paddle wheel effect.

the navigator will want to know the course actually being steered.

When out of sight of land the yacht has to be steered by compass. This is a more tiring exercise, at least at first, because the beginner will tend to stare at the compass, to the exclusion of all else, repeating to himself the rules for bringing the yacht back on course. This is understandable, and even the most experienced can easily recall their earliest attempts at compass steering. This initial mesmerism is soon overcome and steering by compass becomes a joy, so much so that some people prefer it even within sight of land.

Binnacle and porthole compasses

Steering compasses on small boats are of two main types. One is viewed obliquely from above so that the whole compass card is in view. This is a binnacle compass and is normally mounted on top of the steering wheel pedestal (Photo 14). The other, more commonly found on tiller yachts, is viewed from the side and is usually fitted as a pair on either side of the main hatch companionway. This is a porthole compass (Photo 15). Here, only the near edge of the compass card is normally visible.

On the binnacle compass the card is marked with 360 degrees at magnetic north, and the yacht's course is read at the forward (dis-

Photo 14. Binnacle compass.

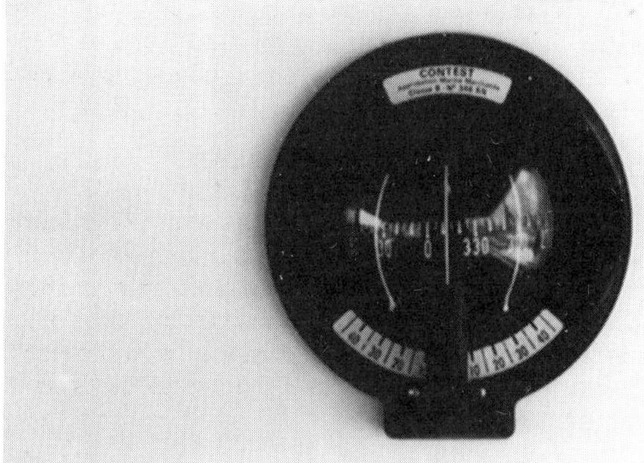

Photo 15. Porthole compass.

tant) edge of the card. However, with the porthole type, where only the nearer edge of the card is visible, the card is deliberately marked 180 degrees out so that the figures on the nearest (rear) edge of the card represent the boat's heading. These different types of compass require different steering corrections to bring the yacht back on course.

Notation

Both types of compass usually have numbered marks every 30 degrees at 030, 060, etc, with unnumbered marks every 10 degrees and smaller marks every 5 degrees. The main points are normally labelled N, E, S and W, and sometimes also NE, etc for the main intermediate points. Compass courses are always read and spoken in three-figure notation, ie zero five five, three four zero, etc. Note that courses to steer are normally given on yachts to the nearest 5 degrees; it is impossible to steer a small vessel to within 1 degree.

Lubber line

From the photo of the binnacle compass you will see that a pointer extends vertically from the central, pivoting point of the compass card. There is also a mark on the furthest side of the compass dome; this latter mark is the lubber line. The compass is installed so that the lubber line and the pivot pointer are along or parallel to the yacht's centreline. In order to reduce parallax errors due to slight movements of the helmsman's head, the compass is read where the lubber line meets the card, with the lubber line and the pivot pointer in line. (The other lines on the compass dome opposite and at right angles to the lubber line are there for the purpose of taking bearings etc.)

With the porthole compass, where there is normally no pivot pointer visible, the parallax problem is overcome by placing the lubber line very close to the edge of the compass card nearest to the helmsman (Photo 15).

With both types the compass card, to which the north-seeking compass needle is attached, is hardly ever 'steady' due to the movement of the boat. The card is delicately pivoted not only for easy response but also so that it will remain horizontal when the boat heels. The bowl is filled with fluid in order to dampen down the natural swing of the displaced needle.

Course corrections when steering by compass

When the boat's head is off course, the required reading on the compass card will have moved to one side or the other of the lubber line (Figs 25 and 26). It is easier to accept that this apparent movement of the compass card is real, though in fact it is the boat which has swung while the compass card remains 'steady', because the needle always points to magnetic north. Do not attempt to visualise what has happened and therefore what is required to bring her back on course. Better by far to remember that:

1 On a **wheel-steered** yacht with a **binnacle compass**, if the required course goes to the *left* of the lubber line, turn the wheel *left* (Fig 25i) and if it goes to the *right*, turn the wheel *right* (Fig 25ii) to bring her back on course.

Or, turn the wheel *towards* the required course when it moves away from the lubber line.

2 On a **tiller-steered** yacht with a **binnacle compass**, when the desired course goes to the *left* of the lubber line, move the tiller end to the *right* (Fig 25i), and when the desired course goes to the *right*, move the tiller to the *left* (Fig 25ii).

Or, in both cases, move the tiller in the *opposite* direction from the required course when it moves away from the lubber line.

3 On a **wheel-steered** yacht with a **porthole compass**, when the

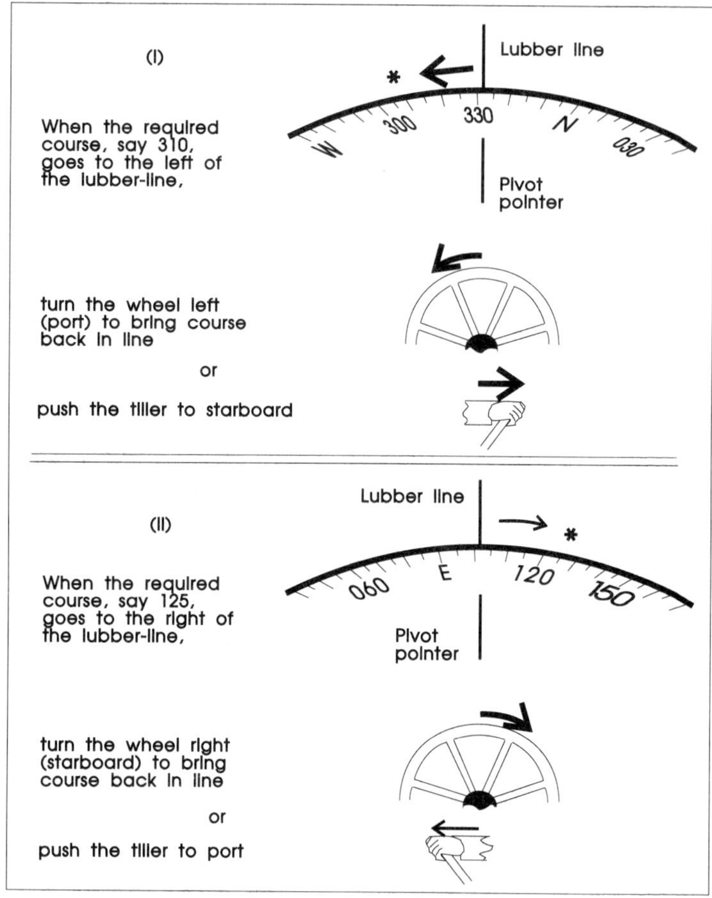

(i)
When the required course, say 310, goes to the left of the lubber-line,
Lubber line
330
300
W
N
030
Pivot pointer
turn the wheel left (port) to bring course back in line
or
push the tiller to starboard
(ii)
When the required course, say 125, goes to the right of the lubber-line,
Lubber line
060
E
120
150
Pivot pointer
turn the wheel right (starboard) to bring course back in line
or
push the tiller to port

Fig 25. Steering by binnacle compass.

desired course goes to the *left* of the lubber line, turn the wheel *right* (Fig 26i) and when it goes to the *right*, turn the wheel *left* (Fig 26ii).

Or, turn the wheel *away* from the desired course.

4 On a **tiller-steered** yacht with a **porthole compass**, when the required course moves to the *left* of the lubber line, move the tiller to the *left* (Fig 26i) and when it moves to the *right*, move the tiller to the *right* (Fig 26ii).

Or, always point the tiller *towards* the required course.

All this may seem confusing, but only one set of rules will apply on any one yacht. Again, as with most aspects of steering, there is no substitute for hands-on experience. After all, when the wrong rudder movement is made, the required course will move even further away

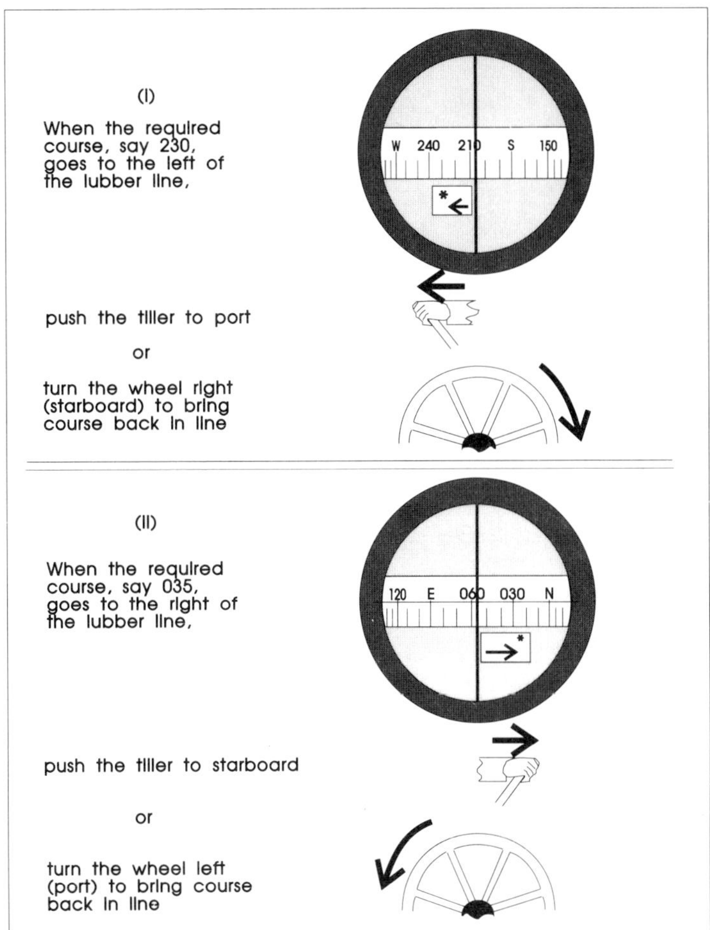
(i)
When the required course, say 230, goes to the left of the lubber line,
W 240 210 S 150
push the tiller to port
or
turn the wheel right (starboard) to bring course back in line
(ii)
When the required course, say 035, goes to the right of the lubber line,
120 E 060 030 N
push the tiller to starboard
or
turn the wheel left (port) to bring course back in line

Fig 26. Steering by porthole compass.

from the lubber line; opposite rudder will bring her back.

No helmsman, no matter how experienced, can be expected to keep the yacht exactly on course all the time. Steering a small boat is a process of repeated corrections when her head wanders off course. As a consequence, the course will wander 5 to 10 degrees either side of a mean which should be the required course, though the bow should be on this mean for most of the time in order to produce a reasonably straight wake. It is important that this mean course is the course which you have been asked to steer. If for any reason you have been unable to maintain the required course and your mean course is 5 to 10 degrees or more from it, you must tell the navigator. Anything less than absolute honesty here may endanger the yacht.

In rough seas, say winds of force 6 or more, even a good helmsman will find it difficult to keep the boat's head within 10 degrees of the

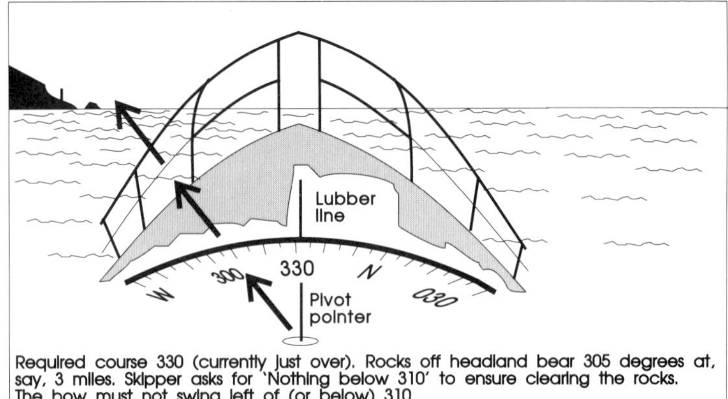

Required course 330 (currently just over). Rocks off headland bear 305 degrees at, say, 3 miles. Skipper asks for 'Nothing below 310' to ensure clearing the rocks. The bow must not swing left of (or below) 310

Fig 27. 'Nothing below 310'.

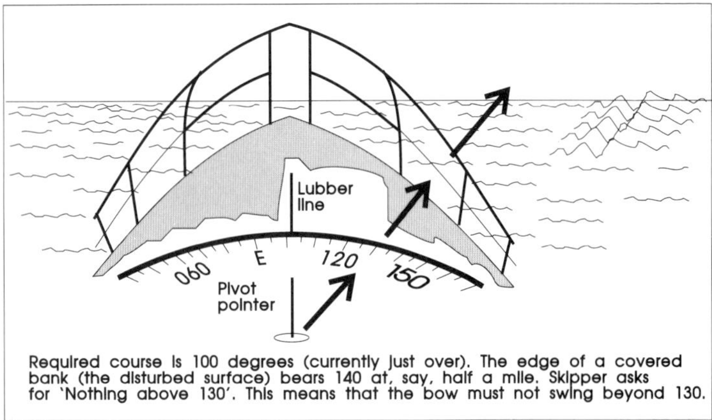

Required course is 100 degrees (currently just over). The edge of a covered bank (the disturbed surface) bears 140 at, say, half a mile. Skipper asks for 'Nothing above 130'. This means that the bow must not swing beyond 130.

Fig 28. 'Nothing above 130'.

required course, though his mean should equal it. Here it must be accepted that the yacht's head will swing up to 20 degrees either side of the mean. Such departures are purely momentary, for even as these extremes are approached the helmsman will already be correcting the swing to bring her back.

'Nothing above' and 'nothing below'

In these rough conditions, especially, with rough seas causing the boat's head to wander up to 20 degrees either side of the mean, the skipper may qualify a given course, say 320 degrees, with 'nothing above 340' or 'nothing below 300'. These limits (one only for any given heading) are given in order to clear a hazard lying fairly close to the required course. They denote that the boat's head must not be allowed to swing beyond the given limit. 'Above' and 'below' in this sense have strictly numerical definitions. (See Figs 27 and 28.)

Fig 29. Steering by cloud patch.

The 'clearing' limit, which may be 20 degrees or even more, should allow a sufficient margin to avoid the hazard. The situation is obvious enough when the hazard is visible, but it is not so apparent when the hazard is a covered bank or reef. It is even more important then to concentrate on the compass course and the clearance limit in order to avoid any tendency to creep towards the hazard.

Concentration

Obviously much more concentration is required when steering by compass than when steering for a fixed object. For this reason, tricks at the helm at night and in rough seas are normally reduced to 15 minutes or so even for experienced helmsmen. Anything less is not practicable since it takes each relief helmsman a few minutes to settle down to the conditions.

Novice helmsmen tend to become mesmerised and subsequently confused by the compass, especially at night. This fixation may be broken in several ways. Experienced hands will glance up when exactly on the required compass course and, choosing a distinctive cloud patch in line with part of the mast rigging (Fig 29), will steer by

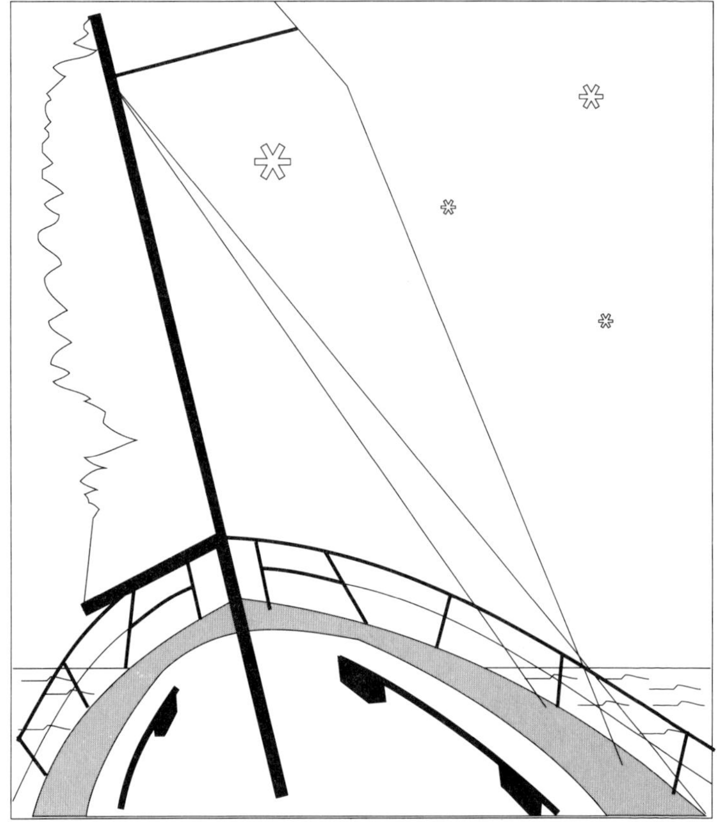

Fig 30. Steering by a star.

that for a minute or two with occasional glances at the compass to check on the course. When the original cloud patch has moved off line, another may be selected against a different part of the rigging. The main reference point is thus transferred, if only temporarily, to a distant object almost at eye level, away from the close-up, eyes-down, compass reference point within the cockpit. This is a great relief to the eyes (and also to the stomach!).

By night, choose a star situated in the triangle between the yard-arm, and the lower and cap shrouds (Fig 30). Since stars appear to move very slowly, it may be possible to use the same star for ten minutes or even more. Most helmsmen never forget their first experience of steering by a star.

On overcast nights or on cloud-free days, shroud telltales (black ribbons can be seen even on the darkest night) may be used as a steering aid, by keeping them streaming in the same direction for a few seconds of relief before returning to the compass. In their absence, use the relative wind indicator dial or, by day, use the wave pattern and try to maintain their relative direction. On cloudy nights just look ahead for a few seconds. After all, as helmsman you should be used to the wave effect and should be anticipating the fairly regular wanderings of the boat's head. In any case, it is surprising how quickly one acquires the art of 'feeling' when the boat is exactly on the required course. This 'feel' arises from a combination of the yacht's speed, heel and wind and wave noises. It is peculiar to each heading, and differs with changing wind and wave conditions.

STEERING · ON THE WIND ·

It has already been said that steering downwind is one of the two most difficult points of sailing for the novice helmsman. The other is sailing close-hauled or 'steering on the wind'. When the destination lies directly upwind, the yacht will have to tack, first one way and then the other (see pages 29–33) at about 45 degrees to the true wind.

There are other expressions for this point of sailing. The most common are 'beating' and 'sailing on the wind'. The latter describes the difference between steering in these close-hauled conditions and in all others when, because the wind is free, the yacht may be steered directly to its destination.

THE VARIABILITY OF THE WIND

When steering on the wind, the sails are sheeted in as close as possible and the yacht is sailed as close as practicable to the wind direction. This point of sailing, more than any other, demonstrates that the wind is never exactly steady – it is constantly changing in direction and speed, by as little as 15 degrees and 15 per cent, respectively, every half minute or so and often by much larger amounts when gusty. These short-term variations are quite different in character from the more 'permanent' changes lasting several hours rather than just fractions of a minute.

When sailing to windward, it takes much longer to reach your destination than when sailing a direct course (Fig 31). It is therefore important to keep the yacht sailing as close to the wind as practicable in order to make the best time towards the destination. Any delay may mean missing a favourable tide or being unable to enter a safe harbour due to lack of water depth.

If the yacht is sailed too close to the wind, boat speed will drop and leeway (sideways drift) will increase (Fig 32i). If she is sailed off the wind, the speed may be maintained but each tack will take the yacht less distance to windward (Fig 32ii). In both cases it will take much longer to arrive. But how is the beginner to know when the yacht is being sailed at the closest (optimum) angle to the wind, often called 'sailing to advantage'?

FORESAIL LUFF

There are several aids to steering on the wind. The first and simplest is the luff (forward edge) of the foresail. When the yacht is being

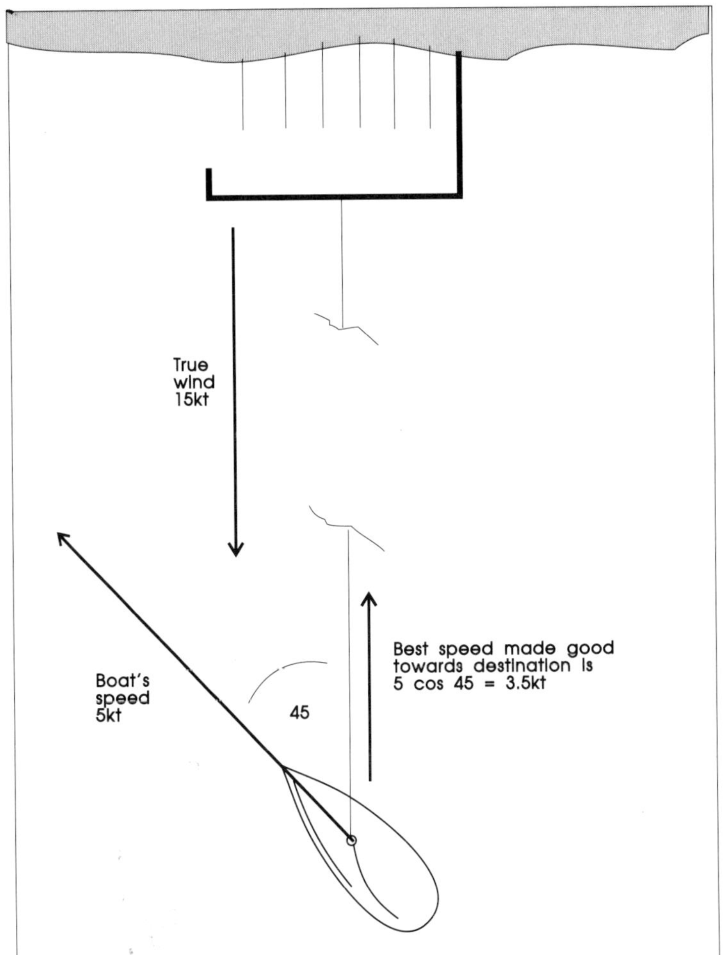

Fig 31. Sailing on the wind.

sailed correctly on the wind, the close-hauled foresail will adopt a smooth, aerofoil curve, concave when viewed from the cockpit (Fig 33i). If it is sailed too close to the wind, ie **pinching**, the foresail luff will assume a reverse convex shape throughout its height as the wind gets into the 'back' of the foresail (Fig 33ii). This reverse curve or **backing** of the luff is known as **lifting**. If the bow is allowed to swing even closer to the wind, the whole foresail, and also the mainsail, will flap or **flog** with increasing noise, finally inducing vibrations throughout the yacht. At the first sign of lift in the foresail luff, the bow should be gently eased back away from the wind until the lift just disappears. The yacht is now sailing to windward 'to advantage'. The mainsail luff is not nearly as sensitive to lifting as the foresail due to

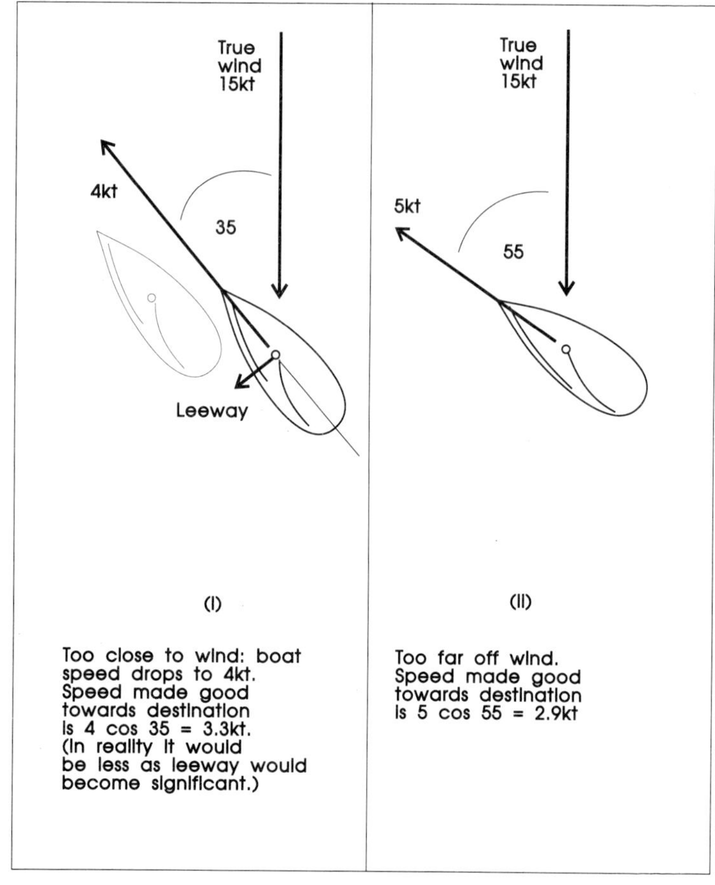

Fig 32. Inefficient sailing on the wind.

the deflection of the wind around the mast and so it is not used as an aid.

The lift in the foresail luff will be seen first in the area just above the mitre seam (see Fig 36, page 66) and so the helmsman should stand or sit so that he can easily see this area of the foresail as well as the horizon ahead. This reference point on the foresail will be the chief focus of his attention, with occasional glimpses to either side (and astern if alone in the cockpit) and at the compass, for the navigator will need to know the course being steered.

Every half minute or so the bow should be gently eased up or **pointed up** towards the wind until the luff just begins to lift once more and then as gently eased back until the lift just disappears. This is to test for any small favourable shift in the wind direction which otherwise may not be detected by the helmsman from his position in the cockpit.

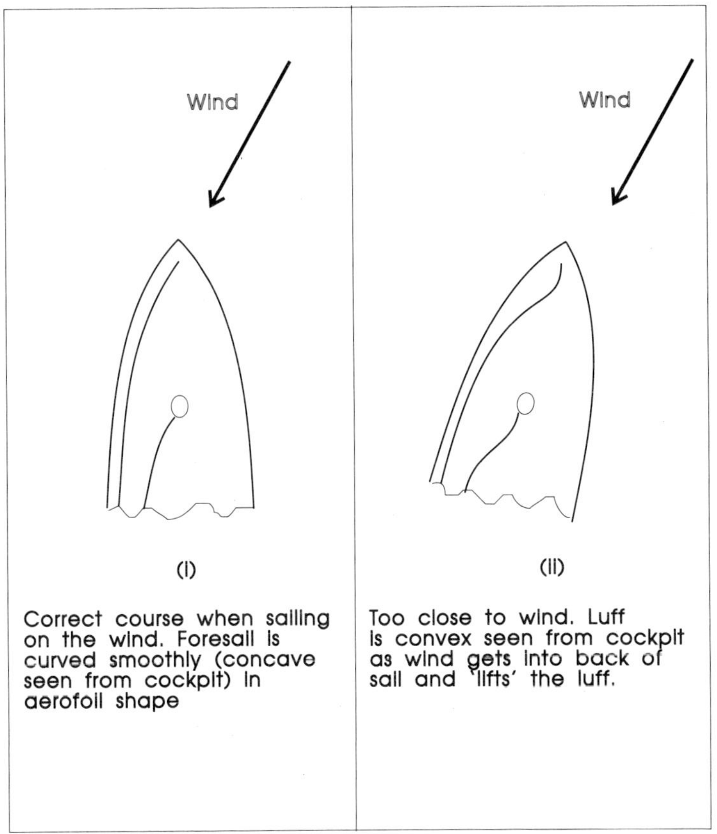
Wind
Wind
(i)
Correct course when sailing on the wind. Foresail is curved smoothly (concave seen from cockpit) in aerofoil shape
(ii)
Too close to wind. Luff is convex seen from cockpit as wind gets into back of sail and 'lifts' the luff.

Fig 33. The foresail luff.

CHANGES IN THE WIND DIRECTION

It may be that a lift appears in the luff of the foresail even though the boat's heading has remained constant. This is because the wind itself has changed to come more head-on to the yacht. The bow will therefore have to be eased away from the wind until the lift disappears. Such a change in the wind direction is known as a 'heading' change, or, more commonly, a **header** (Fig 34i).

A change of wind in the opposite direction means that the wind has become 'free' or has **freed**, so the yacht should be pointed up towards this new wind direction. This change of course to windward – and therefore towards the destination – is called a **lift** (Fig 34ii).

There is now some ambiguity between the 'lift' of the foresail luff and a 'lift' due to a freeing wind change. Though this may seem confusing, in reality the term is related either to the foresail or to the wind, and so the context removes any ambiguity. A lift from a wind change is a help, whereas lift in the foresail is a hindrance.

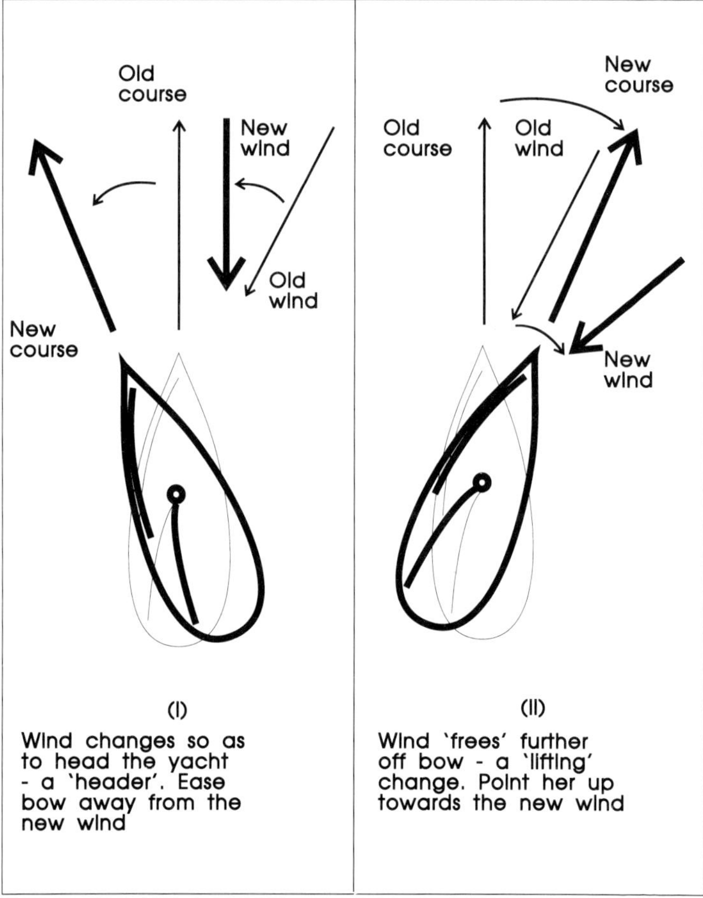
Old
course
New
wind
Old
wind
New
course
(I)
Wind changes so as to head the yacht - a 'header'. Ease bow away from the new wind
New
course
Old
course
Old
wind
New
wind
(II)
Wind 'frees' further off bow - a 'lifting' change. Point her up towards the new wind

Fig 34. 'Heading' and 'lifting' wind changes.

Burgee and shroud telltales

There are other indicators to assist the beginner to acquire the ability to steer on the wind. The burgee at the masthead, kept parallel to the top of the mainsail, is a fair guide but is tiring on the neck! Another clue is telltale ribbons attached to the shrouds (Fig 35) a little above eye level. The windward telltale only is used, and on many yachts it so happens that this streams directly towards the helmsman when the yacht is being sailed correctly on the wind. When pinching (a little too close to the wind) the telltale will point more towards the stern of the yacht and when sailing too far off the wind, it will stream more across the boat.

THE FEEL OF THE YACHT

The beginner will soon feel when the yacht is being sailed correctly on the wind. When pinching, the angle of heel will decrease until the

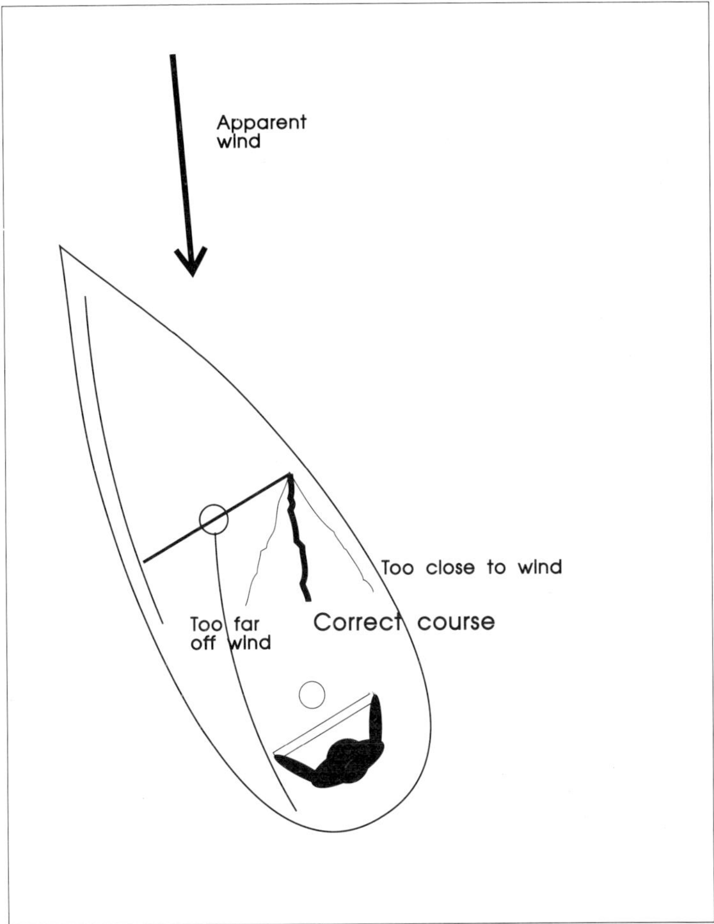

Fig 35. Shroud telltales.

yacht becomes upright with the sails eventually flogging noisily. As the bow is gently turned away from the wind to the correct course, the yacht will heel over and accelerate, producing much excitement from the crew, especially the helmsman who will feel a detectable tremble from the rudder as the water surges past it.

If the yacht is then allowed to turn further off the wind, she will remain heeled over (the angle may even increase) but the sails will be 'stalled' as they now present an inefficient angle to the wind. The boat's speed will therefore slowly decrease. Stalled sails remain 'asleep', ie the curve looks right, but the telltales or burgee will show that the sails are not driving the yacht at best speed to windward. It will also be much quieter as the yacht will be riding the waves more easily.

With only a little experience, the feel of the wind on the face will also become a useful aid to steering on the wind.

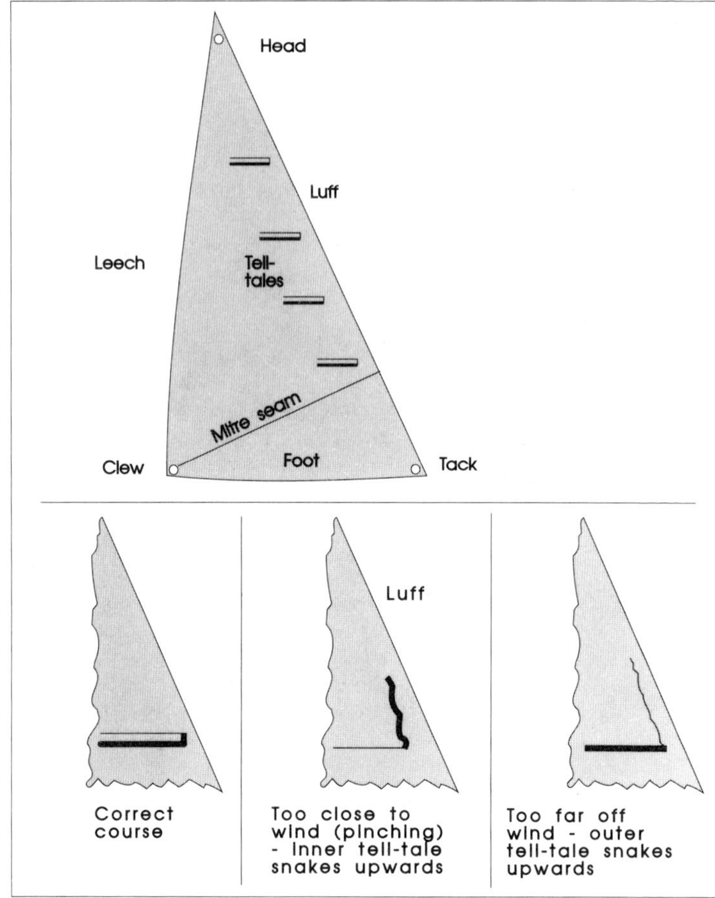

Fig 36. Foresail luff telltales (beating).

Foresail luff telltales

The novice, then, should begin by using the foresail luff, backed up by the shroud telltales and soon followed by feel, to indicate in these early days that the boat is being sailed efficiently. With further experience he will be able to draw on other valuable guides.

The most useful of these, since it is the most sensitive, is a refinement of the lifting luff. This aid takes the form of a series of pieces of natural wool (man-made wool sticks to the sails) each about half a metre long, threaded through the foresail about half a metre in from the luff and spaced about two metres apart starting near the mitre seam (Fig 36). With the sails close-hauled and the yacht being sailed correctly on the wind, each pair of telltales will stream horizontally (the shadow of the hidden part behind the foresail is easily seen in daylight).

If the bow wanders a little towards the wind (pinching), then the nearest, inside, part of each telltale will start to snake upwards even before the luff begins to lift (Fig 36ii). The telltale just above the mitre seam will normally react first. Ease the bow away from the wind until they fly true once more. Conversely, if the bow is turned too far off the wind, the shadow of the outer telltales will be seen to snake about with increasing vigour. The bow should then be turned or pointed up to windward until the telltales fly parallel once more. On some yachts, ribbon-type telltales are attached to the leech (after edge) of the mainsail. These are used for adjusting sail trim and are not to be used for steering.

Electronic wind instruments

Some yachts are fitted with wind instruments; these provide an accurate method of indicating the wind (see Photo 13, page 28). The main 360 degree dial shows the apparent wind direction. When the wind lies within 45 degrees of the bow, the adjacent, close-hauled dial is activated. This gives an expanded scale from 0–45 degrees on each tack. The port or starboard side is used according to which tack is being sailed (the main direction dial will remind you). The pointer on the close-hauled indicator is kept on the optimum angle which is normally about 30 degrees off the apparent (not the true) wind. When the pointer angle increases above this optimum angle it shows that the bow is too far off the wind, so point her up to get her back on course. Conversely, when the angle decreases below the optimum you are pinching, so turn the bow gently away from the wind. The yacht's speed dial is usually situated next to the close-hauled indicator in order to gain best performance to windward. When sailed correctly, the yacht's speed will increase to a maximum.

Masthead Windex

The last type of wind indicator is a Windex, fitted at the masthead in undisturbed air (see Photo 12, page 27). This instrument is set up so that the arrow flies parallel to one arm or the other, according to tack, when the yacht is 'beating' correctly. Though a good system in many ways, it suffers from the disadvantage of being sited too far above the helmsman's normal eye level.

Wind indicators at night

Most of the indicators just described will be invisible at night. However, apart from the wind dials which are illuminated, the shroud telltales, perhaps surprisingly, are still useful. The small amount of light which is always present even on the darkest night, is enough to throw these into silhouette, especially if the telltales themselves are black.

Exceptionally, a torch may be used to illuminate the foresail luff or the burgee. If this is done, however, the night vision of those observing the illuminated area will be drastically affected. The helmsman must screen his eyes for the few seconds this takes, relying on someone else's observation of the luff, because his night vision must not be impaired.

NIGHT VISION

On this vitally important point, great care must be taken in order to avoid affecting the night vision of those on deck. Cabin lights should be turned off before the hatch is opened from below. Smokers should warn everyone before lighting up, and should do so as far aft as possible. A torch should be shone through closed-up fingers, again after a warning, and never pointed at anyone's face.

As a general point with windward sailing, you will have noticed by now that steering orders are not given in terms of left or right, but in terms of the wind. On the one hand the instructions 'towards the wind', 'to windward', or more commonly 'point her up', and on the other hand 'away from the wind', 'to leeward' (pronounced loo'ard), 'take her off' or 'ease her off' are the expressions most frequently used. The order 'keep her footing along' is sometimes given. This means keep the yacht going at best speed just off close-hauled, to avoid pinching, so as to keep a good bow wave (known as a bone in her teeth) where the **forefoot** meets the water. This point of sailing, nearer to close-hauled than to 'close-reaching', is sometimes called **full and bye**. Strictly speaking, the sails here should be eased out slightly from the close-hauled trim.

TACKING

The favoured tack

Windward work consists of sailing relatively long tacks or 'boards', each roughly at 45 degrees to the true wind. When the destination lies exactly upwind, the boards will be of the same length, all other things such as tide being equal (Fig 37i). However, when the destination is not quite dead upwind, the one tack will make more distance towards it than the other. This 'closer' tack is called the **favoured tack** and the other tack the **cross tack** (Fig 37ii).

In an equal tack situation, a wind change will make the one tack or the other the favoured tack. If this wind change is a header so that the bow has to be turned away from the wind, the same wind change will be a lift on the opposite tack which now becomes the favoured tack (Fig 37). When racing, the yacht will be tacked on to the favoured tack immediately, but when cruising it is normal practice to see if this wind change is more than just temporary before tacking.

It is worth repeating: *a heading wind shift on the one tack is a lift on the other*. This is another reason for pointing her up a little every half minute or so; to test for a lift.

Time to tack

Whether after a wind change, at the edge of a channel or to avoid a collision, the time to tack is the skipper's decision. Only in extreme cases will the helmsman tack the boat without first referring to him.

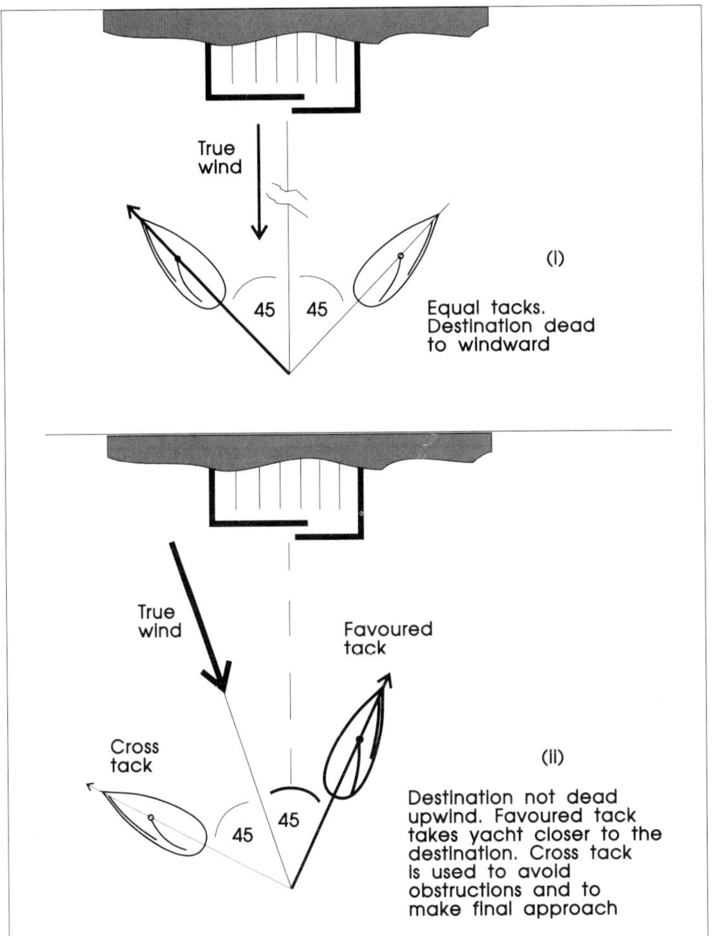

Fig 37. Equal, favoured and cross tacks.

The skipper will ask the helmsman to tack the boat when he is ready (that means in no more than a minute), or in a definite time (say five minutes) or, when approaching a familiar shore, when the echo sounder depth decreases to, say, 3 metres. **Tacking** the yacht, ie turning the bow into and through the wind to bring the wind on to the other bow, is then the helmsman's responsibility.

Tacking procedure

When told to tack the yacht, other than in an emergency, the helmsman should look around to see that the process of changing on to a new course will not hamper another craft in the near vicinity. The most dangerous sector is that between the windward beam and dead astern because the new course will lie along the direction of the old

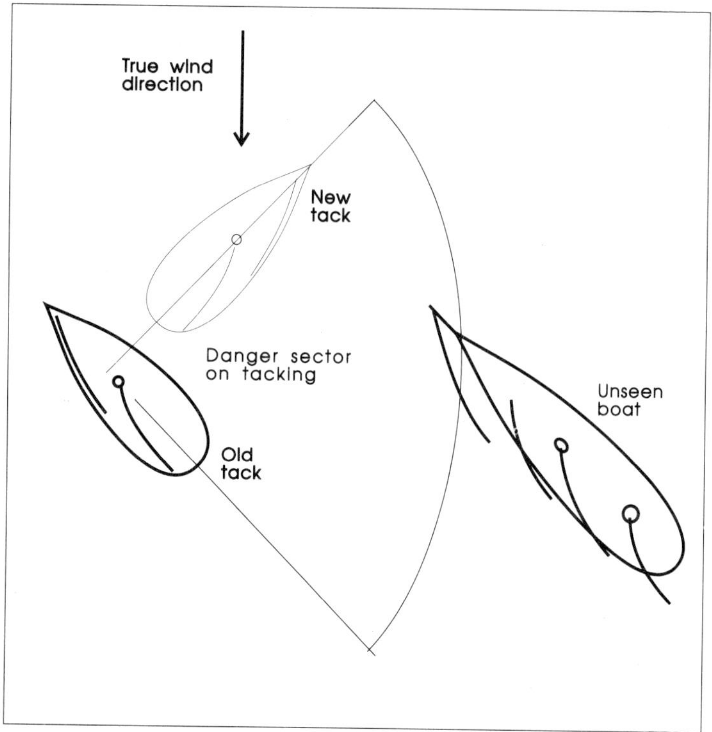

Fig 38. Danger sector on tacking.

tack windward beam (Fig 38). The helmsman must always make sure it is safe to do so before tacking the yacht, even though he is aware that the skipper has just checked; it *must* become a routine part of the tacking procedure.

Since many beginners become temporarily disorientated when tacking, it is useful first to look out in the direction of the windward beam, for this will be the new course. (After all, each tack will be 45 degrees to the true wind ie at right angles to each other.) Choose a suitable object or a distinctive patch of cloud on the windward beam as an initial guide to steer the yacht towards on the new tack before settling down to sailing on the wind using telltales, etc (Fig 39).

If steering by compass, add or subtract 90 degrees according to tack. A change from starboard to port tack will require the *addition* of 90 degrees to the old course, while a change from port to starboard requires the *subtraction* of 90 degrees (Fig 40, page 72).

Having checked that it is clear to tack and having selected a useful marker for the new course, the next step is for the helmsman to cry out 'ready about' loud enough for the benefit of anyone down below who is not safely stowed away in a bunk. On calling 'ready about' the helmsman continues along the original course, but the crew will be preparing the foresail sheets for tacking (the mainsail looks after itself). In this interval the helmsman should have a further look all

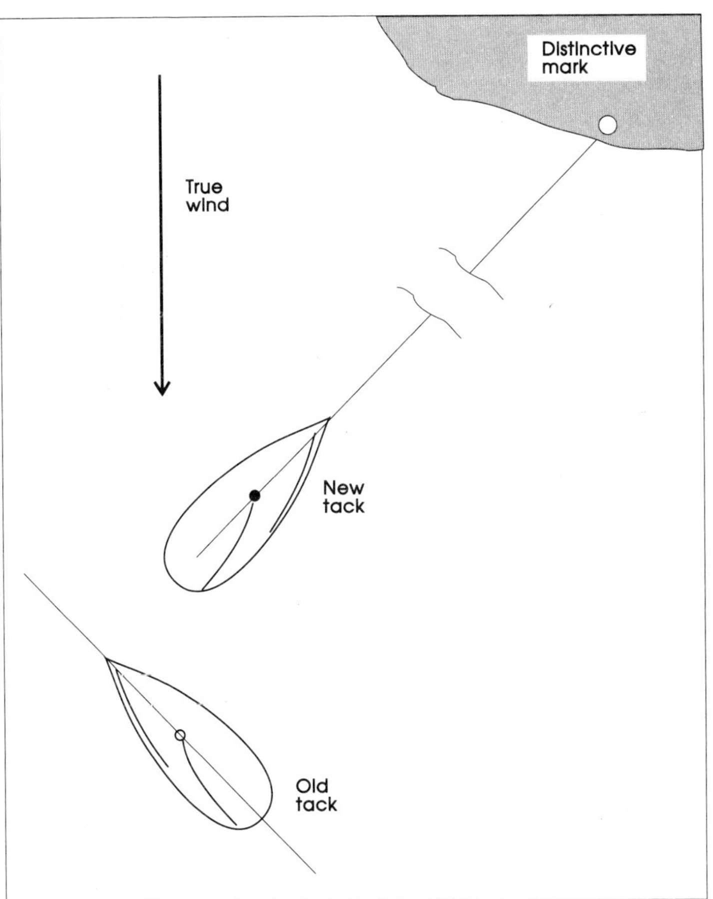

Fig 39. Choosing a mark before tacking.

round and also, if necessary, re-identify his 'mark' for the new course. This will also serve to remind him that he will be altering course by turning the bow into and through the wind, and not by turning the bow away from it. When the crew have the foresail sheets ready for tacking they will reply 'ready'.

The helmsman then cries 'lee-oh' or 'helm's-a-lee' (meaning tiller down to leeward) and proceeds to turn the bow steadily towards and then through the wind. The dinghy sailor will be used to slamming his boat through the tack in three seconds or so, but the process must be carried out much more slowly on a yacht to allow time for handling the foresail sheets. The mainsail sheet moves across to the other tack of its own accord as the apparent wind changes direction. With tiller steering, push the tiller down to leeward steadily to a maximum of 30 degrees from the original position in about two or three seconds. With wheel steering, steadily apply about half a turn over the same period to arrive at the same rudder angle.

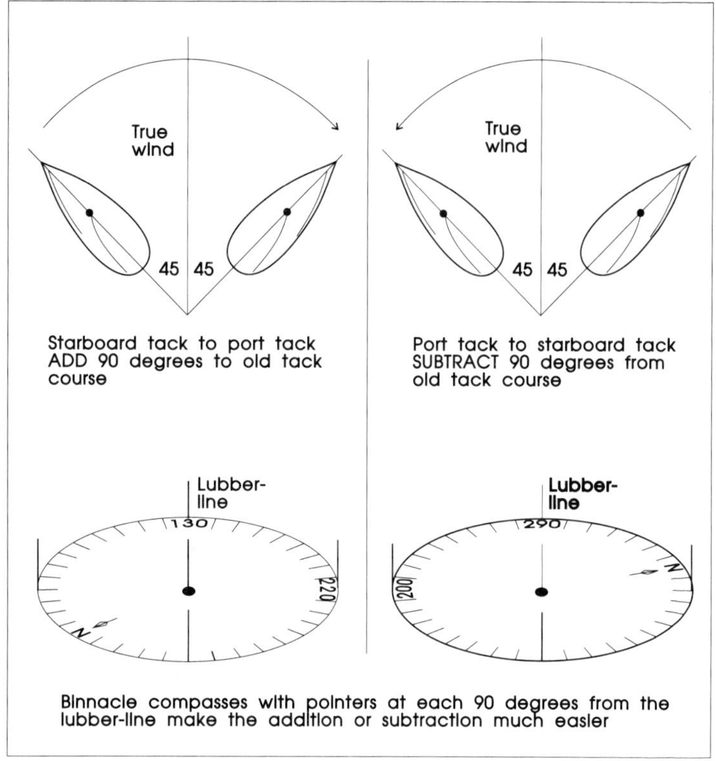

Fig 40. Tacking when steering by compass.

As the yacht's bow turns up into the wind there will be much hustle and bustle as the sails flog noisily and the crew slave away at the winches, but wave noise will decrease as the speed drops and the yacht sits upright. This swing of the bow from 'lee-oh' to head-to-wind should take a little more than five seconds.

On coming head-to-wind, the rudder angle should be held at about 30 degrees. Even so, the bow's rate of swing will have decreased as boat speed drops, but it must not be allowed to become zero or the yacht will 'stall'. As the bow goes through the wind, the rate of swing will suddenly increase. Now quickly bring the tiller or wheel midships to reduce the rate of swing. On bringing the rudder back to midships on a tiller yacht, the helmsman now transfers the tiller to his other hand (behind his back so as not to lose forward vision) ready to move to the new windward side of the cockpit as the yacht heels on the new tack. Anyone in the way must be bundled off unceremoniously; the novice, especially, *must not* be distracted by looking down to see if there is room to move. As the bow swings away from the wind on the new tack, the helmsman should identify his new mark or compass course and adjust the rudder angle to 'home in'. Luff or shroud telltales, etc are then used to sail the yacht to advantage.

Winch crew notwithstanding, the helmsman is the busiest crew member during the tack. His eyes must remain on the bow to monitor the swing, with occasional glances at the chosen mark or compass course to assist him in steadying up for the new course.

The success of the tack depends to a very large extent on the rate of swing as the bow approaches head-to-wind. If the swing becomes too slow the bow may fail to go through the wind; too quick and the crew will have insufficient time for sheet handling. The bow will probably also swing through the new course with even further delay before settling down on the new tack. To assess the correct rate of swing at this critical stage clearly demands the ability to recognise the head-to-wind position. This may not be as obvious to the beginner as it may seem. The wind direction is nearly always where the waves are coming from; this can normally be identified easily before beginning the tack. When head-to-wind, the yacht's heading will be perpendicular to the wave crests, and the yacht will sit upright with the sails flogging. Further, the shroud telltales and the burgee will stream aft and the pointer of the wind direction dial will come on to the bow.

The best and easiest way for a beginner is to use the shroud telltales if you have difficulty in reading the wind direction from the waves. Focusing on to a close-up wind dial is too limiting at this stage.

If the winds are strong, say above force 5, the resultant fairly large waves will stop the yacht surprisingly quickly as she comes head-to-wind. Care must be taken to maintain a slightly faster rate of swing in these conditions to carry the bow through the wind. As a sideline, the only way to stop a yacht, apart from anchoring and bringing her up 'all-standing' in an emergency, is to bring her head-to-wind.

Should you lose the new mark or new compass course as the bow goes through the wind, the only recourse is to transfer attention to the shroud telltale on the new windward side and settle the yacht down on the new tack with the telltale streaming towards you. The helmsman must concentrate on steering the yacht and should not allow himself to be distracted by the furious and sometimes hilarious activities of those operating the winches. However, if a sheet or part of the foresail becomes snagged during the tack, the boat's head should be returned to near head-to-wind until the snag has been cleared.

In normal circumstances, the helmsman should attempt to arrive at head-to-wind in about seven seconds; the natural reaction of the beginner is to arrive there in two or three (and sometimes less!). The whole process from 'lee-oh' to just settled on the new tack should take about half a minute.

SHOOTING THE WIND

Paradoxically, more experienced helmsmen will take a little longer than this since most will attempt to 'shoot the wind'. The purpose of this is to gain as much distance as possible directly to windward (the whole aim of windward sailing) before turning the bow through the wind on to the new tack (Fig 41).

The technique begins as before, except that the initial rudder angle

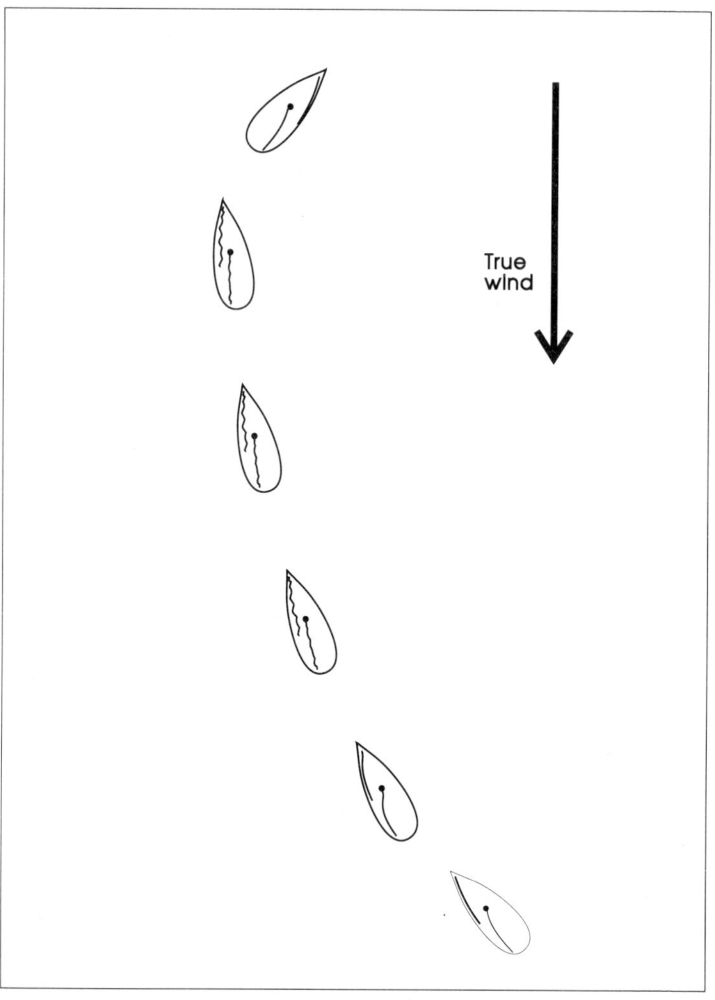

Fig 41. Shooting the wind.

is a little less and is progressively reduced to near zero as the yacht approaches head-to-wind. The boat is then held on this near windward course as long as possible, carried along by her own momentum, making valuable gain upwind, before the bow is finally turned through the wind to bring her on to the new tack.

The manoeuvre requires more than a little skill in judging the right moment to complete the turn. If it is left too late there will be insufficient momentum to carry her through the wind (ie insufficient steerage way) and she will remain head-to-wind with the sails flogging noisily. This is called being caught **in irons** or **in stays** or **missing tacks** (Fig 42).

It is difficult for the beginner to judge when there is just enough steerage way left. The log may not record the boat's speed accurately

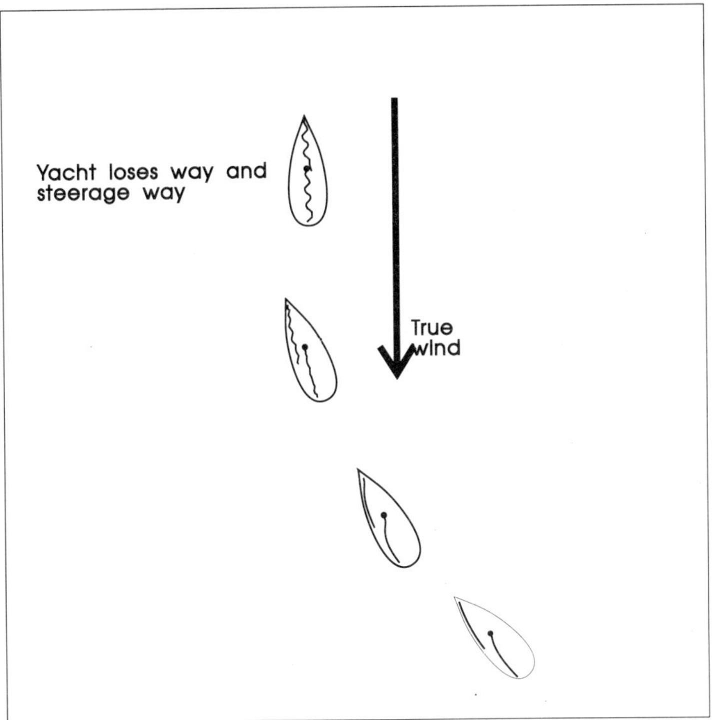

Fig 42. 'In irons' or 'in stays'.

when near the 'stall', and wind and wave noises will combine to give a confusing indication of movement. The judgement is really based on the feel of the rudder which trembles a little as the water continues to flow past it. The remaining steerage way is also tested momentarily at short intervals by small increases in the rudder angle. A glance at the water itself for bubbles or seaweed, etc close to, but clear of the yacht's disturbance, will also give an indication of the yacht's deceleration.

If the turn through the wind is made too soon, the object of the exercise – which is to gain distance to windward – will not be achieved. With strong winds and high seas it is not possible to 'shoot the wind', since the waves will soon stop the yacht.

When carried out correctly there is a gain of several boat lengths directly to windward. This may make all the difference when racing, but even when cruising it is a practical, seamanlike manoeuvre and it is well worthwhile acquiring the skill. Even a beginner should be able to make a reasonable attempt within a few days of general sailing.

Remedial action when caught 'in irons'

When caught in irons the rudder will feel light and will be totally ineffective. The yacht will remain head-to-wind with the sails streaming aft and flogging noisily as they keep the yacht 'weather-cocked'.

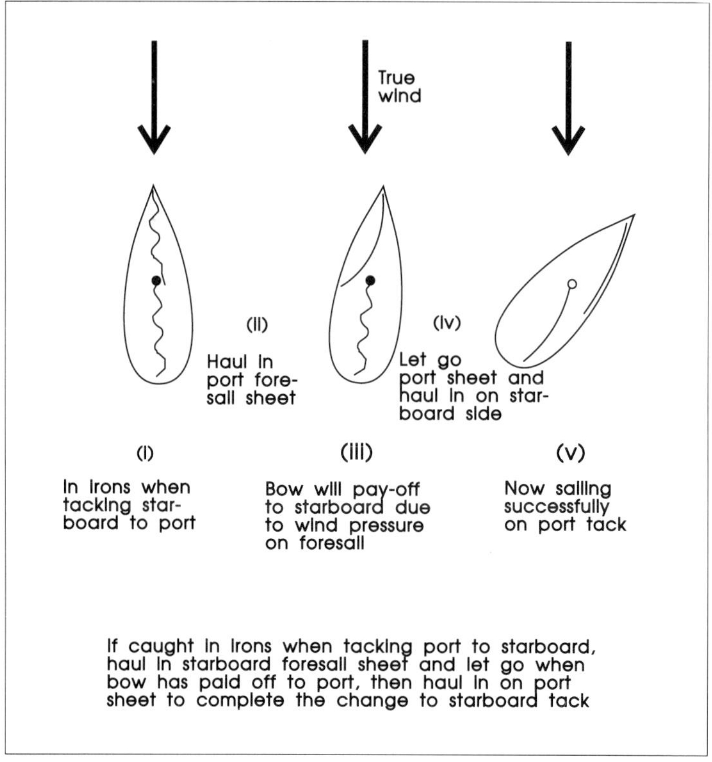

Fig 43. What to do when caught in irons.

Some positive action has to be taken to break the stalemate.

The correct action is to pull in one or other foresail sheet to **back** the foresail, so that the wind will push the bow off, then let go of this sheet and haul in on the other one to sail off on the new tack (Fig 43).

Which sheet is initially pulled in depends on which will be the new tack. If caught in irons when changing from port to starboard tack, haul in on the starboard sheet until the bow has turned towards the new tack direction, then let go and sheet in on the port side to sail off on starboard tack. If changing from starboard to port tack then the port sheet is hauled in first (Fig 43). Meantime, in both cases, the rudder should remain midships until the bow has been turned away from the wind.

EMERGENCY TACK

Sometimes the yacht has to be tacked instantly in order to avoid a collision or going aground. In these circumstances, the urgency will be indicated in the skipper's order 'tack now!' There is no time for a 'ready about', nor should any attempt be made to shoot the wind. Here, exceptionally, the bow should be swung through the wind as quickly as possible even as the helmsman is calling 'lee-oh', leaving the crew to sort out the sheets after the tack when the yacht is no longer in danger. These circumstances normally arise through someone's neglect, either on your yacht or the other vessel.

HEAVING-TO

A variation of this manoeuvre occurs when it becomes necessary to stop the boat, without the sails flogging in the head-to-wind position, in order to sort out some problem or even to have a quiet cup of tea! The requirement may or may not contain an element of urgency and so may be carried out briskly or in a more gentle fashion. In order to heave-to, the helmsman simply calls out 'heaving-to'. After checking around for other vessels in the vicinity, he then calls 'lee-oh' and turns the bow steadily through the wind as if tacking the boat. No

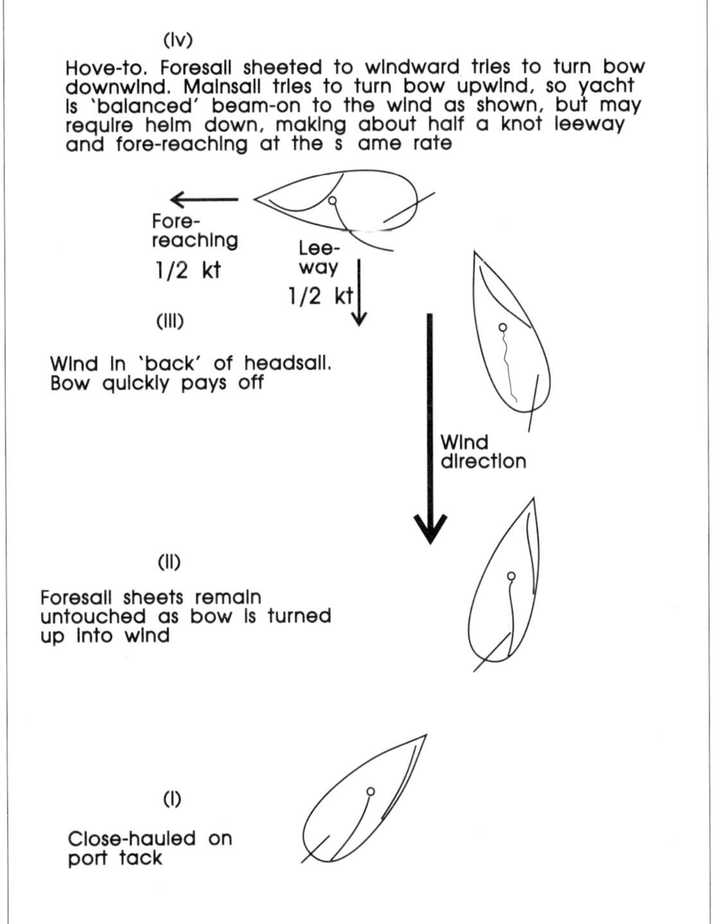

(iv)
Hove-to. Foresail sheeted to windward tries to turn bow downwind. Mainsail tries to turn bow upwind, so yacht is 'balanced' beam-on to the wind as shown, but may require helm down, making about half a knot leeway and fore-reaching at the s ame rate
Fore-reaching
1/2 kt
Lee-way
1/2 kt
(iii)
Wind in 'back' of headsail. Bow quickly pays off
Wind direction
(ii)
Foresail sheets remain untouched as bow is turned up into wind
(i)
Close-hauled on port tack

Fig 44. Heaving-to from port tack.

action is required on the foresail sheets. As a consequence the foresail will 'back' as the bow goes through the wind (Fig 44). Wind pressure in the backed foresail will accelerate the rate of turn and there is little that the helmsman can, or need, do to reduce this because the sails have now taken over control of the turn.

The yacht will stop turning when the wind lies more or less on the beam. After the bustle of the beat, all is now almost silent with the boat apparently stopped, the foresail attempting to turn the bow further off the wind, while the mainsail provides the balancing, opposite effect. This balanced state is normally only achieved by easing out the main and putting the helm down (Fig 44). In practice, the yacht will not be stopped but will be **fore-reaching ahead** at about half a knot and will be making a similar amount of leeway.

Rights of way still apply when hove-to. If there is a choice, the yacht should be hove-to on starboard tack – boom out to port – to retain right of way over port tack vessels. When finished with heaving-to, let go the foresail sheet and haul in on the other to sail away on a new tack or gybe round to sail away on the old tack.

FEATHERING

A yacht is stopped dead by turning head to wind in order, say, to avoid a close-call collision situation and allow the other vessel to get clear. With more distance to spare, a variation of this drastic

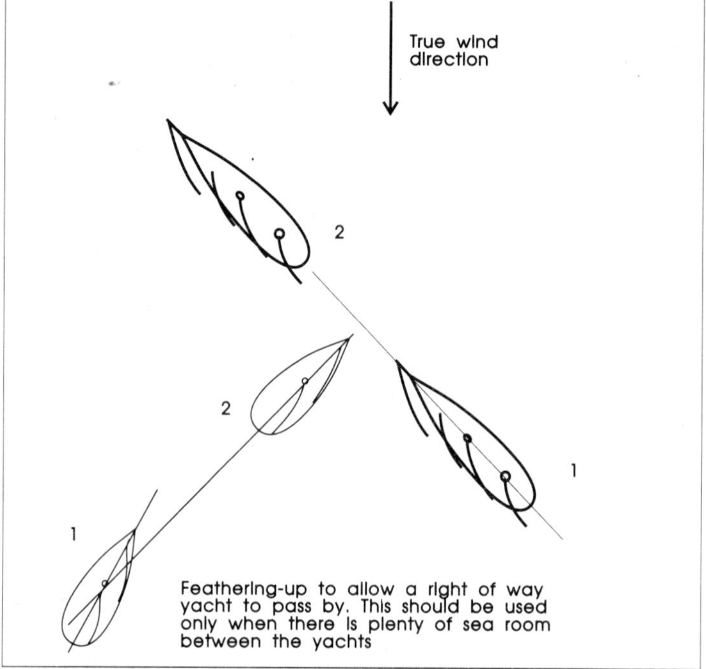

True wind direction
2
2
1
1
Feathering-up to allow a right of way yacht to pass by. This should be used only when there is plenty of sea room between the yachts

Fig 45. Feathering.

manoeuvre is to **feather-up** towards the wind in order to slow the yacht to allow a right of way vessel to pass clear ahead (Fig 45). The technique is to ease the boat up into the wind a little beyond the pinching position, so that she begins to sit more upright and the luff of the foresail 'lifts' along its whole length; then hold her there. The yacht's speed will be reduced by about half.

The manoeuvre should not be used to allow a vessel to pass close to leeward, because when feathering-up the helmsman has less control of the steering, and his only way to regain control quickly is to bear away to leeward – which would develop rather than avoid a collision risk. The decision to stop or feather-up is the skipper's.

It is also bad seamanship to feather-up in order to pass to windward of a buoy or similar object. Wind and tide may combine to set the yacht on to the object anyway. Better by far to warn the skipper some time beforehand that you are unlikely to 'weather' the buoy. You will then normally be directed to pass on the downwind or downtide side of the buoy.

In a man overboard situation the helm will be immediately taken over by the most senior person on deck, so the helming procedure is beyond the scope of this section. However, the sail and deckwork, together with a brief account of how the boat is steered back, is given on pages 120–122.

WEATHER HELM AND LEE HELM

No account of steering a sailing yacht could be complete without describing weather helm and lee helm. It has already been mentioned that the setting of the sails alone may influence the steering of a yacht. In fact, it is possible to tack and gybe a yacht using sails alone and thus turn her through a complete circle, but this too is beyond the scope of this book.

It is vital on any point of sailing, but none more so than when sailing to windward, that the sail rig should be balanced, ie there is no net turning effect from the sails. A well-balanced sail trim will allow a yacht to sail on the same course for some time without touching the helm, no matter what her keel configuration may be. Figure 46 shows the relevant forces acting on the sails. Though both sails drive the boat forward, each produces an athwartships component of the wind force. Both these components try to turn the boat, but in opposite directions; the foresail tries to turn the bow **away from**, while the mainsail tries to turn it **towards** the wind. This may be demonstrated easily when reaching across the wind by first letting out the mainsail sheet and then, after sheeting the main in again, easing out on the foresail sheet (Fig 47).

If the sail plan is not balanced, one sail or the other will produce a net turning effect. If this turns the bow towards the wind (mainsail dominant) then continuous helm will have to be applied to keep the yacht on the correct course. This is inefficient since the rudder will be acting as a brake, so boat speed will decrease. Further, in strong winds the amount of rudder angle required will soon exhaust the

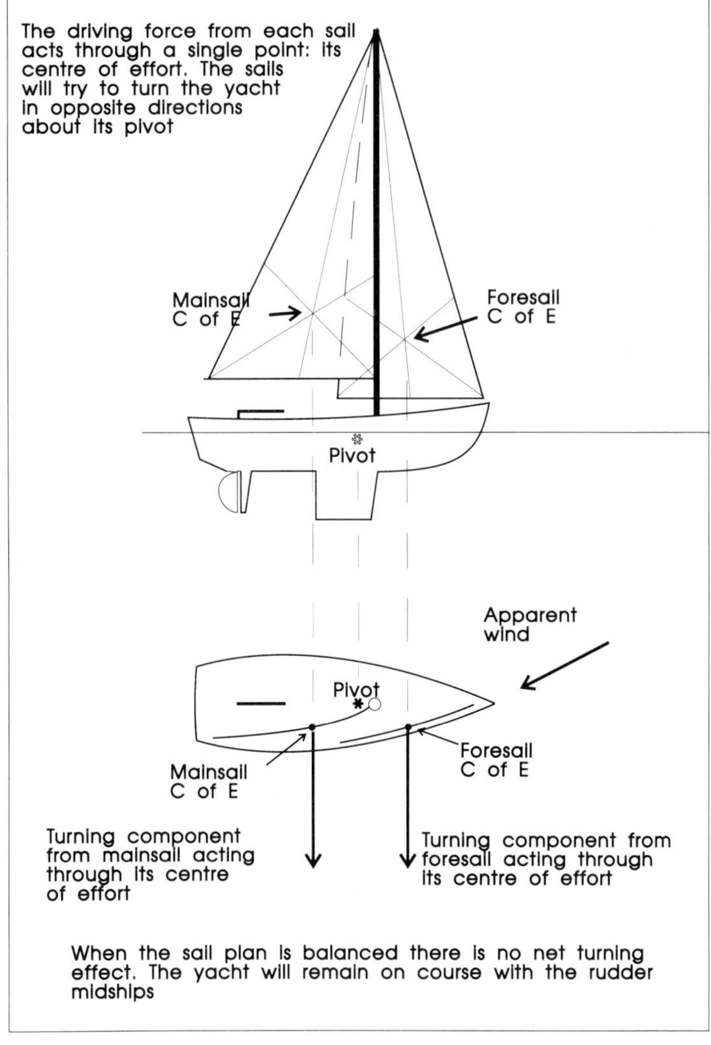

The driving force from each sail acts through a single point: its centre of effort. The sails will try to turn the yacht in opposite directions about its pivot
Mainsail C of E
Foresail C of E
Pivot
Apparent wind
Pivot
Foresail C of E
Mainsail C of E
Turning component from mainsail acting through its centre of effort
Turning component from foresail acting through its centre of effort
When the sail plan is balanced there is no net turning effect. The yacht will remain on course with the rudder midships

Fig 46. Balanced sail plan.

helmsman. On a tiller yacht, in the example just given, the tiller would have to be held up to windward, or to **weather**, in order to prevent the bow from turning up into the wind. This is **weather helm** (Fig 48). With wheel steering, the top of the wheel would have to be constantly turned away from the wind.

If the foresail effect is dominant, then correcting helm would have to be applied to prevent the bow from turning away from the wind. The tiller would have to be held down to **leeward** (Fig 49) or the top of the wheel turned towards the wind. This is **lee helm**.

The effect experienced by the helmsman is thus:

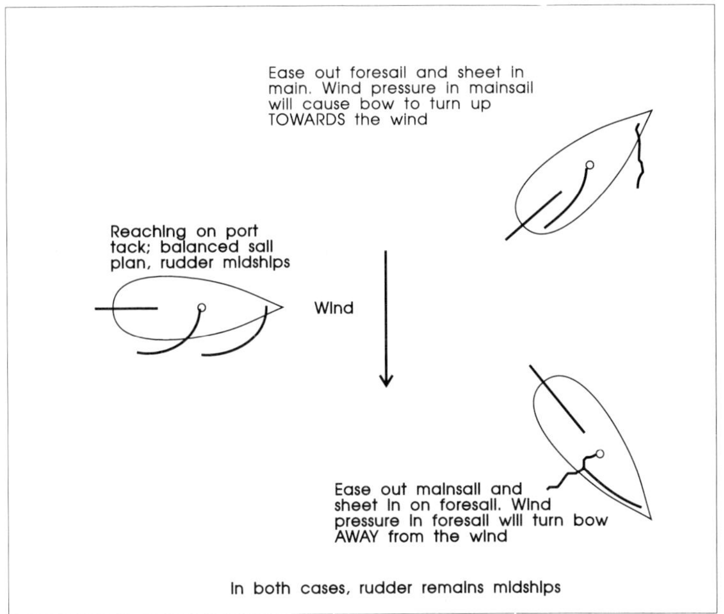

Ease out foresail and sheet in main. Wind pressure in mainsail will cause bow to turn up TOWARDS the wind
Reaching on port tack; balanced sail plan, rudder midships
Wind
Ease out mainsail and sheet in on foresail. Wind pressure in foresail will turn bow AWAY from the wind
In both cases, rudder remains midships

Fig 47. Using sails to turn the yacht.

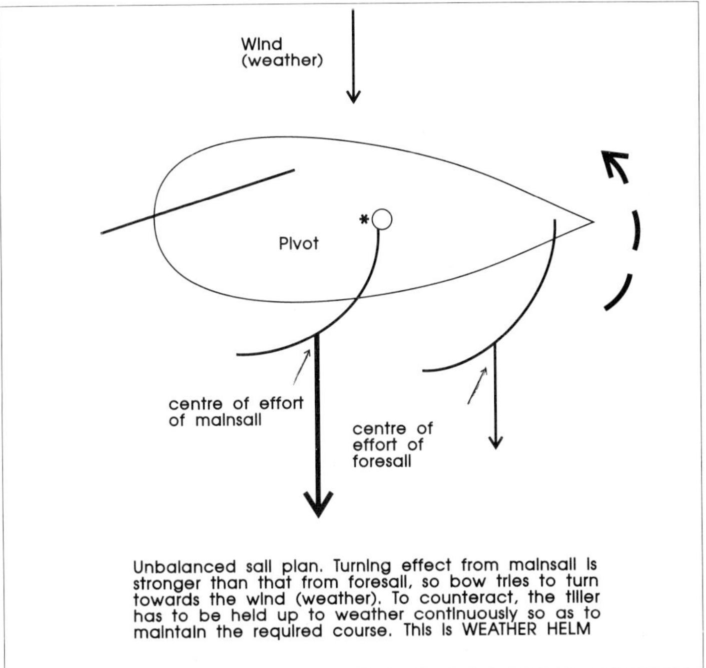

Wind (weather)
Pivot
centre of effort of mainsail
centre of effort of foresail
Unbalanced sail plan. Turning effect from mainsail is stronger than that from foresail, so bow tries to turn towards the wind (weather). To counteract, the tiller has to be held up to weather continuously so as to maintain the required course. This is WEATHER HELM

Fig 48. Weather helm.

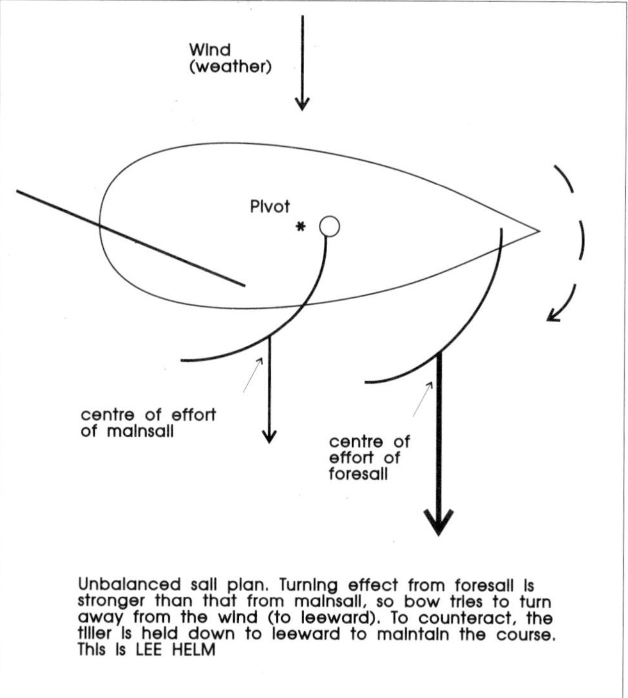
Wind
(weather)
Pivot
centre of effort
of mainsail
centre of
effort of
foresail
Unbalanced sail plan. Turning effect from foresail is stronger than that from mainsail, so bow tries to turn away from the wind (to leeward). To counteract, the tiller is held down to leeward to maintain the course. This is LEE HELM

Fig 49. Lee helm.

If the wheel has to be turned *away* from the wind, or the tiller held up to **windward (weather)**, in order to maintain the correct course, the yacht is carrying **weather helm**.

If the wheel has to be turned *towards* the wind, or the tiller held down to **leeward**, in order to maintain the correct course, the yacht is carrying **lee helm**.

The removal of either effect is beyond the scope of this book, though essentially the remedy is to reduce the foresail area if lee helm is carried, and to reduce the area of the mainsail if weather helm is present.

Though some of this is outside competent crew work, the effects will have to be understood since the skipper will want to know whether the yacht feels right and the best person to assess these effects is the helmsman.

But enough of this plodding theory on ropes, knots, sailing theory and steering. It is time now to prepare for leaving harbour at the beginning of our cruise.

LEAVING · HARBOUR ·

The yacht is already prepared for sea (see pages 11–14) so the skipper gathers the crew down below to brief them on the day's cruise from a chart spread out on the navigator's bench. We are in Gosport and the overall plan is to sail across to the Isle of Wight, anchor for lunch in Osborne Bay, then sail on to Yarmouth. At dusk we shall leave Yarmouth for a few hours of night sailing before mooring at the marina in Cowes (Figs 50 and 51).

The charts may seem confusing at first but there will normally be several occasions during a 5-day cruise to discuss the vast amount of information they reveal. The chart colours cannot be reproduced in this book but you should know that permanent land is coloured yellow, land which is uncovered by the falling tide is green, shallow water is blue and deeper water is white.

Depths are given in metres and tenths. These may be interpreted as minimum depths to which we need to add the height of the tide for the particular time. The black lines are depth contours and they are labelled in metres. Some of these lines are edged in blue. The nature of the seabed is indicated by initial letters, eg 'm' for mud; this is important for anchoring. There is no common scale for charts as there is with many road maps. However, the latitude scale on the two side edges of the chart automatically gives the scale since one degree of latitude equals 60 nautical miles, so one minute of latitude equals one nautical mile. A knot is a speed of one nautical mile per hour.

The weather forecast is favourable with a fresh north westerly breeze backing south by this evening, and strengthening from the west or south west for a time this afternoon. The weather is expected to remain fine and the visibility good. So the skipper has decided that we shall use the full mainsail and our largest foresail (the No 1 genoa). It is as well here to pause for a moment to note foresail names, because they are numerous.

Generically, they are commonly called **foresails** and almost as commonly **headsails**. The largest are known as **genoas**, numbered from large to small. Smaller headsails are called **jibs** and are similarly numbered. This simplified account is displayed in Fig 52, page 86.

We shall also need a Tidal Stream Atlas for the area (Fig 53, page 87) to show us how the water is moving at any given time.

Besides the skipper and the mate, there are three other novice crew and you.

After clearing Camper and Nicholson's marina, the plan is to turn head-to-wind to hoist the mainsail, then proceed out of the harbour under engine using the small boat channel on the western side, and

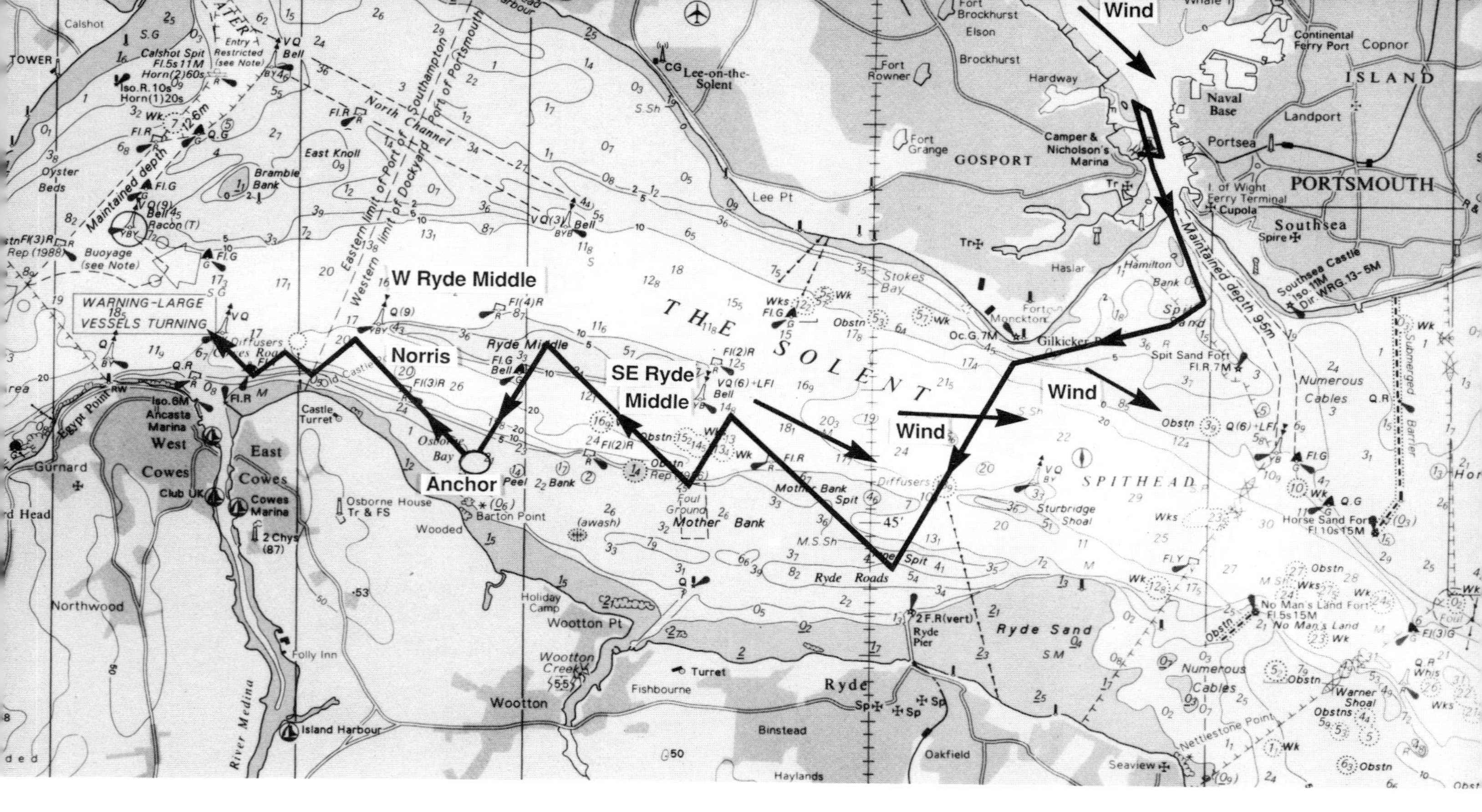

(Above) Fig 50 East Solent, morning

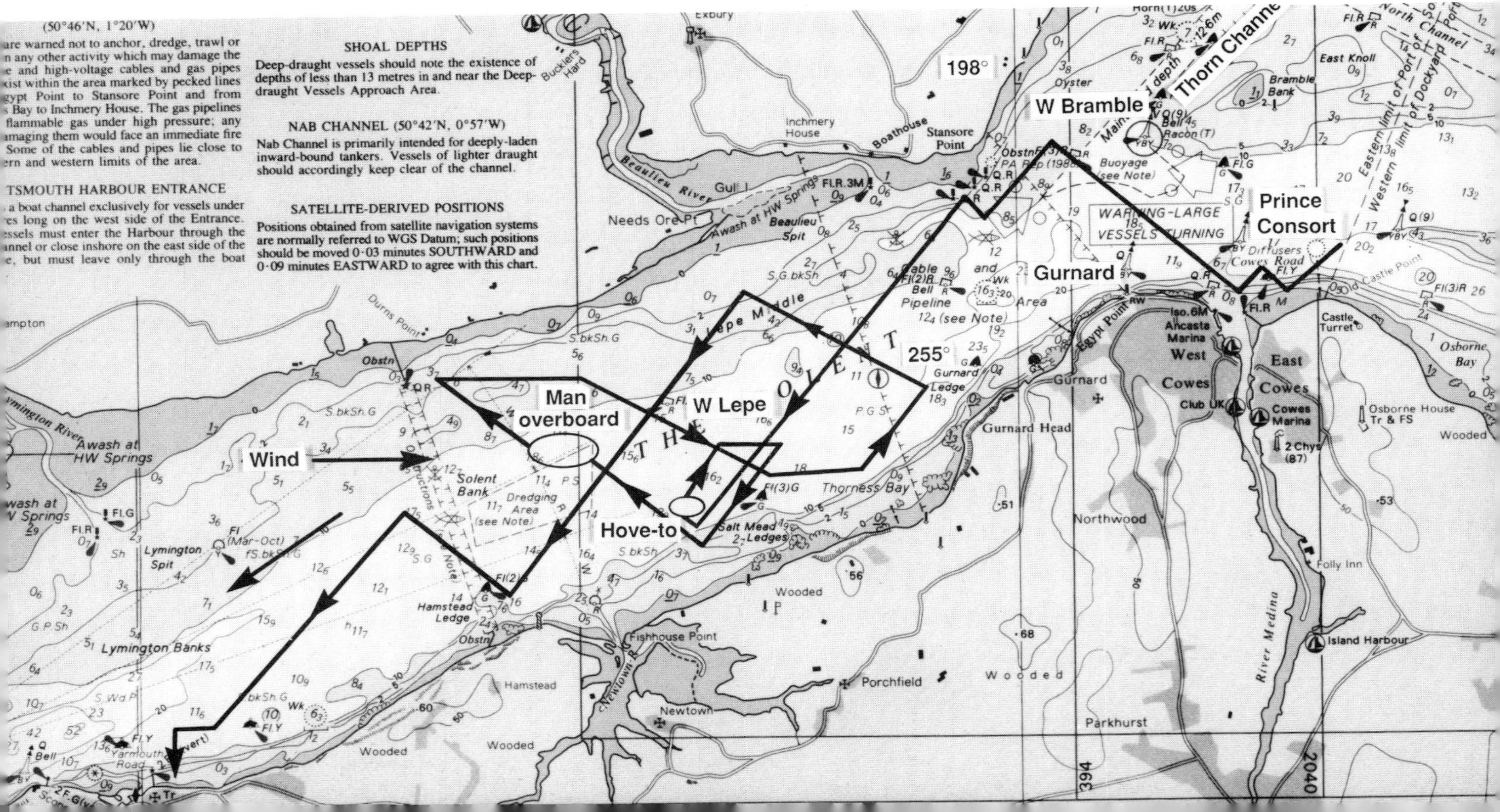

(50°46'N, 1°20'W)
are warned not to anchor, dredge, trawl or
n any other activity which may damage the
e and high-voltage cables and gas pipes
xist within the area marked by pecked lines
gypt Point to Stansore Point and from
s Bay to Inchmery House. The gas pipelines
flammable gas under high pressure; any
amaging them would face an immediate fire
Some of the cables and pipes lie close to
ern and western limits of the area.
TSMOUTH HARBOUR ENTRANCE
a boat channel exclusively for vessels under
es long on the west side of the Entrance.
essels must enter the Harbour through the
annel or close inshore on the east side of the
e, but must leave only through the boat
SHOAL DEPTHS
Deep-draught vessels should note the existence of depths of less than 13 metres in and near the Deep-draught Vessels Approach Area.
NAB CHANNEL (50°42'N, 0°57'W)
Nab Channel is primarily intended for deeply-laden inward-bound tankers. Vessels of lighter draught should accordingly keep clear of the channel.
SATELLITE-DERIVED POSITIONS
Positions obtained from satellite navigation systems are normally referred to WGS Datum; such positions should be moved 0·03 minutes SOUTHWARD and 0·09 minutes EASTWARD to agree with this chart.
198°
W Bramble
Thorn Channel
Prince Consort
Gurnard
255°
W Lepe
Man overboard
Hove-to
Wind
WARNING-LARGE VESSELS TURNING
THE SOLENT
Beaulieu River
Stansore Point
Needs Ore Pt
Inchmery House
Exbury
Bucklers Hard
Durns Point
Lymington River
Lymington Spit
Lymington Banks
Hamstead Ledge
Hamstead
Newtown
Fishhouse Point
Porchfield
Thorness Bay
Salt Mead Ledges
Gurnard Ledge
Gurnard Head
Egypt Point
Northwood
Parkhurst
West Cowes
East Cowes
Cowes Road
Castle Turret
Osborne Bay
Osborne House
Cowes Marina
Ancasta Marina
Club UK
Folly Inn
Island Harbour
River Medina
Bramble Bank
East Knoll
North Channel
Eastern limit of Port of Dockyard
Western limit of Port
Solent Bank
Dredging Area (see Note)
Cable and Pipeline Area
Lepe Middle
Oyster
Yarmouth Road
Wooded
394
2040

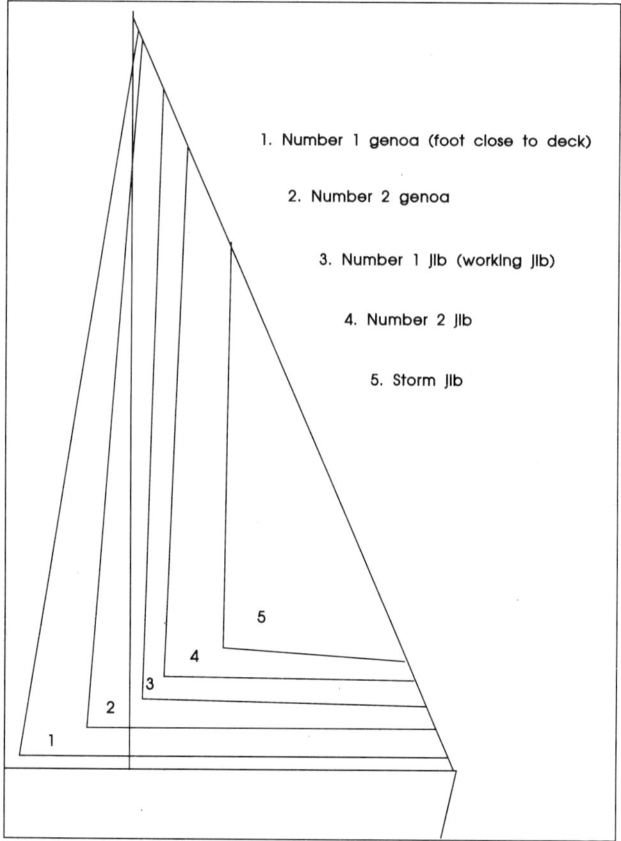

Fig 52. Typical range of foresails.

only then hoist the foresail in the buoyed channel outside the harbour. (The foresail would restrict visibility too seriously in the busy narrows at the entrance. Further, the foresail is always hoist after the main, otherwise it would hinder the crew around the mast when the yacht is head-to-wind.) As it will then be only a little past low water, we shall proceed down the main channel before turning right into the channel between Hamilton Bank and Spit Bank (Fig 54). The north westerly wind will then allow us to sail directly towards Osborne Bay but as it backs into the west we shall have to tack during the latter stages.

The yacht being in all respects ready for sea, we shall first ensure that we are wearing the right clothing for the trip and that all our gear is safely stowed in lockers, etc and not left on bunks, shelves and the like, because the motion of the boat will throw any unstowed item on to the cabin sole. The sun is shining and there is little cloud so, since the forecast is for dry weather and since wind speeds are not expected to be strong enough to generate rough seas in the Solent, it is probably sufficient to wear warm trousers and sweater for it is late autumn

CAUTION:— Due to the very strong rates of the tidal streams in some of the areas covered by this Atlas, many eddies may occur. Where possible some indication of these eddies has been included. In many areas there is either insufficient information or the eddies are unstable.

4	**BEFORE** HW PORTSMOUTH
	3h 30m before HW DOVER

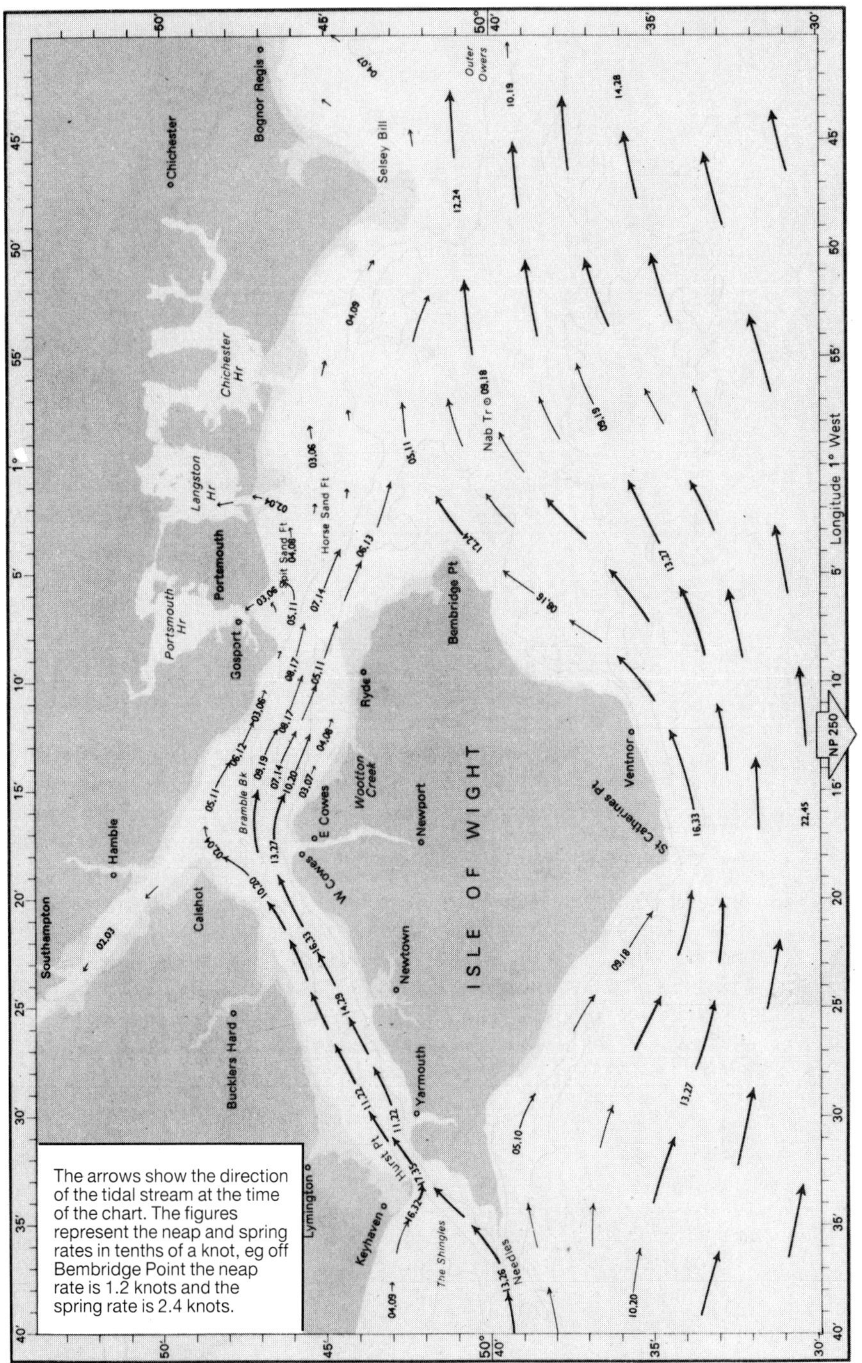

The arrows show the direction of the tidal stream at the time of the chart. The figures represent the neap and spring rates in tenths of a knot, eg off Bembridge Point the neap rate is 1.2 knots and the spring rate is 2.4 knots.

Fig 53. Tidal Stream Atlas – Solent.

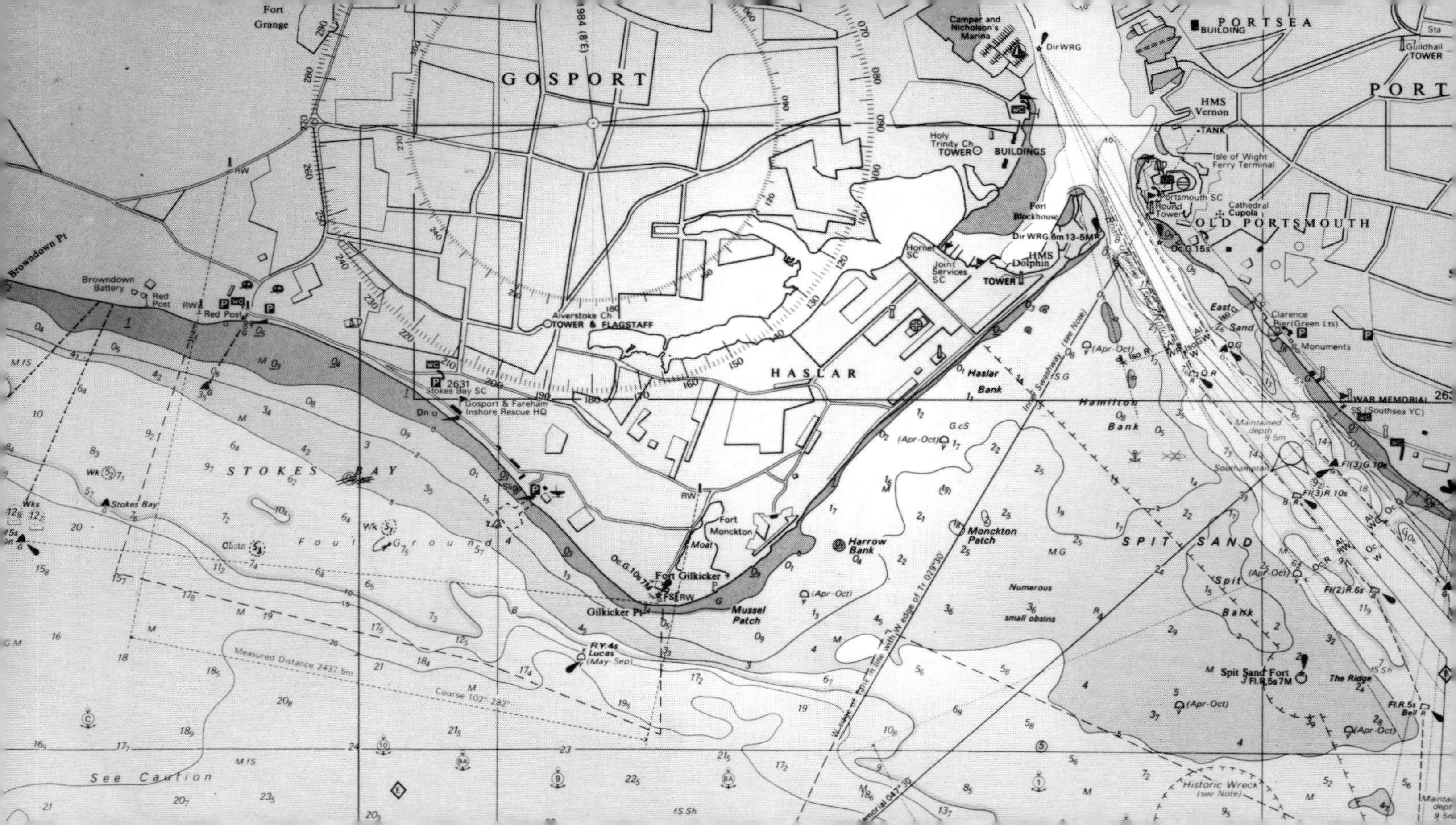

GOSPORT
PORTSEA
OLD PORTSMOUTH
HASLAR
STOKES BAY
SPIT SAND
Fort Grange
Browndown Pt
Browndown Battery
Red Post
Alverstoke Ch TOWER & FLAGSTAFF
Stokes Bay SC
Gosport & Fareham Inshore Rescue HQ
Holy Trinity Ch TOWER
BUILDINGS
Camper and Nicholson's Marina
HMS Vernon
Isle of Wight Ferry Terminal
Portsmouth SC
Round Tower
Cathedral Cupola
Fort Blockhouse
HMS Dolphin
Hornet SC
Joint Services SC
Clarence Pier (Green Lts)
Monuments
WAR MEMORIAL
SS (Southsea YC)
Guildhall TOWER
Haslar Bank
Hamilton Bank
Inner Swashway (see Note)
Fort Monckton
Moat
Fort Gilkicker
Gilkicker Pt
Mussel Patch
Harrow Bank
Monckton Patch
Numerous small obstns
Foul Ground
Spit Bank
Spit Sand Fort
The Ridge
East Sand
Historic Wreck (see Note)
Measured Distance 2437.5m
Course 102°-282°
Lucas
Fl.Y.4s (May-Sep)
See Caution
Maintained depth 9.5m

and the sea is still relatively warm. However, oilskins and yachting boots should be left tidily to hand in case they may be required, for when the yacht has to beat, it is surprising how much spray comes over her, even as far astern as the cockpit.

All hands are summoned to watch the engine starting procedure and the engine will be given a few minutes to warm up. Meantime, the skipper will appoint various crew members to the mooring lines. The departure is straightforward with the yacht being driven astern, once all the mooring lines are clear, out of a U-shaped basin formed by the pontoons.

'Standby springs!' alerts those responsible to prepare to let go the springs. At the order 'let go springs!' they remove them and stow them after coiling up. The yacht is now held by the bow and stern mooring warps which have already been doubled-back on to the yacht (see pages 13–14, page 27). You have been detailed to look after the bow mooring warp so you will already be on the foredeck when 'standby fore and aft lines!' is called. Both you and the stern warp hand will then see that your warps are ready to run. When both these warps were earlier doubled back from the pontoon, the one end of each was left fairly short over its own separate cleat. The figure of eight turns on this end are now removed from the cleat but the initial round turn is left on to take any strain. Having done this look back to the skipper to await his casting-off order. He will interpret your gaze as being ready.

Since the yacht will leave using stern power, the stern warp will now be let go. The skipper may well ask you to 'haul in gently forward' in order to ease the stern away from the pontoon to facilitate the departure. Take the round turn on the short end of the warp off the cleat and gently haul in. Keep looking back at the skipper who will shout 'let go forward!' when the clearing angle is sufficient. Let go the short end of the warp immediately and haul in hand-over-hand on the doubled-back part; shout 'all gone!' when the end is back on deck. (If it has snagged on the pontoon fitting then you must shout 'snagged!' immediately so that the departure may be aborted with some dignity.) Once clear, the warp is coiled and stowed away.

On leaving the pontoon other crew members will have been detailed to fend off as necessary since yachts are sometimes difficult to steer astern until there is reasonable stern-way. Once in the main channel within the marina, the yacht is swung round and ahead power is engaged. The mate is detailed to act as lookout on the foredeck for we are still within the marina and small tenders crossing ahead of the yacht will probably be invisible to the skipper at the helm. The remainder of the crew are asked to stow the fenders. Bring the fender inboard, then grasp the lanyard with one hand and undo the knot with the other before stowing the fender in its locker.

By now the yacht has cleared the marina and is out in the relatively open space of Portsmouth harbour. A large ferry is just leaving the terminal on the other side of the harbour. Once it has passed clear

Fig 54. Entrance to Portsmouth harbour.

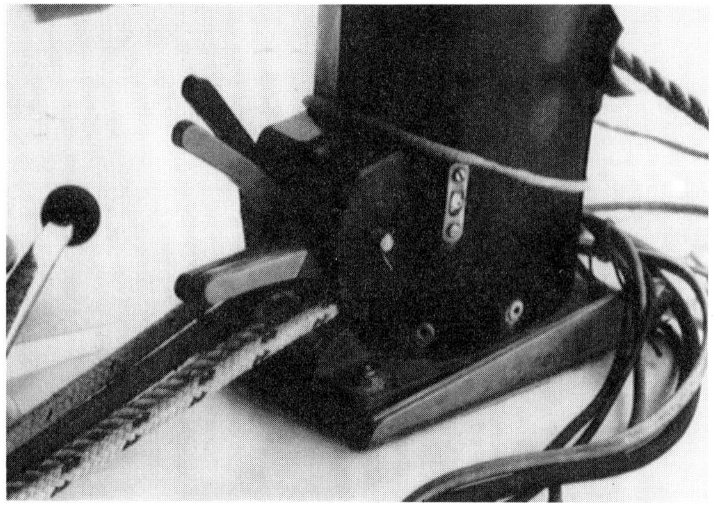

Photo 16. Jamming cleat.

ahead, there being no other large ship movements, the skipper orders 'stand-by to hoist the main!' and turns the yacht head-to-wind. This manoeuvre is necessary to prevent the luff of the sail jamming in the groove in the mast. You have been detailed as the halyard winch hand, and while the others are removing the ties securing the furled sail to the boom and attaching the halyard shackle to the head of the mainsail under the mate's supervision, you, in the cockpit, will ensure that the fall of the halyard is released from its jamming cleat (Photo 16) and that its winch is clear.

When the order 'hoist!' is given, haul away swiftly hand-over-hand, and keep looking up to see that the luff is running smoothly up

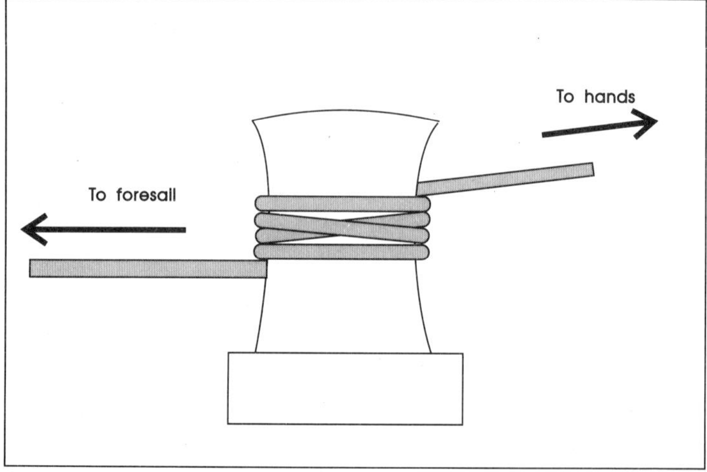

Fig 55. A riding turn on the foresail sheet.

the mast. The hauling will gradually become more difficult as the halyard takes on the weight of the sail. When the effort begins to become too great, take a turn round the winch and continue to haul away by hand. Eventually this also becomes too heavy, so take another two turns around the winch, making sure the strain is kept on as these turns are made and also checking that each turn sits properly above its predecessor on the winch barrel so that there are no overlapping riding turns (Fig 55).

Engage the winch handle and crank away steadily until the skipper is satisfied with the tension in the sail's luff. Then lock the halyard in its jamming cleat and, after stowing the winch handle, remove the turns from the winch to free it for its next task. (The jamming cleat will hold the halyard in place.) Check that the stopper (or figure of eight) knot is pulled up tight about 30–50 cm from the end, then loosely coil the fall of the halyard, without securing turns, and place it on the cockpit sole or in a convenient cockpit pocket if there is one.

While you have been tidying up the halyard, the mate will have supervised the easing away of the topping lift (see Fig 1b) because the weight of the boom is now carried by the mainsail. Since the boat has been head-to-wind so far, the mainsail will have flogged noisily as it was hoist, causing the outer end of the boom to jerk up and down because the mainsheet has been free. The next step is to haul in on the mainsheet to stop most of this fuss. The skipper has directed you to do this since you are already in the cockpit, so quickly locate the free end of the sheet, and disengage it from its cleat. Then pull in hand-over-hand until the slack is taken up.

Now that the mainsail is under control, the skipper, still at the helm, will turn the yacht round through the wind to head for the harbour entrance. He asks for the mainsheet to be eased out as the bow passes through the wind; as you are the nearest you will uncleat the main and ease it out steadily until the skipper calls enough. As you look up you will observe that an inverted black cone has been hoist at the yardarm; this indicates that the yacht is still a power-driven vessel even though a sail is hoist.

We are now broad-reaching on starboard tack through Portsmouth harbour. Though there are a few frigates and destroyers in the dockyard, the eastern side of the harbour is dominated by the masts and rigging of Nelson's *Victory* and there are numerous other signs of the long history of this important dockyard. But this is not a harbour cruise and there is work to do as we approach the harbour entrance, because there are many shipping movements towards the narrows.

The yacht is already in the small boat channel on the western side of the entrance. There are other outbound yachts ahead and astern, as well as a few inbound yachts which are using the eastern side of this restricted small boat channel. The skipper has temporarily altered course a little to allow the Gosport to Portsmouth ferry to pass clear ahead, and is now back on course, but there are three Isle of Wight ferries which would appear to converge on the harbour entrance just as we arrive there. He has decided to slow the boat down by first sheeting the main right in, thus presenting a smaller sail area to the wind, and then reducing engine power. The passenger ferry for Ryde has already accelerated clear of our area, the incoming car ferry has turned into its basin and the outgoing car ferry is already turning to make its exit some 100 metres ahead of us. Increased engine power accelerates the yacht towards the exit, but, since the wind is often 'fluky' in the lee of Fort Blockhouse, the mainsail remains sheeted in and firmly under control.

All of a sudden we are out of the confines of the harbour and into the expanse of the eastern Solent, but because it is near low water, we shall remain within the buoyed channel for a while rather than cut the corner using the Inner Swashway (Fig 54). We can easily see that the deep water channel is marked by a line of red can-shaped buoys on our right hand and by a line of green conical-shaped buoys on our left. The convention for these buoys is that they are arranged with green buoys on the starboard side of the channel and red on the port *according to the direction of the incoming tide*. We, of course, are going against this direction, so the buoys appear on the opposite side for us.

The mainsail is now eased out to the broad-reaching position as before, and there being no other vessels in our vicinity, the skipper calls 'standby to hoist foresail!' Your job is to assist with this task on the foredeck, so you climb out of the cockpit (either side will do as the boat is almost level). Crouch a little as you move forward (in order to keep your centre of gravity as low as practical so as to reduce the risk of falling overboard) with one hand holding on to grabrail, shroud or mast – or even the top lifeline, though this is not entirely reliable. Do not hold a sheet or halyard for these may be adjusted without notice. The No 1 genoa is already bent on and secured along the lifelines on the starboard side (see page 13). But we are still on starboard tack, and so the foresail, when hoist, will set on the **port** side. The safe thing is to move it across to the port side before hoisting so as not to endanger the foredeck crew.

So, under the mate's direction, you remove the ties securing the sail, stuff them in your pocket or secure them to the lifelines, then carry the sail across to the port side. The mate hands you the shackle end of the foresail halyard and asks you to attach it to the head of the sail. After calling for a little slack in the halyard from the cockpit hand, you walk forward, still slightly crouched, ensuring that the halyard remains reasonably taut, so that it will not foul up on the yardarms nor become twisted around the forestay, and secure the shackle to the head of the sail. Check that the shackle is closed properly. You are now crouched in the bows with the head of the foresail in your hand, held low to maintain some strain on the halyard as before; your next task is to see that the sail runs smoothly on hoisting. The forestay is covered with an aluminium foil which contains a groove to take the luff of the sail. Feed the head of the luff into this groove and look astern to await the hoisting instruction. When this comes, let go the head of the sail and stand back to see that the first few metres of the luff run up smoothly before retiring to the cockpit, where another novice is hauling away at the halyard. (On some yachts there is no foil so the foresail is hoist directly on the forestay by means of a series of clips called 'piston hanks' which would be attached to the forestay, in the correct order, when the sail was bent on.)

When the sail is fully hoist and its halyard made up, the foresail sheets will have to be seen to for they, as well as the sail itself, will be flogging noisily. Since the wind is blowing from the starboard quarter, the foresail will be controlled by the port sheet. Grab this and, taking a turn round its winch, haul away to remove the slack. As the load becomes heavier, take successive turns and let the winch take the strain. Never attempt to fight the full strain with only one or two turns on the winch.

As we are broad-reaching, the sail will be properly set after only a little hauling in, so there is no need to resort to the winch handle. When the skipper is satisfied with this set, maintain the strain on the fall of the sheet as you secure this to the nearest cleat; one round turn and one figure of eight is enough. The engine is turned off and the black cone lowered from the yardarm.

Suddenly it is very quiet, just a few rigging sounds, and the swish of the water against the hull. We are sailing! This is what it is all about!

· CRUISING ·

Spit Sand, the bank on the western side of the channel, is interrupted by a shallow channel, or swashway, which we shall use, opposite the war memorial at Southsea (see Fig 54). This swashway is not buoyed, but the transit (see pages 42–3) of the war memorial and St Jude's church spire provides a safe leading line. Numerous yachts ahead of us are turning into the swashway.

As the transit marks begin to close up more quickly, the skipper calls 'standby to sheet in on both sails!' You have been allocated the foresail sheet, so you place one hand on the taut sheet close to the cleat to prevent it slipping round the winch, and take the turns off the cleat. When the transit marks are almost in line, the skipper steadily turns the yacht through about 90 degrees and calls 'sheet in!'

The sails will flog almost as soon as the yacht is turned closer to the wind. When broad-reaching, the strain on the sheet is much less than when closer to the wind, so at first you will be able to haul in the sheet by hand. Since there are three or four turns on the winch, it is important that you begin hauling in as soon as the sail and the sheet begin to shake and then haul in progressively to keep them 'quiet', otherwise a riding turn on the winch will almost certainly occur and the sheet will jam. A further tip to avoid a riding turn is to see that the direction of pull on the tail of the sheet is slightly above the perpendicular to the winch barrel (Fig 56).

When the turn has been executed and there is no more shaking of the sails, take a turn round the cleat, but still hold the tail and look back. You will see the skipper steering the yacht by looking astern to keep on the transit line. Once across the narrow bank he will abandon the transit and set a course to clear Gilkicker Point by a few hundred metres. This alteration will bring the yacht a little closer to the wind so further sheeting in will be required. There will be much more wind pressure on the sail so the winch handle will have to be used. Take the turn off the cleat and, holding the sheet taut in one hand in a line slightly above the perpendicular to the winch barrel, place the handle carefully into the socket on top of the winch, lock it in by turning the knob on the winch end of the handle and then wind away until the shake in the luff of the foresail just disappears. Then bring the woollen telltales on the foresail luff parallel, tale with tale (see Fig 36). If the outer tales are snaking upwards, then wind in gently until they fly parallel with their partners. If the inner (nearer) tales snake upwards, then the sheet will have to be gently eased out until the tales are parallel.

To ease out the sheet, hold it in the forward hand (you will always be facing outboard) and then curve the palm of your after hand around the turns on the outboard side of the winch. This ensures that the fingers of the after hand are away from the standing part and the

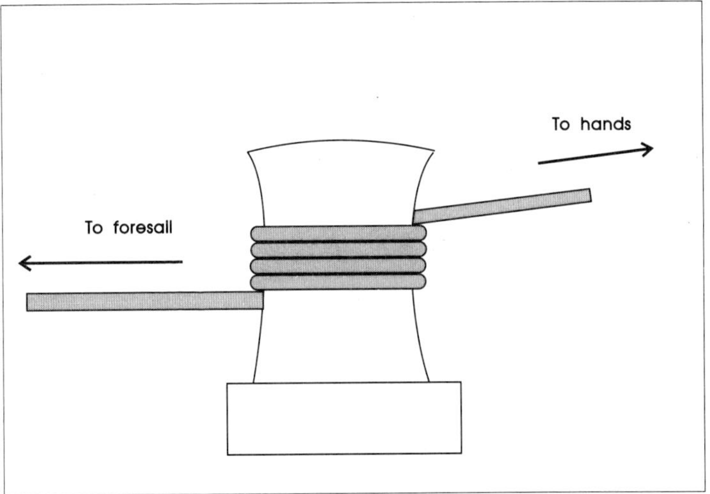

Fig 56. Correct pull on foresail sheet.

fall of the sheet. Now, using this hand, gently coax the turns to slide slowly round the winch while the 'sheet' hand eases the strain. Do not allow any slack in the fall of the sheet for this will soon result in its 'surging' round the winch, with attendant risk to the fingers of the 'winch' hand.

This whole procedure, especially easing out the sheet, will always be done under supervision at first: you cannot be expected to trim sails correctly in the first few days. The foresail now being correctly trimmed, cleat the sheet and then remove and stow the winch handle. Always treat these handles with care, for they are prone to leap overboard from their vulnerable position and they are expensive to replace. Another crew member will have been handling the mainsail sheet in the meantime, though the final trimming of the main is made only after the foresail has been set, since the flow of air around both sides of the foresail will affect the trim of the mainsail.

We are now close-reaching (see pages 29–33) and still on starboard tack. The yacht is heeled over by about 10 degrees and the speed has increased, as this is the fastest point of sailing. Though the waves are still less than 30 cm (wind force 3: about 9 knots) there is now more sea noise, and foam from the bow wave can be seen rushing past the hull.

There are no other vessels in our close vicinity so it is a good time to have a look around and take in the scene. The transit is roughly astern and the entrance to Portsmouth harbour, already a mile away, lies on our right hand. Gilkicker Point lies almost ahead, again about one mile distant (see Fig 50). Ahead lies the northern corner of the Isle of Wight. Our intended anchorage, Osborne Bay, lies almost dead ahead at about six miles. To the left on the island shore we are able to identify Wootton Creek, more from the position of a departing car ferry than the land feature. Further left, on our port bow, we can readily distinguish Ryde church spire which sits high above the town, and just to the west, Ryde pier with an approaching passenger ferry. The end of the pier lies about three miles away.

While there are numerous navigation buoys and vessels of varying size, all of which require our consideration, there are three substantial, stone-built features in the Solent which demand our attention. These are the forts (of Napoleonic vintage) at Spit Sand, about half a mile on our port quarter; at Horse Sand about two miles just aft of the port beam; and at No Man's Land, just forward of the port beam at the same distance. The appropriate chart is brought up into the cockpit so that these various landmarks may be identified on it. The exercise of relating what is seen with the eye to what is displayed on the chart, and vice versa, is vitally important. Though it may seem a little confusing at first, the skill is soon acquired. (The secret is first to establish the scale of the chart, which is given by the latitude scale on the vertical edges.) As the skill of reading charts is acquired, so the skill to estimate distances of sighted objects develops. For both purposes, it is vital to establish the relative bearing of these objects from the yacht's bow. The terms used are displayed in Fig 57.

'Yacht dead ahead!' is heard from a lookout. She is approaching us on almost a reciprocal course to our own at a distance of about 300 metres. There is a definite collision risk. She carries her main boom (and her sails) on her starboard side, ie the wind is blowing over her port side, so she is on port tack. We are still on starboard tack. By long-standing, internationally agreed collision avoidance rules, a

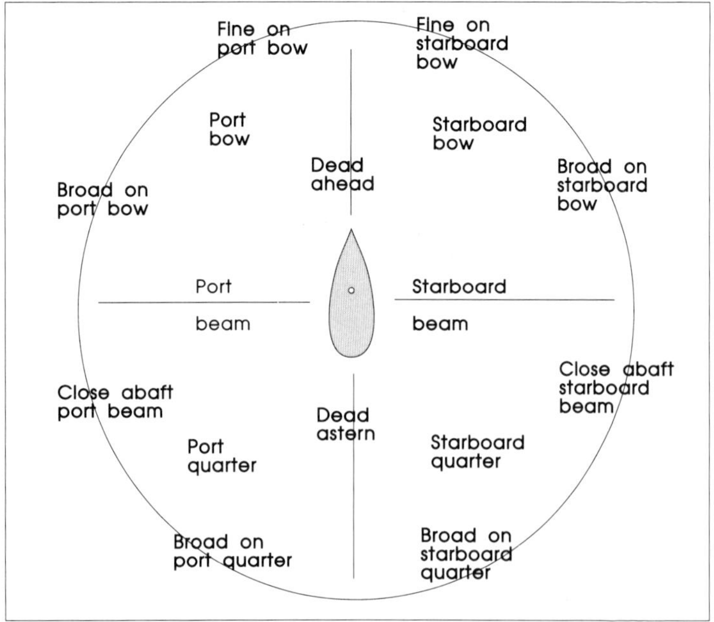

Fig 57. Relative bearings.

vessel on port tack *shall* give way to another on starboard tack. It is mandatory. So the approaching yacht is the 'give way' vessel and we are the 'stand on' yacht. (The skipper is fully aware that a few vessels fail to keep a proper lookout and even fail to respond to the call 'starboard', the usual hail to give way, so that ultimately the right of way vessel is obliged to take action to avoid the impending collision.) But, as is nearly always the case, the approaching yacht gives way in good time by altering course to her starboard so that she eventually passes by on our port side at about 50 metres. A raised hand from our skipper acknowledges the give way manoeuvre; the courtesy is returned in like fashion.

It is interesting to note that although there are similarities in her rig in that, like our yacht, she has one mast, she differs in that she carries two foresails instead of our one. She is, therefore, a **cutter** whereas our yacht is a **sloop**. Moreover, unlike our triangular Bermudan mainsail, hers is held aloft by an extra spar called a gaff (Fig 58). She is, then, a **gaff-rigged cutter**.

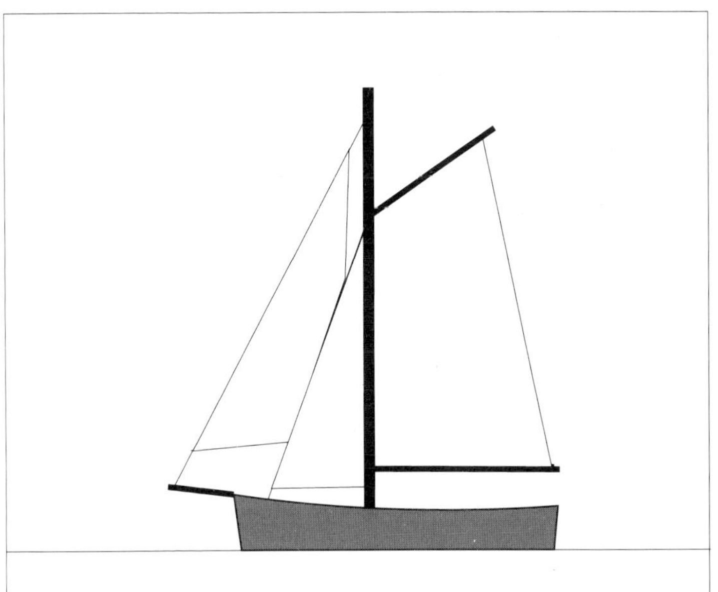

Fig 58. Gaff-rigged cutter.

A cry of 'coffee up' brings the focus back on board. There are very few places on a yacht at sea where mugs are safe, they must be held in the hand until the drink is finished and then passed down below. If some manoeuvre requires crew involvement, then the mugs must be passed down to the galley; a bowl in the sink is normally the best stowage. Never leave them on deck.

During the coffee break the skipper gives a brief summary of the most relevant collision avoidance regulations. We have just seen an example of the opposite tack case where starboard tack has right of way. With yachts converging on the same tack, the yacht which is to windward of the other shall give way. In general, power-driven vessels give way to sailing vessels. However, in channels where a large vessel may not be free to manoeuvre due to her great draft, they have right of way over sailing vessels. Within buoyed channels, all vessels shall keep to their starboard side so as to pass oncoming vessels port to port. (When using busy channels most small vessels voluntarily navigate just outside the line of buoys, where there is normally still ample depth, to allow the larger vessels more freedom of movement.)

But how do we determine that a collision risk exists? There is one golden rule, which is:

If the relative bearing of the other vessel remains constant, then a definite risk of collision exists.

If you line up an approaching vessel with a part of the yacht, such as a staunchion or shroud, then providing you do not move your head and also that your yacht remains on the same course, a very real collision risk exists if this relative bearing does not alter. But to be sure, it is better to take repeated bearings with a hand-bearing compass (Fig 59). If these bearings do not alter then the vessels will collide.

Both sails suddenly lift and flog, indicating that there has been a further 'heading' wind change. 'Sheet in!' calls the skipper. All mugs are instantly passed below to the galley sink. You have the foresail sheet, so you grab the winch handle and secure it on the top of the winch, then remove the sheet from its cleat (maintaining the strain). Then, holding the sheet in the after hand, wind in with the forward hand. Most sheet winches are double geared so that when the load becomes too heavy when winding in the one direction, the lower gearing is automatically selected by reversing the rotation of the winch handle. You should be watching the headsail luff to remove the lift and also finally to make the woollen telltales fly parallel. The mate will be overseeing the operation with some gentle advice.

The sheet is hauled in almost completely by the time the telltales fly parallel. The foresail now set, the mainsheet is also hauled in to trim the main. We are close-hauled (still on starboard tack) and we are still holding the course. So, providing there are no further wind changes, we should **lay** our destination – the Osborne Bay anchorage.

The yacht is now heeled over noticeably further, and the water rushes past the boat only a few centimetres below the lee rail. Rigging, wind and wave noises have increased, and there is an occasional crash from below as some item not properly stowed is flung across the cabin. The crew assume different postures in an attempt to seek some comfort from the strange, heeled attitude of the boat. Those on the leeward (downhill) side have some support from their side of the cockpit but those to windward will have to brace themselves by placing their feet against the opposite side benches. In either position, muscles will be used which have probably never been used before. This will become apparent next day! Try not to 'tense up' all over but relax as much of the body as possible.

The skipper calls you for a trick at the helm. The yacht is wheel-

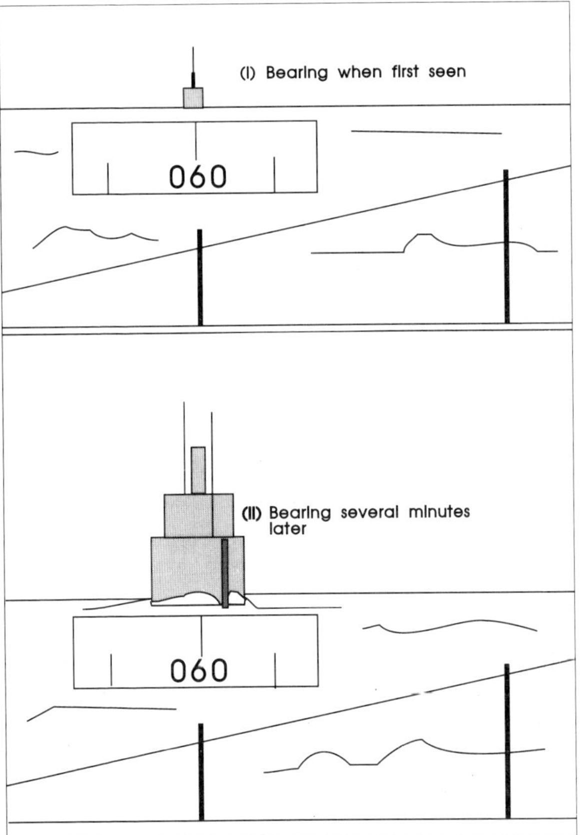

Fig 59. Constant bearing, definite collision risk.

steered, so the process is much the same as steering a car; when you want the bow to turn right, turn the wheel right, and so on. Just before the wheel is handed over to you, the skipper points out a small indentation on the skyline just above Osborne Bay; this is what to steer for. He also hands on the compass course, 270 degrees, though there will be little reference to this during the first part of your half-hour trick. Any vessels in the immediate vicinity will also be pointed out to you, particularly those which may constitute a collision risk in the near future (fortunately there are none) together with the fact that Gilkicker Point lies 500 metres off the starboard bow.

The wheel is now handed over to you. Place your hands at the ten to two position and look up for your steering mark above Osborne Bay. It is not dead ahead (the yacht normally wanders off a little during the handover stage) but lies a little to the right of the bow. So you correct by turning the wheel to the right to bring your mark back in line (see pages 39–42). In a short time you have settled down to keeping the yacht on course, and it all seems plain sailing.

As the yacht arrives off Gilkicker Point, the wind suddenly backs into the west. The flogging sails immediately set up a vibration through the mast that can be felt throughout the yacht. The yacht sits upright and the speed drops back for we are now almost head-to-wind. For a moment you are unsure what to do, but help is not far away and the mate quietly but firmly asks you to turn left. As the sails fill again, still on starboard tack, the yacht begins to heel and accelerates. The mate advises you to 'hold her there' when close to the correct angle off the wind. The flogging has stopped as the sails assume a smooth curve. The last few centimetres are hauled in on the sheets, for we are now beating. You must resist the urge to look at what is going on with the sheets for this will cause the yacht to wander off the wind. Look instead at the windward shroud telltale and keep this pointing towards you (see Fig 35).

When the sails are finally trimmed, transfer your attention to the foresail luff telltales and keep these flying parallel (see Fig 36). You will probably have to move yourself a little to the right (uphill) of the wheel in order to see the foresail luff. The yacht is sailing well and you can feel through a slight tremble in the wheel the surge of water past the rudder. The yacht is no longer pointing towards Osborne Bay but towards Wootton Creek (see Fig 50). With the yacht heeled, it is difficult to see what lies on our port bow, for this area is completely screened by the foresail. The skipper has appointed a crew member sitting forward in the port side of the cockpit to look out beyond the foresail every 15 seconds or so and report back on anything on the port bow which may require attention. This may vary from a large liner two miles away charging towards us at speed, to other yachts much nearer but moving much more slowly, and even to large baulks of timber or crab pot markers 20 metres away which also pose a threat.

You are concentrating on the course to windward by sailing to the luff telltales and responding to the constant small scale variations in the wind direction (see pages 61–7). With 'heading' wind changes the inside telltales snake upwards to give the first indication, so you react by coming off the wind a little (turning left) until they fly parallel again. Within a minute or so a small lifting change will follow, causing the outer telltales to react, so you respond by bringing her up closer to the wind to counter this effect. Between times you have time to glance ahead at other vessels and at the Wootton Creek shoreline, and also to starboard to see what lies abeam. You have even had time to make a quick mental note of the mean compass course in case the skipper calls for it.

Ahead at about half a mile a vehicle ferry is approaching at a very oblique angle, and to starboard a yacht is approaching on a constant bearing. These have been reported to the skipper who decides that the ferry will soon cross ahead at a safe distance to pass down on our port side, but there is a definite collision risk with the yacht on our starboard side. As she is still half a mile away there are a few minutes before any avoiding action has to be taken, so the skipper asks the crew to determine on which tack the other vessel is sailing. She is a ketch, a two masted sailing vessel with the forward mast being the taller (Fig 60). We can see that most of her sails are carried on her

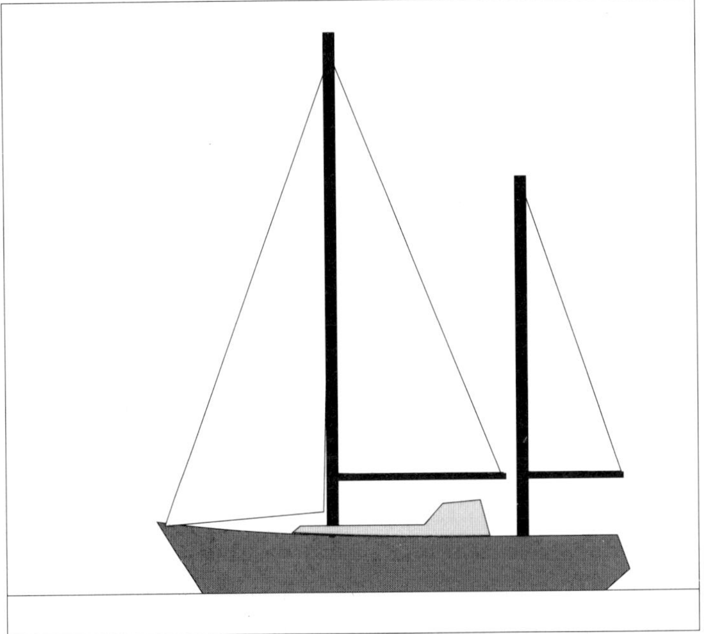

Fig 60. Ketch.

starboard side, though her foresail is set out to port as she is running downwind. The main boom, which determines the tack, is out to starboard so she is on port tack, as most of the crew have judged. Her bearing, taken by hand-bearing compass, remains steady, but at a distance of several hundred metres she alters course to her port to pass close astern of us.

As you look at the island shore dead ahead you note that now we are closer to it, the yacht is no longer heading for Wootton Creek but for a point some distance to the left of it. This is because the tide is setting eastwards through the Solent and has carried us along on its 'conveyor belt'. We are now half a mile north west of Ryde Pier and the skipper asks you to tack the boat when you are ready. (This means within a minute or so.)

You call 'ready about' to alert the winch hands and also to warn anyone down below. When tacking you will turn the bow through the wind to sail away on the new tack at about 90 degrees to the old one.

In the interval till the winchmen are prepared, you check that it is safe to tack, there being no other vessel in the close vicinity – at least 100 metres for yachts and much more for larger vessels – especially in the sector between dead astern and the starboard beam (see Fig 38) and the area hidden behind the genoa. You also pick a new tack marker on the starboard beam, for this is near enough where you will point the bow when settled down on the new tack (see Fig 39). The centre line of Southampton Water is as good an obvious mark as any (see Figs 50 and 51).

The winch hands call 'ready' and so after a further quick check for other vessels, you call 'lee-oh' and turn the wheel slowly to the right about a half turn to generate a steady swing of the bow to starboard. As the boat comes towards head-to-wind the yacht sits upright and there is a noisy flogging from the sails. There is also much activity from the winchmen in front of you, but you must ignore this as you concentrate only on the steering aspect of tacking the yacht. Still holding the half turn of the wheel, you observe the bow swinging steadily through the wind (using wind dials, Windex but, best in the circumstances, the shroud telltales) and as the foresail comes across to set on the other side you begin to undo the half turn on the wheel. Now you make a quick glance at your new tack marker (no longer on the starboard beam but roughly 30 degrees on the starboard bow) still undoing the wheel turn slowly so that it comes midships with the bow still pointing 5–10 degrees to the left of your marker. The remaining momentum of the swing then carries the bow on to the mark.

By this time, about 20 to 30 seconds from lee-oh, the foresail will be close-hauled on the new tack and you can then settle down to steering by the luff telltales. You note the new compass course and the completely different coastline now seen ahead and on both beams, as well as the new relative positions of surrounding vessels. We are now on port tack.

After a few minutes the skipper asks someone else to take over the steering. You hand on the fact that you are 'sailing on the wind' on port tack (and therefore not steering for a specific mark or a compass course) and the pattern of other relevant vessels. Your duties are not over, however, for you are now the starboard lookout. There is nothing in the close vicinity but there is a cargo vessel which appears to be slow moving about a mile away on the starboard bow and another at the same distance on our starboard beam; both heading west north west. They may present a problem later.

Mother Bank buoy (red can) lies right on course and is now only 100 metres away. The helmsman asks the skipper on which side he should pass the buoy. The tide is setting from the west north west according to the Tidal Atlas and this is confirmed by the wake we can now see streaming downtide from the buoy. Since we are beating (westerly wind), there is no scope for 'weathering' the buoy, ie passing it on its windward side. Any attempt to do so by pinching would be foolhardy since the tide would eventually carry us on to the buoy. So the skipper asks the helmsman to come off the wind a little so as to pass on the safe, downtide side of the buoy, thus keeping it on our port side.

The cargo vessel earlier sighted on our starboard bow is now broader on the bow and the other vessel appears to be about to overtake it – both at a distance of about half a mile. The latter has obviously moved fairly steadily and this is supported by a substantial bow wave; a 'bone in her teeth'. The former vessel has no such bow wave; she appears to be stopped. The skipper points out a black ball hoist above her foredeck. This signifies she is at anchor, so she need not concern us further. Successive compass bearings on the moving vessel are changing rapidly and indicate that she will soon pass clear ahead.

Southeast Ryde Middle buoy (Fig 50) lies a few hundred metres almost dead ahead. Unlike the red can and green conical, channel-marking buoys of the 'lateral system' which have top marks of the same shape and colour as the buoy, this navigation mark is much larger, is coloured black and yellow and the top mark is significantly different. It belongs to the 'cardinal system' which identifies the direction of a nearby navigation hazard such as a sandbank or reef. Figure 61 explains the cardinal buoyage system. In the case of SE Ryde Middle, a south cone buoy, the hazard lies to the north; the hazard is the eastern end of Ryde Middle Bank and the clearer, safer water lies to the south.

Whilst taking all this in, you are still lookout on the starboard side

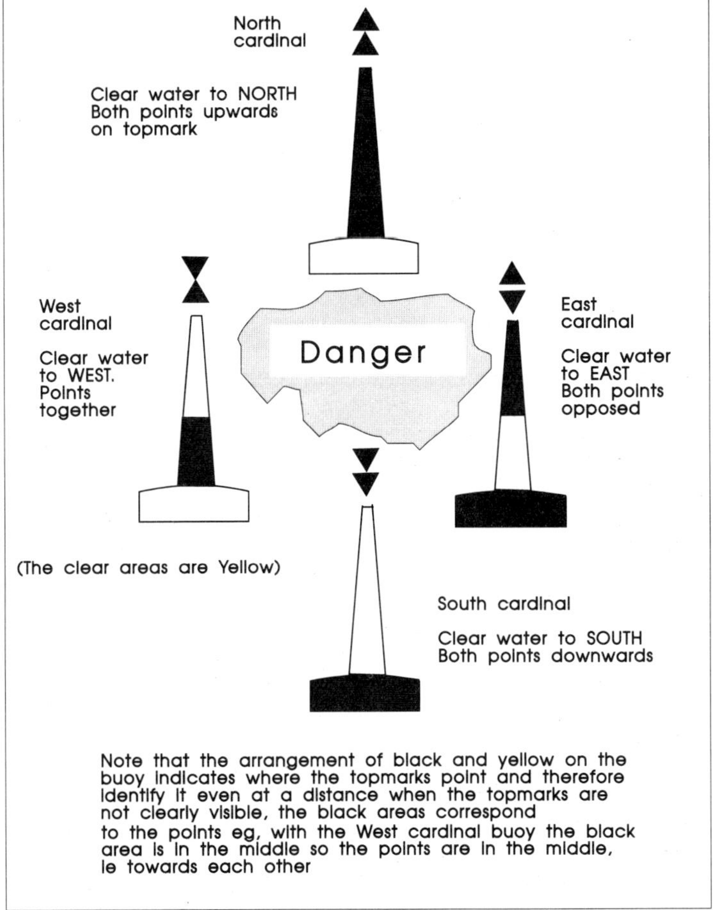

Fig 61. The cardinal buoyage system.

and, on looking around the genoa foresail, you notice a yacht on a crossing course about half a mile away on the starboard bow. She is heeled over to port, so she is on starboard tack. You call out 'starboard tack yacht, starboard bow, about half a mile!' This is acknowledged by the skipper, but both he and the mate are concentrating on a large cargo vessel which has rounded the western end of Bramble Bank and has turned east towards us. She will use the main deep water channel on the south side of Ryde Middle Bank and will pass south of SE Ryde Middle buoy in about ten minutes or so.

The collision risks are now compounding; the buoy lies almost dead ahead at a few hundred metres; the starboard tack yacht lies only a little further away, and since she is still on our starboard bow we are on a collision course, so we must give way. But by far the most dangerous threat is the large vessel still about two miles away. The skipper's solution is to turn on to a south westerly heading which will take the yacht safely over Mother Bank (where, due to the rising tide, there is now ample depth) and clear of all three problems. 'Tack as soon as you're ready' is given to the helmsman who responds with an immediate 'ready about!'

You are the starboard side winchman so you clear the tail of the sheet from its cleat, holding the tail taut all the while, place both hands close together about half a metre from the winch, check that the fall of the sheet is free to run, and call 'ready!' Following 'lee-oh', you do nothing at first other than transfer your attention to the luff of the foresail. When this lifts (and once it starts the whole luff will become 'backed' fairly quickly) raise both hands still holding the tail taut until they are almost over the winch. The turns will then soon fly off one by one. Relax your grip and let the tail slide through your palms. (You have no choice here, for once the first two turns are off you will not be able to hold the tail.) Now ensure that the sheet is running freely and finally check that the stopper knot in its tail is still pulled up tight. Your opposite number on the other winch will still be winding in. All crewing tasks should be shared in a team spirit whenever practicable, so you lean across and take the tail from him, holding it slightly above the perpendicular (see Fig 56), to leave him with two clear hands to finish winching. Figure 62 shows the sheet handling procedures on tacking.

The tack has removed the risk of colliding with the buoy and also with the other yacht. We are now crossing the line of the large vessel, which is still about one mile away, so the collision risk there will also soon disappear. A few minutes later we cross Mother Bank and shortly afterwards the large vessel passes clear about half a mile away.

Even at that distance she looks enormous and completely eclipses a large sector of the Hampshire coastline as she passes by on our northern side. The skipper points out a black cylinder hanging from the yardarm above her bridge. This signifies that this large vessel is constrained by her deep draft from manoeuvring with any freedom in restricted channels. She therefore has right of way over our sailing vessel and we must keep clear.

The mate calls out 'three metres and shoaling!' He has been

watching the echo sounder dial and has noticed that the depths over Mother Bank are now decreasing a little more steadily even though the coast is still about one mile away. Our yacht draws 1.8 metres (ie there is 1.8 metres of hull and keel below the water line). The orders for tacking are given and you still have the task of handling the starboard sheet – the lazy sheet on the current tack. You take up most of the slack in the lazy sheet and take one turn around the winch (in the correct direction) and call 'ready!'

Your next action is triggered audibly, for after 'lee-oh' you wait until the foresail flogs and, more especially, until you have heard the turns come off the other winch. Then haul in hand-over-hand, taking an occasional glimpse forward to see the foresail moving across the foredeck by your action. As it begins to stream aft and is still flogging noisily, take two further turns, haul in a little more, and then take a further, fourth turn around the winch before winding in the remainder of the sheet using the winch handle. The secret here is to get the further turns on to the winch before the 'weight of the wind' on the new tack gets into the sail. Once it does the flogging dies down very quickly. So get the turns on, one above the other allowing no slack,

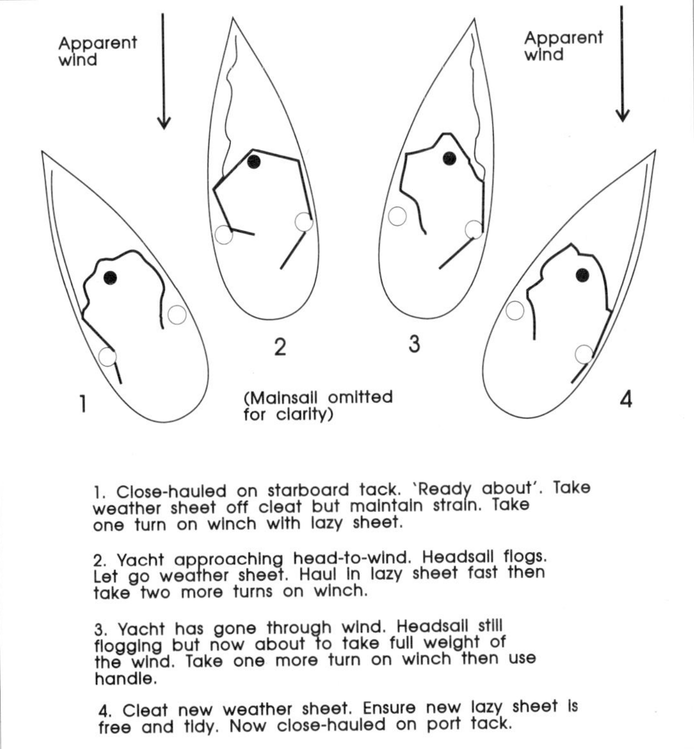

Fig 62. Winch action on tacking.

while the foresail is still flogging. And don't forget to hold the tail slightly above the perpendicular from the winch barrel while hauling and winding in to avoid a riding turn which will ruin the whole performance. If a riding turn does occur, then say so and the helmsman will return the yacht towards the head-to-wind position which will allow sufficient slack on your sheet to remove the riding turn. Replace the four turns and complete sheeting in.

Never carry on winding in until there is no further scrap to be sheeted in. With larger foresails this will probably mean that the foresail leech (its back edge) will be speared by the yardarm. Look up and ensure that there is a small gap between the two. Next secure the tail to the nearest cleat (one round turn and one, or even half, a figure of eight is enough for the winch carries all the strain) then stow the winch handle and tidy up the fall of the sheet.

We are once again on port tack, heading roughly towards Southampton Water and all is clear about us. This is only the third tack and already the essential crew team spirit, especially between the helmsman and the two winchmen, is showing through. It has gone well and the skipper lets us know.

We are now well on towards our planned anchorage for lunch. Southampton Water, almost dead ahead, has assumed a broader aspect but even it is dominated by the huge chimney at Fawley power station on its western flank. Gilkicker Point is now on the starboard quarter. Beyond that we can see some of the large buildings in Portsmouth, though the transit is no longer discernible at this range – almost five miles. Coming further right, the Spithead forts are easily recognisable. Ryde Pier lies almost dead astern at about two miles and the conspicuous church spire on the skyline above the town lies a little to the right of the pier. Osborne Bay itself is almost abeam and the anchorage is identified by Osborne House, once the island home of Queen Victoria and her family.

But we cannot tack yet for the anchorage as the tide is still setting against us at about ¾ knot, so we are 'standing on' until we are across Ryde Middle Bank. In a few minutes the echo sounder reveals that we have crossed the bank, so the orders are given for tacking the yacht. You are still the starboard sheet man so you clear the sheet from its cleat, ensure the sheet is ready to run, stand back from the winch with the hands close together about half a metre from it and call 'ready!' After 'lee-oh', you wait until the foresail luff begins to back as the bow swings closer to the wind, then you raise your hands above the winch and let the tail run through as the turns fly off the winch. When the sheet has cleared the winch you tidy up the tail, checking that the stopper knot in its end is tight, before turning to see if you can assist with the sheeting in on the other side. Someone else is already tailing for the winchman there, so you reassume your duties as lookout.

We are once again on starboard tack. Cowes and its approaches can just be seen clear of Old Castle Point but these soon disappear as we run on south westwards towards Osborne Bay. It will soon be time to prepare the yacht for anchoring there.

· ANCHORING ·

With the whole crew gathered in the cockpit, the skipper takes over the wheel and gives a quick brief on the overall plan for anchoring. We shall be in the area in about ten minutes, and we shall be anchoring when the depth decreases to about 3 metres on the echo sounder. Water levels are still rising due to the incoming tide though high water will not occur until just after we leave the anchorage in just over an hour's time. In order to leave the foredeck clear for anchorwork and to allow easier manoeuvring at the time of anchoring, we shall lower the sails and approach the anchorage under power. The foresail is always handed first so that it will not hinder the deck crew, especially those near the mast, when they hand the mainsail with the yacht head-to-wind. Tasks are allocated, ties for the handed sails are passed up to those who will require them, and we are sent to our positions. Now that we are closing the shore there are no other vessels around except for two other yachts well inshore which are already at anchor. The engine is started and allowed to warm up.

'Standby to lower foresail!' activates the crew. You are on the foredeck with the mate to hand the foresail; someone else will see to the halyard and the sheets from the cockpit. When he sees that all is ready, the skipper turns the yacht head-to-wind so that the foresail will drop directly on to the foredeck. You are right in the bows by the forestay. 'Lower!' is ordered and the sail begins to come down with a rush as the halyard hand takes the turns off the winch in much the same manner as they come off the sheet winch. But he checks the rate of fall as necessary to assist the foredeck crew.

Your job is to see that the foresail luff slides nicely down its groove while another crew member, kneeling near the mast, controls the flogging leech of the foresail by stuffing it under his knees as it comes down. When the sail is down, you remove the halyard shackle from the head of the sail, ensuring little slack and pass this to the other foredeck hand who will secure it in its place on the mast. The halyard will then be secured tightly in the cockpit. You then remove the head of the foresail from the luff groove (the remainder of the luff has already left the groove as the sail came down), gather up the whole luff and secure it to the lower lifeline on the port side using a reef knot or 'reef bow' for easy release. The other crewman has stretched out the lowered sail, having left the sheets bent on, and has secured the clew area with a tie to the same lifeline. One or two further ties are then used to secure the main body of the foresail to keep it tidy and under control should the wind increase, and also to keep it out of the way. In all this, both of you have taken care not to step on to the lowered sail.

With piston hanks on the foresail luff the procedure is similar.

The hanks remain on the forestay and the sail is secured to a lifeline with ties.

Meantime, the halyard hand in the cockpit has already eased out the mainsheet a little and has raised the boom a touch by hauling in and securing the topping lift which, alone, now carries the weight of the main boom. The mainsheet is once again hauled in taut to prevent the boom from swinging about, because those handing the mainsail on the coachroof will use the boom for support.

You are at the mast end of the boom, with feet spread for balance and, as the halyard is run out following the command 'lower', you assist the luff of the mainsail to run smoothly down the mast groove (the yacht is still head-to-wind). Two other crew members, both on the same side, are meantime gathering the body of the mainsail as it comes down into a 'bag' formed by the lowest metre or so of the sail itself. When the head of the mainsail comes to hand you remove the halyard shackle and secure it to its fitting on the mast then lay the head into the 'bag'. Starting away from the boom, you roll up the 'bag' into a tight sausage, taking care that the sail battens lie flat within it, until the sausage is finally rolled over on to the top of the boom. The sail is now secured with at least four or five ties around sail and boom, again using a reef knot or bow. (It is much more convenient and probably safer to leave a 'slab stow' (see page 13) until the yacht is in the marina.) All is now set for anchor preparation.

The mate has already removed the hatch from the anchor locker on the foredeck and asks you to lift out the anchor. It is fairly heavy, weighing 15 kg, and it is shaped like a double sided ploughshare; it is a CQR type of anchor. The 'ploughshare' is attached by a swivel fitting to the shank and the chain is attached to the other end of the shank by a shackle. Before lifting out the anchor check that this shackle is up tight. The shackle pin is normally 'seized' with wire, so you also examine the wire for corrosion. Now lift it out, take it forward into the bows, and pass the anchor out through the space between the forestay and the pulpit on the starboard side of the forestay. Someone else reaches over the pulpit and takes the anchor from you then brings it back inboard, still *on the starboard side of the forestay*, and places it on the port side of the foredeck. The chain therefore now runs from the hawsepipe forward and through the space on the starboard side of the forestay, then over the top of the pulpit and back inboard to the anchor.

A roller fitting is now pointed out to you right in the very bows of the yacht. This is the **stemhead fitting** and it is fitted on the starboard side of the yacht's centreline since the forestay is already on that line. The mate explains the action of a pin which prevents the chain from coming out of the stemhead fitting, moves the pin to allow you to place the chain in the fitting and then asks you to secure the pin once more. It is clear now why the anchor had to go out on the starboard side of the forestay. This is also why the foresail has been secured to the lifeline on the port side, clear of the foredeck.

Now for the preparation of the anchor chain. The skipper has already said that he will be anchoring in 3 metres of water. Since the tide is still rising a little, we shall reckon on a mean depth of 3.3 metres during our one hour stay for lunch. In quiet conditions without rough seas or strong tidal streams, it is sufficient to lay out enough chain to give three times the expected depth of water. So we have to prepare 10 metres of chain.

One crew member is positioned at the hawsepipe through which the chain passes from the chain locker; another is near the mast and you forward – the last two on the starboard side. Chain is fed out to the man near the mast until there are 2 metres lying straight and tidy on deck, parallel to the toerail. This man then turns the chain back to you after placing his foot on the 'turn'. You lay 2 metres alongside the first and return the chain to the man near the mast. The process, called flaking down, is repeated until there are five lengths of chain lying side by side on the deck. The hawsepipe end of the chain is now secured to the large cleat in the centre of the foredeck by taking a round turn then passing a 'bight' of the chain under its standing part and bringing the bight over the cleat. Figures of eight are not turned round the horns of a cleat as with a rope because the chain links will jam.

The skipper suggests a little leadline practice as we run in towards the anchorage. This is a thin throwing line with a tapered cylindrical lead weight attached to it. In the days of the sailing ship, tallow was placed in the hollowed out end of the weight, to which the bottom substance, sand or mud, etc, would adhere. This was not only useful for anchoring but was an aid to navigation in well-known waters in poor visibility. The mate demonstrates the lead swinging operation and now it's your turn. As you are left handed you move over to the port side, facing forward, hold the line about a metre from the weight in your left hand with the remainder of the line neatly coiled in your other hand and ready to run. The inner end of the line is held between the palm and thumb of the right hand.

Now you swing the lead fore and aft, easing out a little as you increase the swing, then at the forward end of the third swing, you let the line slip through the fingers of your left hand and open the fingers of the right (palm up) to let some of the coils run. You count the metre markings on the line as they disappear below the surface. If judged correctly the weight reaches the bottom directly underneath the thrower. The moment of striking is clearly felt as the line suddenly becomes light. Note which mark has just disappeared at this instant, and check this as you quickly recover the lead. You call 'four metres!' as the lead becomes visible, then neatly and quickly coil the line ready for another sounding.

The exercise over, the skipper calls 'standby to anchor!' You lift the anchor and carry it over the pulpit on the starboard side of the forestay, check that the chain is free to run and that your feet which have to straddle the chain are well clear on both sides, and that everyone else is clear. Then lower the anchor slowly until it is about ⅓ metre above the water. You look back for the skipper's 'let go'. Because of the engine and wave noises, and also the distance between the skipper in the cockpit and the action forward in the bow, he has already briefed you that he will signal with his arm instead of shouting.

When anchoring it is important that the vessel is moving slowly, usually astern, so that the chain will not pile up on top of the anchor to foul it. The skipper has turned the yacht head-to-tide (west north westwards) and has now selected astern power. By means of a transit between a tree near the beach and the higher ground behind it, the skipper is ensuring that the yacht is actually going astern over the ground before giving the signal. (We will be going astern over the ground when the background moves to the left of the foreground tree.)

The signal is given (a quick downward 'chop' with the forearm) and so you quickly lower the anchor into the water and let go. The chain rushes out with a great noise. When about 6 metres of chain have run out (there is a little more than 3 metres water depth so the anchor is now on the bottom) the mate asks you to stamp on the chain and keep your foot there. This 'snubbing' action stops the chain from running out and, since we are still going astern, encourages the anchor to dig in. At the mate's signal you remove your foot and the remainder of the chain runs out until it comes up sharply on its cleat. In a minute or two the yacht will have settled down to riding to her anchor. The tide is still running at a little over half a knot and so she streams downtide from the anchor. The yacht is **tide rode**. (With little or no tide effect she would lie to the wind and so be **wind rode**.)

A black ball shape is now brought up to the foredeck, and hoist on the forestay using the foresail halyard with a lanyard from the ball secured to a foredeck cleat to prevent the ball from riding up and down the forestay. This signifies that we are at anchor. The skipper has chosen a suitable transit on the shore abeam formed by a post on the beach and a tree several hundred metres dead behind it. If the anchor should drag then the tree would appear to move to the left of the post. We shall keep an eye on this transit from time to time.

During lunch the skipper runs quickly through the new skills that have been acquired. You have bent on the sails, cast off springs and mooring lines, hoist the sails, trimmed sheets, and handled them during a tack. You have also steered the yacht, both towards a given object and, more challengingly, on the wind including tacking her, and also learnt quite a lot about lookout duties, buoyage systems and rights of way. Finally you have handed the sails, prepared for coming to anchor and have carried out the tasks of foredeck crew during anchoring. And we have been at sea for less than four hours – there is still half of the first day to go!

Even now, as you make short work of lunch (for your appetite will have increased), you may not relax completely for the anchor transit requires monitoring every few minutes. You will also be watching out for other vessels nearby possibly dragging their anchors and for new yachts coming into the anchorage.

The plans for the remainder of the day are now discussed, starting with the intention of sailing away from the anchorage using sail rather than power, though the engine will be running as a standby just in case. The foresail will not be hoist until we are underway in order to leave the foredeck clear for anchor work. The tide will soon become slack for a short while after our departure, before it turns to set westwards, now ebbing, through the Solent. The wind continues from the west at about force 3 but is expected to back (an anti-clockwise shift) into the south west and to freshen a little during the afternoon. It will still be a beat through the west Solent to Yarmouth but we shall make better time to windward as the tide will be setting in our direction – this is a fair tide. Moreover, the Tidal Stream Atlas shows that its rate will be stronger than that of the foul tide we experienced this morning. We shall be doing man overboard drills, turning to sail downwind so that we can gybe the yacht, pole out the foresail and, if time permits, hoist the spinnaker before continuing the beat to Yarmouth.

While another crew member is detailed to wash up and stow from lunch, the remainder of the crew will prepare the yacht for sailing off the anchorage. 'Standby to hoist the main!' starts off the afternoon's sailing. Two of you with the mate climb up on to the coachroof and remove and pocket the sail ties. The mate assists in keeping the furled sail 'asleep' while you attach the halyard shackle to the head of the sail and feed the top few centimetres of the luff into the mast groove, all the while ensuring very little slack in the halyard in order to avoid a snag aloft. Following the hoist you see that the luff continues to run smoothly up the mast groove before retiring aft to assist in the cockpit. Once the halyard has been cleated by the halyard hand, you locate the main boom topping lift (the skipper identifies its colour code to you) and you ease this out now that the sail is carrying the weight of the boom. Cleat the topping lift and then, at the skipper's request, ease out the mainsheet sufficiently to take the drive out of it (until it flogs) for we are still at anchor.

'Standby the anchor!' takes the mate and two crew forward to the foredeck ready to haul in the chain and anchor. With strong tides or strong winds this is a heavy task, and normally the yacht would be motored up to the anchor to reduce this effort. But today there is only a little tide still running and the wind is relatively light so the task should be carried out easily with two crew.

You remove the bight of chain from the horns of the foredeck cleat but keep the round turn on it. The other crew member straddles the chain right up in the bows, ready to haul in when ordered. When the skipper sees that all is ready he calls 'up anchor!' You remove the turn round the cleat and both of you haul away with two-handed pulls on the chain. As it comes in you ensure that it is fed into its hawsepipe to run into its locker below the foredeck.

The mate has been looking over the bows as best he can without getting in the way, and sweeps his arm up and down to signal that the chain is vertical and that we are now over the anchor. (Chain, sail and engine noises preclude voice communication.) The crew in the bows will normally feel the anchor break free at this stage; it certainly becomes lighter once it has broken out for there is then less chain to haul in. When the mate sees the anchor coming up he swings his lowered arm to signal that the anchor is free. It is brought in through the pulpit and laid on the starboard side of the foredeck, away from the foresail. As the chart suggested, it is covered in mud and will have to be scrubbed down before stowing in its locker. Bucket and scrubbing brush have already been passed up.

Meantime the skipper has sheeted in the main and we are now sailing away slowly on port tack under that sail alone. There are no other vessels in the near vicinity but we must not dawdle on the foredeck for the skipper will want the foresail hoist as soon as possible to regain maximum manoeuvrability.

You are the bucket hand so you face forward, hold the end of the lanyard attached to the handle, invert the bucket and throw it down. The forward movement of the yacht encourages the bucket to fill with water as it rights itself, aided by a steady pull from you to bring it clear. With greater yacht speeds, this pull has to be carefully timed, and needs to be more of a snatch in order to bring the bucket out when only about half full; a full bucket will soon be dragged aft, and the handler with it if he doesn't let go in time!

Several bucketfuls are required to scrub off the anchor and, when it has been stowed, finally the foredeck. The skipper has been looking on, and as soon as the bucket and brush are passed aft he calls 'standby to hoist the foresail!'

Both crew hands remove the ties securing the foresail and pocket them, before carrying the foresail over to the starboard side. (We are on port tack, so the headsail will fly out on the starboard side as it is hoist.) You attach the halyard shackle to the head of the sail then feed the first few centimetres of the top of the luff into the luff groove on the forestay foil. All is ready. 'Hoist!' sees the cockpit hand leap into action hauling away on the halyard. You see that the luff is running smoothly in its groove (or that the hanks are not fouled) and move quickly aft, crouching and making use of handholds as you go, to assist with the sheets in the cockpit.

The operation is already becoming familiar; you grab the starboard sheet, the one which will soon take the strain, and take a turn round its winch. As soon as the foresail halyard is secured, haul away hand-over-hand on the sheet, place another turn on the winch, haul a little more then place a further two turns on before the sail stops flogging; once it stops there will be too much strain on the sheet to allow further turns. Haul in what you can by hand, remembering that the pull on the tail should be just above the perpendicular from the winch barrel to avoid riding turns. Now wind in using the winch handle until the sail is sheeted home, but glance aloft before cleating to ensure that the leech is just off the yardarm.

The yacht is heeled over on port tack and sailing fast. The second part of the cruise is just beginning.

CONTINUING · ON PASSAGE ·

Norris buoy (red can) has just been left on our port hand at 50 metres and as we continue close-hauled on port tack towards the north west, the entrance to Cowes opens up and suddenly the scene ahead becomes busy. A gathering of yachts near the entrance to the Medina River suggests that a race is about to begin there. A ferry from Southampton has just rounded Bramble Bank heading for Cowes, while the passenger hydrofoil is streaking southwards across the bank (it is high water) on a more direct route. Once again the skipper and mate seem more concerned with a large vessel, an ocean liner, now rounding Calshot Spit light float. It is not yet clear which track she will take after rounding Bramble Bank. She may continue westwards for the Needles Channel or she may turn sharply for the East Solent and the Nab. There is no immediate threat but the skipper indicates that there may well be a series of problems if we continue on our present course and has decided to 'short tack', close to the island shore. The first tack is to begin when West Ryde Middle buoy is abeam.

The wind freshens a knot or two as we come out of the lee from the island, but the sea has become much more choppy in the last few minutes, out of all proportion to the small wind increase. This more agitated sea state is due to the fact that the tide has turned to run westwards. All morning the tide was running with the wind; now it is running against it. Wind against tide always roughens up the sea surface.

We are abeam West Ryde Middle buoy and the skipper prompts the helmsman to tack when ready. We have several tacks already under our belts and this one shows the result of our experience. The helmsman turns slowly towards the wind while the sheet hand waits until the luff backs before he lets fly his sheet. The bow is turned equally slowly through the wind while the new sheet hand hauls in furiously as the foresail comes across. He has got his turns on in good time and has finished sheeting in by the time the yacht settles down on the new tack. The helmsman has chosen a good new tack mark and has immediately settled down on his course towards it without letting the bow come too far off the wind; a common fault with beginners especially if they become disorientated.

The vehicle ferry is now entering Cowes and the hydrofoil is already alongside her berth. The gathering of yachts suddenly assumes more order and purpose as they start their race; a few seconds later the starting gun can be heard even at our distance. They are heading westwards, away from us, and so present no problem.

The liner has rounded Bramble Bank and is turning for an East Solent exit. She will pass between Prince Consort, a north cardinal buoy, and West Ryde Middle, a west cardinal buoy, in the next few minutes. We are heading south west on starboard tack, and already the tide has carried us clear of Old Castle Point. But we soon run into shallower water and, with the prearranged 3 metres on the echo sounder, the helmsman cries 'lee-oh!' There is a little more urgency about this tack and there is little room for mistakes. But once again it is carried out smoothly, though with the mate and skipper closely supervising each stage.

We are now on a converging course with the liner which looks enormous. The skipper's 'tack in one minute' is immediately followed by the helmsman's 'ready about!' Both winch hands leap into action and their 'ready!' is heard simultaneously within a few seconds. 'Tack!' is followed on the instant by 'lee-oh!' and the bow swings away from the towering liner ahead. She is still half a mile away and her course and speed are such that she would have passed clear ahead even if we had not tacked away from her. But the skipper knows he should give as much room as possible in good time to large vessels in narrow channels.

Now that we are heading south west once more, there is an excellent view of the liner as she majestically crosses astern of us. It is sobering to think that each of the 30 lifeboats on her upper deck is almost as big as our yacht! The mouth of the Medina River, the entrance to Cowes, lies dead ahead; besides numerous small vessels entering or exiting the river, the hydrofoil can be seen just rising on to her foils for the return journey. She is obliged to keep clear of all the craft, small and large, in the vicinity and presents no threat as she planes away for Southampton.

Since we do not wish to go into Cowes just yet, another tack is called for and is almost executed satisfactorily. However, with a measure of over enthusiasm, the new sheet winch hand has allowed the second turn on the winch to ride over the third, and with subsequent hauling the sheet has jammed. To his credit, he calls out 'riding turn!' immediately. The skipper instantly takes the wheel, for we are almost in the river entrance and there are other yachts around us. He luffs up to almost head-to-wind to provide the necessary slack for the riding turn to be replaced by four proper turns and then sheeted home as the yacht settles on to the new tack. This tack will carry us out into the western Solent.

During the relatively long board (tack or leg) to the Hampshire shore, the mate asks you to make coffee. On your way down the companionway to the galley in the main saloon, you ask for the gas to be turned on in its locker on the after deck. The motion down below feels quite different but there are plenty of handholds around the galley. The water system is pressurised so you fill the kettle directly from the cold tap, and place it on the cooker which is 'level' since it is on gimbals. It also has guardrails or 'fiddles' around its edge to prevent the kettle or saucepans from falling off. Identify the knob for the burner you are going to use (if in any doubt ask), hold a lighted match to that burner and turn on the knob. Ignition should follow instantly; if it has not within two seconds then turn the knob off and seek advice before trying again. After placing the kettle over the lit burner you now turn your attention to the coffee cups.

The only practical place for mugs when brewing up at sea is in a bowl in the sink. Take care not to spill any coffee or sugar; spilt sugar especially on the cabin sole is an awful nuisance. Now all is set.

It has taken longer than you think, for as you stick your head out into the main hatch and say 'coffee up', the skipper asks you to wait a little longer for a change of tack is imminent. You turn off the gas and try to visualise what will happen 'down below' when the yacht is tacked. The kettle will be perfectly safe on the cooker, the mugs are snug in the bowl in the sink and all else is stowed away. Following 'lee-oh' you grab two handholds and brace yourself as the yacht first comes upright then heels over in the opposite direction. You take a few seconds to adjust to the opposite heel then, when the tack is completed, you ask for the gas to be turned off in its locker, before carefully pouring the near-boiling water into the mugs to a little over half full. When the milk has been added, the mugs should not be more than two-thirds full (in rough seas half full) to avoid spilling. Stir them and hand them up into the cockpit.

The general conversation in the cockpit quickly focuses on sailing matters for the racing fleet are now rounding a buoy and the leading yachts are on a course converging with our own. They are running downwind under spinnaker, some on port tack and some on starboard. We are on starboard tack so we have right of way over those yachts on port tack. With yachts on the same tack, those to windward of the others shall give way. So we have right of way over the whole racing fleet. However, since they are racing and since there is ample time to make our intentions clear, the skipper has decided, as most do, to give way to the racing fleet by tacking back to the Hampshire shore. He points out that racing yachts fly a rectangular or square burgee instead of the usual triangular one at the masthead, and also that while they are racing they do not fly their national ensign.

'Coffees below!' is called and you place the mugs into the bowl in the sink as they are passed down, including your own, before climbing out into the cockpit to assist with the tack which is already underway. There is little you can do for the winch hands are now quite skilled so you take a look at the racing fleet before retiring to the galley. You return the mugs to their owners (colour coding helps here). Later, when you have washed up and stowed away, following yet another tack to come away from the Hampshire shore, you are given another trick at the wheel. The yacht is heading south west, close-hauled on starboard tack and it is clear all round in our immediate sailing area. Due to the orientation of the west Solent (see Fig 51) starboard tack is the favoured tack (see Fig 37) with a westerly wind, since we shall make more distance down Solent on this tack than on port. The board is a long one from the vicinity of Stansore Point to near Salt Mead Ledges. It calls for considerable concentration for the wind, as usual, is never constant. Just when each pair of foresail luff telltales is flying parallel, the wind changes and the telltales respond immediately, one of each pair, dependent on the change, snaking upwards. You mutter to yourself: *Inner, bear away*: *outer, luff up* (see pages 66–7).

All too soon, however, it is time to tack away from Salt Mead Ledges. You ensure that it is safe to tack, pick a distinctive copse on the Hampshire skyline abeam as your new tack mark, give the orders and tack the yacht. Half a minute later, with a minimum of fuss, the yacht is being sailed to advantage on port tack. It all seems so familiar. But it was a well executed tack, by you and the winchmen, and you gain the skipper's praise. A lookout calls 'large vessel approaching starboard beam, one mile!'

At this early stage the skipper decides that there is a collision risk and in planning avoiding action, decides to heave-to until the large vessel, which is still in a relatively narrow channel, has passed by. The skipper stands behind you to talk you through the manoeuvre. Since, for the most part, the sheets remain untouched, the usual 'ready about' is replaced by 'heaving-to!', by way of forewarning. You are going to turn the bow through the wind then let the boat settle down as she will, almost beam on to the wind, so there is no requirement for a new tack mark. You call 'lee-oh!' and bring her through the wind a little more quickly than when tacking. Once through the wind, the backed foresail takes charge and accelerates the swing; no amount of opposite wheel will have the slightest effect here. Suddenly the rate of swing almost ceases but we are still moving at about 2 knots.

The skipper asks for the mainsail to be eased out and the speed drops considerably. Then, to stop the swing entirely, the foresail is eased out a touch and the helm put down. As we are on starboard tack, boom now out to port, this means that you turn the wheel to the right about half a turn and then lock it in this position with the clamping ring near its centre. (A tiller would be put over to port and temporarily secured to a cleat with a spare sheet end.) We are now hove-to (see Fig 44). All is quiet and stable, but the boat is not quite stopped as the sail plan causes us to forereach ahead at about half a knot towards the island shore and also to make about half a knot leeway. The latter is not noticeable, however, as the tide is setting us towards Yarmouth at about 1 knot. A shore transit confirms a drift towards the west with the skyline moving to the right of a building on the coast.

The mate hands around generous portions of plain chocolate as we watch the world, and the large vessel, go by.

To return to normal sailing we can either let go the foresail sheet and haul in on the other to sail away on our present tack, or we can gybe the yacht by turning the stern through the wind to sail off on the previous tack. The skipper decides to gybe then run downwind because almost all our sailing so far has been windward work, ie beating.

Once again the skipper stands behind to see you through the manoeuvre. You call 'ready to gybe!' This alerts one hand to man the mainsheet, and everyone else that the boom is about to swing across above the cockpit. Anyone standing on the cockpit lockers or on the side decks should crouch, or better still move into the cockpit, clear of the swinging boom. You check that there are no other vessels in the immediate vicinity and then search for a new course mark. The yacht is heading south towards the island shore and the wind is still from the west. In order to turn the stern through the wind you will have to turn the wheel left which will turn the bow back up the Solent. Fawley power station chimney is an excellent mark, for it will always remain clearly visible on the yacht's port side. Another check for nearby vessels, then you call 'gybe-oh!' and steadily apply about half a turn of left wheel.

The mainsheet hand is now hauling in furiously in order to have the sail fully sheeted in by the time the yacht comes stern to wind, in order to keep the boom under control. It is important that this is achieved, so you look up at the main boom's progress and further up to the burgee to judge the timing. If you are going to arrive stern to wind before the sail is sheeted in, then turn the wheel right to midships to stop the yacht's swing until the sheet hand has caught up. If he has the sail sheeted in before stern to wind, no matter.

At about stern to wind, the wind will get into the back of the mainsail and move it and the boom across to the other side of the yacht. The process is alarmingly sudden, even under these controlled conditions. It is potentially lethal if the main is not sheeted in. The yacht's rate of swing will temporarily and dramatically increase as the mainsail moves across. But you spot the chimney drawing forward fine on the port bow and settle the yacht down steering towards it.

'Ease out on both!' and the main is run out until the boom is perpendicular to the burgee. The foresail is eased out until the luff begins to lift. However, this point is difficult to determine, for we are broad reaching and the main is beginning to blanket the foresail. The skipper has noted this and asks for the foresail to be cleated up as it is, for when we have sufficient distance from the island shore, he intends to run dead downwind with the foresail poled out to port and a preventer rigged on the main (see Fig 12) to avoid an accidental gybe. The mate takes the wheel while the skipper supervises the rigging of the preventer which can be done early.

The mainsail is temporarily sheeted in so that the snap shackle on one end of the preventer tackle can be secured to its outer end before the sheet is eased out once more. The remainder of the preventer is then taken forward, outside of all rigging and clear of the foresail sheets, so that the other end of its tackle can be secured by another snap shackle to an eyebolt on the foredeck. The long tail of the preventer is then led aft, under the foresail sheets, to the cockpit where it is cleated.

There is now sufficient offing (inshore water clear of hazards) so the mate is asked to steer directly downwind. As he gently turns the yacht on to her new course and the main sheet is eased out, you uncleat the preventer tail and haul in the slack. With the mainsheet now fully eased out, you cleat the preventer. The risk of an accidental gybe is now greatly reduced, and it is much safer for the skipper and three hands to go forward to pole out the foresail on the port side in order to get it to draw, for it is hanging limp in the lee of the mainsail.

The skipper goes through the procedure verbally before allocating tasks. You learn that the spinnaker pole is to be used and that this can be extremely unwieldy on a moving foredeck unless kept fairly rigidly under control. If lost overboard, they are expensive to replace. So, before removing the pole from its securing chocks on the port side of the foredeck, you take the shackle on the end of the **spinnaker pole topping lift** (a halyard fitted with its block on the forward side of the mast near the yardarms) and secure this to a ring fitting on the top of the spinnaker pole. (The spinnaker pole is used so that the jaws at each end always open upwards; this defines the top.) While another crew member holds the forward end of the pole down on the foredeck, you take the after end and, with a crew man in the cockpit hauling on the topping lift which takes the weight of the pole, you secure its after end to its ring fitting on the mast by opening the jaws with the attached lanyard. Another crew member is asked to take the lazy (port side) sheet and place it in the jaws of the forward end of the pole. The downhaul is then attached to the lower side of the pole. This is a rope rove through a block on the foredeck and led aft to the cockpit.

The next stage requires two crewmen other than the helmsman in the cockpit in order that the port sheet may be hauled in as the topping lift hand raises the pole to the horizontal and also eases out the downhaul. You remain on the foredeck and watch these simultaneous operations in response to the skipper's order. On hauling in the foresail sheet, the clew soon arrives at the jaws of the forward end of the pole. Then the combined system, pole plus foresail, is hauled outwards and aft on the port side. The sheet is cleated with the pole just off the port forward lower shroud (Figs 1b and 63). Yacht speed has almost doubled because the foresail is now drawing well.

The skipper goes aft to the cockpit to examine the rig and notices that the pole is not horizontal; the clew end is higher than the mast end. So you are asked to rectify this by going to the mast end of the pole, slackening the locking screw on the ring fitting and sliding this up its track on the mast until the skipper is satisfied that the pole is now horizontal before tightening the locking screw.

Your appreciation of your handiwork is shattered by 'starboard tack yachts approaching, port bow about one mile!' You duck down to look under the foresail and there they are, three abreast separated by about 100 metres; after all this! It is soon decided that at least one of these is probably on a collision course. There is no time to wait and confirm, so the skipper takes over the wheel and asks the mate to take you and another crewman forward to remove the pole so that, after the preventer has also been removed, the yacht may be gybed out of the way, for we are the give way yacht.

The foresail sheet is steadily eased out and the pole swings forward with much flogging from the now unsupported foresail. At the mate's bidding you go forward to the bows and remove the port sheet from the jaws, but still hold the pole end against the forestay. A cockpit

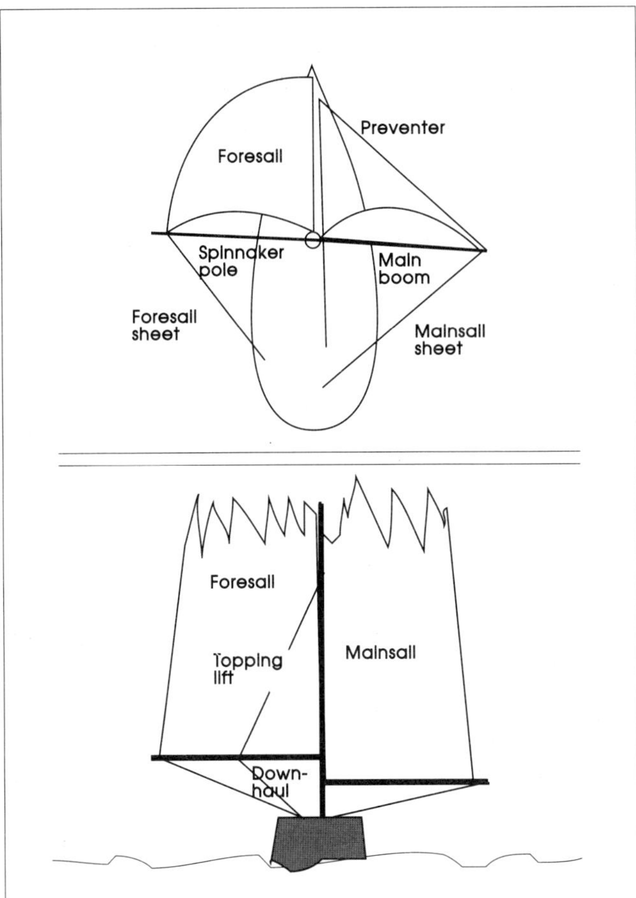

Fig 63. Poled-out foresail.

hand pulls in a little on the starboard sheet – more to encourage the foresail to stay on the starboard side of the foredeck and therefore out of the way, than to get it to draw. Another cockpit crew now eases out steadily on the topping lift at the mate's request, and you allow the forward end of the pole to lower on to the foredeck and hold it there. The other foredeck crew now removes the other end from its mast fitting and the topping lift is further eased to complete the lowering of the pole. Both foredeck crew then secure the pole in its chocks.

The skipper asks you all to come into the cockpit immediately for he is about to gybe the yacht. He details you to handle the mainsheet and someone else to ease out on the preventer at his next order. As soon as he calls 'ready to gybe' you haul in the mainsheet hand-over-hand furiously, for the boom is right out and there is a lot of mainsheet to come in. While slowly turning the yacht's stern towards the wind, the skipper briefs the crew that when he has gybed the yacht he will bring her right round to close-hauled, now on starboard tack, to beat westwards once more. This alerts a winch hand to sheet in on the port foresail sheet, and alerts you not to let the mainsheet run out immediately after the gybe.

As soon as you have the mainsheet hauled in and cleated (the preventer is eased right out and is no longer effective) the skipper calls 'gybe-oh!' and continues to turn the wheel right to bring the stern through the wind. The boom flips across almost immediately and remains close-hauled on the other side as the mainsheet is cleated. Someone else removes, coils and stows the preventer. There is now a dramatic increase in noise due to the wildly flogging foresail and because the yacht is rounding up into the choppy, wind against tide, waves. The foresail is soon sheeted right in as the yacht rounds up to beat, now heeled over to port. A glance astern shows that the other yachts are still several hundred metres away – all is well for we are now all going in the same direction on the same tack.

In a few minutes we are once more off Salt Mead Ledges, the yacht is tacked with pleasing effect and we are heading north west, now on port tack, back across the Solent. A lookout reports that the other yachts have gybed and are now running away from us. It is clear all round so the skipper decides to demonstrate man overboard drill.

After some discussion on other techniques, such as tacking or gybing instantly to sail back, or even lowering the sails and starting the engine to get back, all of which have their drawbacks, he describes the RYA method which relies on the sails for they, unlike the engine, are dependable. This method has the inestimable merit of being a drill which is always the same no matter what the point of sailing. It can also be readily executed by a new night watch who are still a little 'woolly' after their spell below.

Whoever sees a crew member fall overboard will bellow 'man overboard!' to alert everyone including the watch below. He will also immediately throw a lifebuoy and the special sparbuoy, which has a flag and automatic light about 1.5 metres above the float for greater visibility, and then, ignoring any order which will conflict, he will remain on the afterdeck and point continuously to the sparbuoy. The senior man will take over the helm and immediately turn the yacht on to a reach on the same tack; the crew will jump to it and adjust the sheets accordingly. He will glance frequently at the pointing arm and beyond to the sparbuoy and when he judges the distance off is sufficient (and this is usually achieved within half a minute) he will give the tacking orders; the crew's 'ready' should be returned immediately. After the tack, the yacht will be sailed on a broad reach for a time then rounded up to a close reach without sheeting in on either sail. A crewman will be detailed to put a bowline on a warp (the bight big enough to slip easily over the man's shoulders) and to crouch by the shrouds on the weather (windward) side.

The helmsman will now be able to see the sparbuoy, representing the man in the water, and keep this fine on the bow as the yacht decelerates due to the loss of drive from the sails. At the right moment he will turn up head-to-wind, and seconds later the yacht will be stopped alongside the man. The bowline will be slipped over his shoulders and under his arms and the warp will be secured to the yacht. Next comes the recovery aboard stage.

Numerous techniques have been suggested over the years, but most of them take too much time, for the man may be injured and the water cold, or they are just not realistic in a seaway. He will not be able to pull himself up on deck; in fact it would take four men to lift him out, but while they are doing so at least one, if not all of them, risks falling in, thus compounding the crisis. An efficient method is to lower the foresail and sheet in the main. The yacht will then lie 'weather-cocked' head-to-wind without needing attention. Maximum manpower may then be applied to the recovery, which is done by shackling the foresail halyard to the bight of rope around the man in the water; he is then winched aboard with minimum delay.

The skipper recapitulates the 'getting back' technique with the use of a sketch (Fig 64) before giving a practical demonstration. We are still sailing close-hauled on port tack. You are appointed 'observer' so you bellow 'man overboard!' as you go to the afterdeck, remove a lifebuoy from its rack in the after pulpit, and throw it astern to the 'man in the water'. The sparbuoy is then removed from its stowage

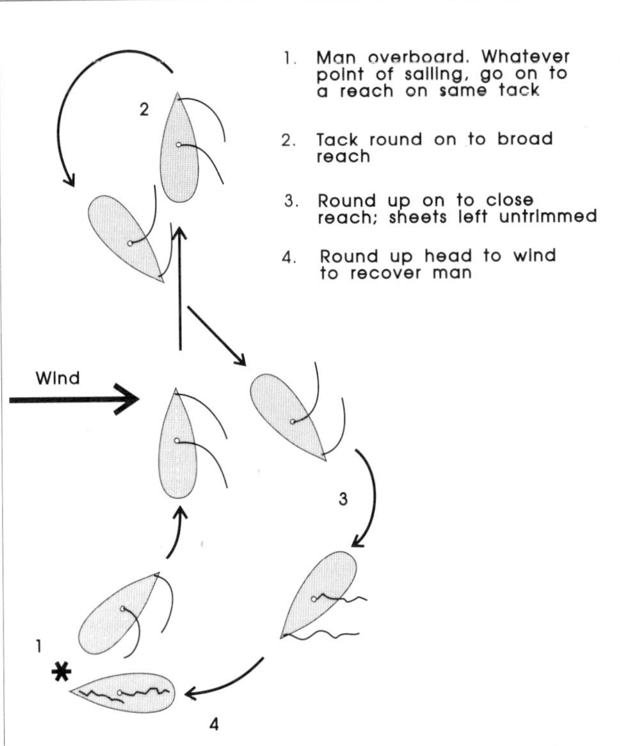

1. Man overboard. Whatever point of sailing, go on to a reach on same tack
2. Tack round on to broad reach
3. Round up on to close reach; sheets left untrimmed
4. Round up head to wind to recover man
Wind
1
2
3
4
*

Fig 64. Man overboard drill.

on the backstay and you quickly lower it into the water. Then you look at and point towards the sparbuoy continuously. Meantime the yacht has been turned off the wind on to a reach. The skipper asks someone to get a short warp from the cockpit locker. You ignore this order and keep looking and pointing. The man's life depends just as much on your maintaining visual contact with the sparbuoy (you will not be able to see his head above the water for long except in calm seas) as it does on the skipper's skill in getting the boat back.

After what seems a very long time, for we are sailing away from the man in the water (and it must seem even longer to him, though it is still just under a half minute) the yacht is tacked right round to a broad reach on starboard tack. With one hand holding on to the backstay and the other still pointing, you turn to maintain visual contact. Because the yacht is being turned through about 150 degrees you lose sight of the sparbuoy, temporarily, behind the No 1 genoa. But you have been monitoring the rate of swing of the bow relative to the sparbuoy and soon pick it up as it reappears on the other side, now broadening on the starboard bow.

Still pointing, you move forward to the region of the mast and sit down, now raising your pointing arm well above the horizontal so the skipper can see it. In a short while the yacht is rounded up on to a close reach, now with the sails flogging as the sheets remain unadjusted. The skipper soon calls 'got him' so you lower your arm, but keep on looking just in case, as you move forward of the mast and out of his vision. The warp with bowline tied is brought up on to the coachroof. The skipper finally rounds up the yacht head-to-wind and, since this is a drill, asks you to recover the sparbuoy. A few seconds later the yacht comes to a stop with the sparbuoy within an arm's length alongside the starboard shrouds. He asks you to drop it back in while we are still fairly close to the lifebuoy, and after sheeting in on both sails the whole technique is repeated, now with someone else in the observer role. It is demonstrated yet again with the mate in command, before all four new crew are given a turn at bringing the yacht back with the skipper advising when to tack and when to round up on to a close reach and again head-to-wind. On the penultimate attempt the lifebuoy is recovered using a boat hook, and finally the sparbuoy is recovered.

All your attempts have been reasonably successful, but since the skipper has been calling the shots, you all ask for another attempt on your own. 'Tomorrow' is promised, for time is passing too quickly and there is some spinnaker work and some reefing still to be done; the latter even if the wind does not freshen.

The yacht is sailed away on port tack towards the Hampshire shore and preparations are made for a spinnaker run. First, the spinnaker sheets have to be rigged. You have the starboard (lee) side and you crouch a little as you work your way forward, carrying the still coiled sheet in one hand and holding on to grabrails, shrouds, etc with the other. You sit down on the foredeck with feet braced against the toerail, undo the securing turns on the coiled sheet and secure the snap shackle on the free end of the sheet to the pulpit. Then you work your way aft, slipping off coils as necessary and ensuring that the spinnaker sheet is passed outside of the foresail sheets and the shrouds. The end of the sheet is finally brought inside the lifelines near a block already secured to the base of the after pulpit. You pass the end through this block, from outboard to inboard, tie a stopper knot in the tail, then coil the fall of the sheet in the after end of the cockpit.

Meanwhile the spinnaker in its 'sock' is brought up on to the foredeck and temporarily secured near the mast. (The sock is one of the best ways of keeping a spinnaker under control at the hoisting and handing stages. Of the other ways, the most common for hoisting is a series of rubber bands fitted inwards from all three corners of the sail as far as possible. These bands break away as the spinnaker fills with the wind when hoisting is nearly complete.) The sock is a long nylon sausage, completely enveloping the spinnaker along its whole length, with a hard plastic 'mouth' at its lower (spinnaker clews) end. An 'endless' rope attached to the mouth runs inside the sock to a block attached to the head of the spinnaker and returns outside the sock to the mouth. This line is hauled one way to release and let fly the spinnaker, or hauled the other way to 'snuff' it prior to lowering.

The yacht is now gybed round on to starboard tack to run downwind; the preventer is fitted to the boom before it is run out. The foresail will not be able to draw, and since it will otherwise be in the way it is now handed and secured to the starboard lifelines. You are assigned the mast end of the spinnaker pole. First you attach its topping lift to the eye bolt in the middle of the pole, upper side, to secure it to the yacht. A cockpit hand then hoists a little on the topping lift and you secure the pole, opening jaws uppermost, to its ring fitting on a track on the forward side of the mast. The other end is raised by hauling on the topping lift so that the other foredeck crewman can secure its jaws temporarily to the forestay. The same crewman now attaches the pole downhaul, a line shackled to the middle of the lower side of the pole, rove through a block on the foredeck and led aft to the cockpit. The pole is under control; now for the spinnaker.

The sail is carried forward to the bows by another crewman and yourself, taking great care not to trip on the preventer, the pole downhaul and any other piece of equipment on the foredeck. The spinnaker sheets are now attached to the rings on the clews of the sail, which are already protruding from the mouth of the sock, ensuring that neither sheet comes inside the forestay. One clew is coloured red (port) and the other green (starboard); the sheets are snap shackled on accordingly. The spinnaker halyard is now shackled to the head of the spinnaker, ensuring there are no twists in the sock, then sock and sail are hoist from the cockpit. The halyard shackle is swivel-mounted to discourage any twisting as the sock is hoist. Now to attach the pole.

We are running dead downwind on starboard tack so the mainsail boom is right out on the port side of the yacht. The spinnaker pole is always carried on the opposite side, so it will be finally set out to starboard. The outer end of the pole is now removed from the forestay and attached to the starboard (green) clew ring which now becomes the tack; the sheet already attached to the tack becomes the spinnaker guy.

The pole is still pointing forward and the spinnaker is still contained within its hoist sock. The next stage requires simultaneous action from you on the sock endless line and two other crew members in the cockpit, under the skipper's direction. One will haul away steadily on the guy to bring the pole and tack aft on the starboard side and the other will steadily haul on the spinnaker sheet, bringing the clew aft and preventing, to a large extent, any twisting in the newly released spinnaker.

'Hoist the sock!' is given when all is ready, so you grab the endless line on the outside of the sock and haul away downwards hand-over-hand to raise the mouth of the sock and thus expose the lower part of the spinnaker. Meanwhile, pole and tack as well as the clew are coming steadily aft on their respective sides, allowing the wind to fill the foot of the spinnaker. Quite suddenly, your efforts become redundant as the wind fills more of the spinnaker and forces the mouth of the sock to accelerate upwards, finally stopping, concertina-shaped, beyond the head of the sail. You take up the slack and secure the endless line to any free fitting on the side of the mast and then sit down on the foredeck, for your tasks here are not yet over. All the while the pole has been hauled aft until it is almost up against the forward lower shroud and the sheet has been hauled aft to keep the spinnaker full but allowing the foot of the sail to float free of the forestay.

The skipper notices that the tack end of the pole is lower than the mast end so asks you to lower the latter in its track until the pole is horizontal. You undo the locking screw and slide the eye fitting down in its track until the skipper asks you to stop and secure. The yacht is still running dead downwind, the pole is as far aft as it can be and is close to the optimum, which is perpendicular to the wind. The sheet is now eased out gently until the starboard side of the spinnaker (the luff since it rises from the tack) begins to lift (or back). This is due to the wind getting into the back, or forward side, of the luff. The sheet is now gently pulled in until the lift in the luff just disappears. The clew hand is required to repeat this testing process every minute or so. You are now given the wheel. Don't worry, the skipper will stand by and advise!

When sailing dead downwind, the general practice is to leave the pole and guy alone (but keep testing on the sheet as above) and sail the yacht to keep the spinnaker drawing well throughout the small fluctuations in direction which occur every half minute or so. These are best indicated by the burgee at the masthead, so a spinnaker run is a neck-craning job, with the main effort concentrated on the luff of the spinnaker and the burgee, with occasional glances ahead (for you will also have a conspicuous mark or compass course to rely on if temporarily disorientated).

The burgee shows a small wind shift from dead astern to very broad on the starboard quarter, ie the burgee now points fine on the port bow, and the spinnaker luff begins to lift. You ease the wheel a little left to bring the bows left until the burgee points dead ahead once more. A glance down shows that the lift in the luff has disappeared. The technique calls for close co-operation between the helmsman and the sheet hand. The former should tell the latter when he is turning the wheel and the latter should cease 'tweaking' the sheet while the boat's heading is being changed.

A further wind shift towards the port quarter follows within a minute or so, with a consequent tremble in the leech of the spinnaker. The burgee is now pointing fine on the starboard bow so you turn the wheel gently right until it flies dead ahead once more. The spinnaker leech is now 'asleep'.

The skipper now requests an alteration of course by 20 degrees to starboard in order to give way to a close-hauled starboard tack yacht. (Same tack. We are clearly to windward. We give way.) So you turn the wheel right on to the new course. The turn is executed slowly so as to allow the spinnaker guy and sheet hands to adjust the sail in unison. The guy is eased out to keep the pole perpendicular to the wind and, simultaneously, the sheet is gently hauled in by the same amount to keep the spinnaker drawing. Meantime the preventer is eased out and the mainsail sheet hauled in to keep the main drawing efficiently with its boom perpendicular to the wind.

Under these new conditions with the wind no longer dead astern, you hold your course and let the cockpit crew trim the spinnaker to the small but frequent wind shifts. The wind shifts further out on the quarter, lifting the spinnaker luff. The guy hand calls 'easing' to the sheet hand as he eases out the guy until the lift in the luff disappears. The sheet hand hauls in on the sheet by a similar amount to keep the spinnaker drawing. Again, there must be close teamwork here. A little later the wind shifts further aft and the leech trembles. The sheet hand calls 'easing' to his teammate, who hauls in by the same amount.

We are now back into the area off Salt Mead Ledges, and the skipper indicates that a gybe would be a useful exercise before the yacht is turned round to beat down the Solent once more. The process is carried out in several stages. You are part of the foredeck crew who will gybe the spinnaker – the skipper has taken over the wheel. When the yacht has been turned dead downwind and all is clear round and about, the skipper calls 'gybe the spinnaker!' You are at the mast end of the spinnaker pole and you release it from the mast by using the lanyard to open the jaws. The pole is constrained vertically by its topping lift and downhaul, but the tack end will attempt to move the pole across the yacht. Allow it to do so under control, for another crew hand will be waiting on the port side of the yacht to secure it to the spinnaker clew ring. Some sideways swinging of the pole can be reduced by the cockpit hands hauling in on the pole's topping lift and downhaul. Nevertheless, the spinnaker foot will swing a little from side to side in its new freedom quite safely as long as the yacht remains near to dead downwind.

Meantime, activated by the skipper's 'ready to gybe the mainsail!', the cockpit crew have eased out then removed the preventer while the mainsail has been sheeted in. Following 'gybe-oh!' the skipper eases the wheel a little to the left, the stern soon turns through the wind, and the close-hauled main flips across to the other side. The preventer is now rigged to the boom on the starboard side of the yacht, for we are now on port tack, and the main eased out as the yacht is turned slightly on to a dead downwind course once more.

The foredeck crew now complete the task of gybing the spinnaker. You pull on the lanyard on the pole's starboard end to release the clew then take this free end of the pole and secure it to its eye fitting on the mast. The pole is now set out to port. New guy, new sheet, topping lift and downhaul are trimmed to make the sail draw efficiently. (On gybing the spinnaker, the old guy becomes the new sheet and vice versa.) The process of gybing when flying a spinnaker is shown schematically in Fig 65.

As we are now about to approach shallow water in Thorness Bay, the skipper advises that he is about to turn on to a broad reach to run parallel with the shore, and calls 'standby on guy, sheet, mainsheet and preventer!' Four crew men jump into action and call 'ready!' The

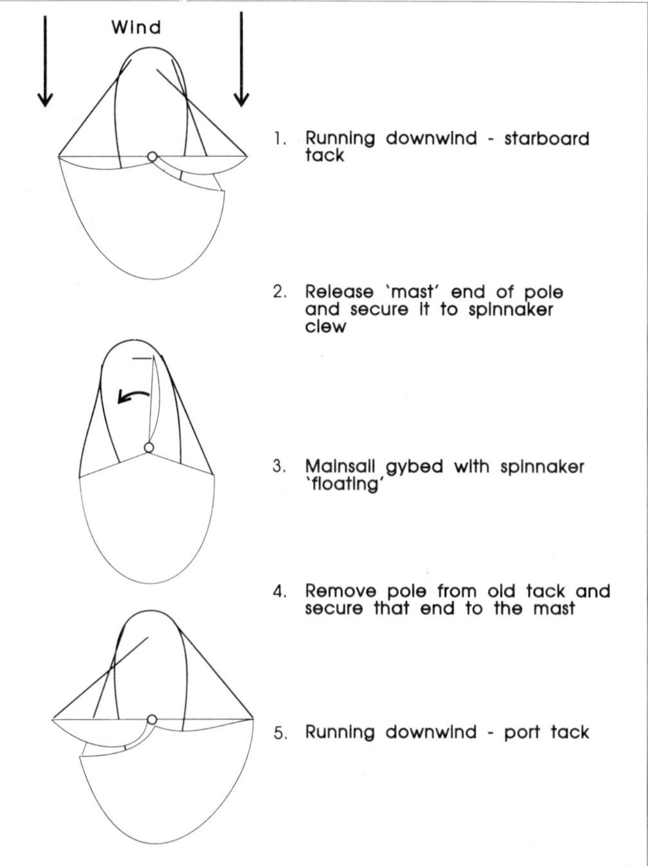

Wind
1. Running downwind - starboard tack
2. Release 'mast' end of pole and secure it to spinnaker clew
3. Mainsail gybed with spinnaker 'floating'
4. Remove pole from old tack and secure that end to the mast
5. Running downwind - port tack

Fig 65. Spinnaker run – gybing.

yacht is steadily turned through about 40 degrees to port while the guy is eased out and the spinnaker sheet hauled in with final adjustment being left until the course alteration is complete. The preventer is eased out to allow the mainsail to be sheeted in until the lift just disappears from its luff. You are asked to remove the preventer since this is no longer required. The boom is hauled in temporarily so that you can remove that end of the preventer. Its block on the foredeck is next removed, then you 'shorten-up' this block to the boom end and coil up the preventer, finishing off with securing turns before you stow it.

The afternoon is now well advanced so the skipper decides to turn the yacht round for the beat to Yarmouth, but first the spinnaker has to come down. Again you are part of the foredeck crew and your first job is to snuff the 'chute'. You remove the sock's endless line from the mast fitting and on the skipper's order you haul away hand-over-hand to bring the sock down. The task is easy enough, for as you are doing this both tack and clew are eased forward to meet as the sock's mouth arrives at the foot of the spinnaker. The endless line needs no further attention as it is now contained by the outstretched sock. The halyard is now run out from the cockpit and the whole sausage falls on to the deck. Someone else detaches the halyard and secures its shackle to the mast.

Since you are already in the bows and the pole is forward against the forestay, your next task is to clear the tack and clew. You lean on the pole to keep it against the forestay, remove the tack ring from the end of the pole, unshackle the guy and secure this to the pulpit, then remove the sheet from the clew and secure its shackle to the other side of the pulpit. The snuffed spinnaker is now completely free and is stowed below. You call for the pole topping lift to be eased out so that you can hold your end of the pole down on the deck. Someone else removes and stows the downhaul, then moves to the mast to remove that end of the pole from its fitting. He calls for the topping lift to be eased out again while you both guide the pole on to its chocks and then secure it. The topping lift is finally detached and its shackle secured to the mast. You are asked to remain on the foredeck to assist with hoisting the headsail. The yacht will remain on this course to make this task easier.

You collect the foresail halyard from its mast fitting and shackle this to the head of the foresail, mindful of any slack, while other hands remove the ties. Since we are on port tack, the sail is already on the correct (starboard) side so, after a quick check on the clew bowlines, the sail is ready to hoist. Someone else feeds the luff into its groove so you go aft along the port side, safely away from the flogging sail and sheet, to the cockpit. Another crew member is sheeting in on the foresail so the skipper hands over the wheel to you and asks you to round up to close-hauled for the beat to Yarmouth. You call 'rounding up!' There is an immediate reaction from the cockpit crew who jump to the sheets and haul away on both foresail and mainsail as you steadily turn left towards the wind. You have already assessed the true wind direction from the waves, visually aimed off to the right at about 45 degrees, and chosen a building on the mainland as a guide.

As you come round towards this, you reduce the rate of turn by decreasing the amount of left wheel, check that the sails are now sheeted right in and then fine tune your windward steering by using the foresail luff telltales. Only a small steering adjustment is required for them all to fly true; and the mainland building is almost dead ahead! This building is near the entrance to the Beaulieu River. As we approach mid-Solent, it appears to have moved a considerable amount to the right of the background. This is because the tide is setting us westwards at an average of 2 knots. So despite the tacking it will not take too long to reach Yarmouth.

Some minutes later, the skipper decides to reef as the wind has definitely freshened and is now at the upper end of force 4, about 15 knots. This means that we shall reduce the area of the mainsail and change down to a smaller headsail. As we shall soon be approaching the Hampshire shore and will have to tack, the skipper decides to change the headsail first. The forestay foil has, in fact, two luff grooves – a racing refinement – so that the replacement sail may be hoist in the spare groove on the concave side of the old foresail (there are two foresail halyards, and the skipper has noted that the spare groove is conveniently on the correct side). The mate takes over the wheel so that the skipper can direct the reefing.

The No 2 genoa is brought up and removed from its bag which is then passed below. (The No 1 genoa bag has also been brought up and is secured to the lifelines.) You (yes, you're foredeck crew again) secure the tack of the new sail, then take the spare halyard as it is passed to you and shackle this to the head of the sail. Still maintaining tension in the halyard, you feed the extreme top of the luff into the spare groove. Meanwhile another crew hand has undone the bowline on the lazy sheet (port side) and secured this to the clew of the No 2 genoa; this will become the weather sheet when we tack. The associated fairlead (Photo 17) is moved forward three holes in its track (a predetermined position) by raising its securing pin. The bulk of the sail is now moved across to the starboard side.

Photo 17. Foresail sheet fairlead and track.

When all is ready, the skipper calls 'hoist!' and the No 2 genoa is run up. The other foredeck hand hauls the clew of the new sail aft so that the No 2 lies happily in the concave side of the No 1 genoa. The foredeck crew is called aft to the cockpit while the mate tacks the yacht. You stand back to let the cockpit crew do their thing, then after the tack you go forward again since the No 1 genoa can now be lowered. At the skipper's 'lower!' the foredeck crew assist the No 1 genoa to run down, one at the luff and the other at the leech. (The mate will have ensured that the correct halyard has been used!)

While the other two kneel on the handed sail to keep it under control, you remove the single sheet from it and secure the sheet with a bowline (and good tail) on the No 2 genoa as the new lazy sheet. Someone else moves the new lazy sheet fairlead forward three holes to match that on the port side. The old halyard has been removed and secured to the mast in the meantime, and the tack freed from its fit-

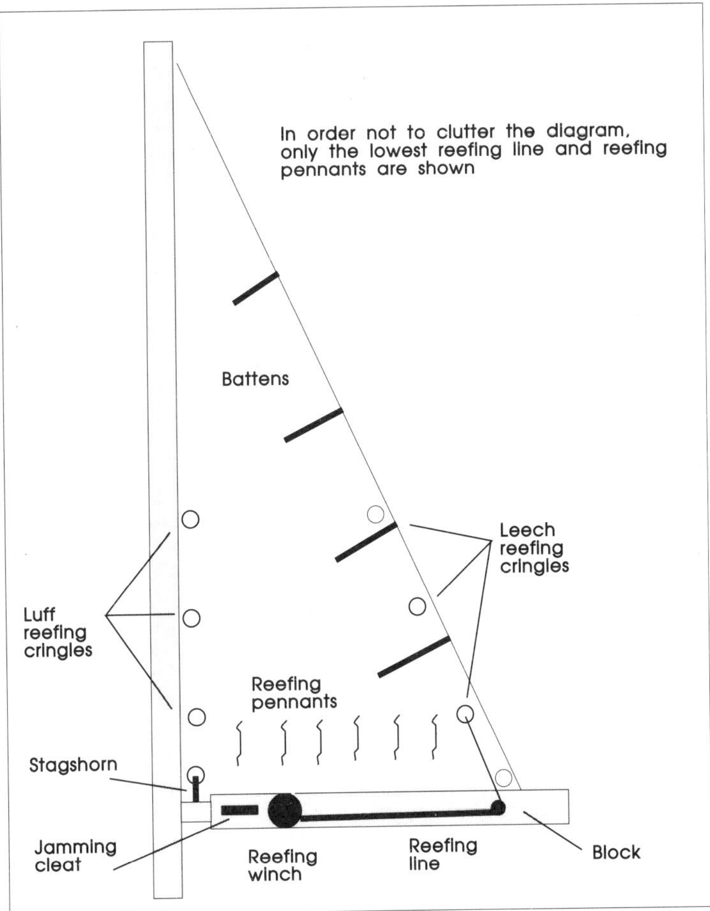

Fig 66. Slab reefing gear.

ting. The No 1 is now stuffed unceremoniously (another advantage of man-made sails) into its bag, but with the tack secured to the lanyard on the mouth of the bag, for quick location next time, and the No 1 genoa is passed down below and stowed. (With single-groove foils or with piston-hanks on the luff (see pages 92–3), the old sail would be handed and stowed, then the new one bent on and hoist.)

The main is now overpowering the foresail and tries to drive the bow up into the wind, ie to the right since we are now on starboard tack. To counteract this the helmsman has to hold the wheel to the left. This is weather helm (see pages 79–82). The constantly angled rudder is now acting as a brake, so the skipper is anxious to reef the main now in order to restore sail balance.

There are several types of reefing gear. The most common type fitted for a number of years now is slab reefing, itself a modernisation of an old method. Our yacht is fitted with slab reefing gear. The main parts are shown in Fig 66. (If not already close-hauled, a yacht is always put on to that point of sailing before reefing its mainsail.)

At the order 'take one slab out of the mainsail!' the skipper takes two of you on to the coachroof, leaving the mate to supervise the steering (we are still close-hauled on starboard tack) and to assist the remaining cockpit hand. The kicking strap (there to hold down the boom, see Fig 1b) is eased out a little by the cockpit hand to allow tensioning of the main boom topping lift. You are the mast man and, after the skipper has asked for the mainsail halyard to be eased out, you assist the bottom of the luff to slide down, grab the first cringle and place this over the spare end of the stagshorn, tack fitting. Meanwhile the other crewman has hauled in on the leech reefing line, finally using the small 'snubbing' winch on the boom itself, until its leech cringle is down on the boom. He cleats this line in the jammer, also on the boom. The skipper cries 'tension the halyard!' then 'ease out the topping lift and tension the kicker!' These are seen to from the cockpit. The slab now hanging at the foot of the sail is rolled up and secured to the boom with reef knots tied in the reefing pennants, before the reefing crew move aft to the cockpit.

On some yachts, the leech reefing lines are also led aft to the cockpit, and on a few, these are even accompanied by similar lines run through the luff cringles. While this undoubtedly leads to greater safety, the resultant spaghetti mountain of rope tails in the cockpit can be an awful mess, despite colour coding. In the relatively quiet conditions obtaining within the Solent, the reefing of the foresail and mainsail was carried out without safety harness. In rougher conditions there, and almost always offshore on novice training, they would have been worn.

The yacht is now sailing under a well-balanced rig, close-hauled on starboard tack (still the favoured tack) at a little over 6 knots. She is heeled over so that the lee rail is about 10 cm clear of the water as it storms past (without reefing, the lee rail would now be just under most of the time).

Two more tacks later, and we are approaching Yarmouth. It is time to prepare for entering harbour.

ENTERING · HARBOUR ·

Yarmouth, a mile or so away to the south west, is almost unique in the Solent area for there is no marina. Instead, yachts moor to **piles** (substantial posts driven into the harbour bed) from the bow and stern. The engine is started and the skipper calls 'standby to hand and bag the foresail!': the latter in order to leave the foredeck clear. You are the halyard main in the cockpit. You have correctly identified the foresail halyard in use and taken four turns round the halyard winch to hold it so that you can open the jamming cleat which is currently taking the strain. When the foredeck crew are ready, the skipper turns the yacht into the wind so that the foresail will drop neatly on to the foredeck. On his 'lower!' you remove the turns from the winch and let the halyard run through your fingers. The foresail drops into the middle of the foredeck and is stuffed away in its bag. The now redundant foresail halyard is secured and tensioned.

The skipper calls 'standby the main!' and, after identifying the various ropes for you, he asks you to 'ease the kicker and mainsheet', 'tension the topping lift' and then 'haul in on the mainsheet and kicker' all in quick succession. This done, the weight of the boom is now taken by the topping lift, and the boom itself largely prevented from swinging from side to side by the mainsheet. It is therefore safe for the handing crew to lean on. You take four turns of the mainsheet around the halyard winch, open its jammer and then, following the lowering order, you remove the turns and let the halyard run through your fingers. While the others roll up the mainsail into a sausage and secure it to the top of the boom, you tidy up the cockpit spaghetti as best you can. As soon as the mainsail is secured, the skipper calls 'long warps bow and stern and three fenders each side!'

You take the stern warp, undo the securing turns, tie a bowline in the free end and place it temporarily over a cleat on the afterdeck. Then lay the warp down, open coiled, in the after end of the cockpit out of the way. It is essential to ensure first that it cannot fall into the water to foul the propeller and secondly to see that it remains tidy for immediate use. Next you go forward, grab the remaining fender and secure it in the 'free' slot. First you lower it over the side until the bottom is a few centimetres above the water and then tie a clove hitch on to the upper lifeline, locking it with a half hitch on the standing part of its lanyard. The fender is now brought inboard until required in harbour. That done, you all retire to the cockpit, except for the bow warp man who sits down in front of the mast, out of the way.

The skipper has turned the yacht round to point directly to the

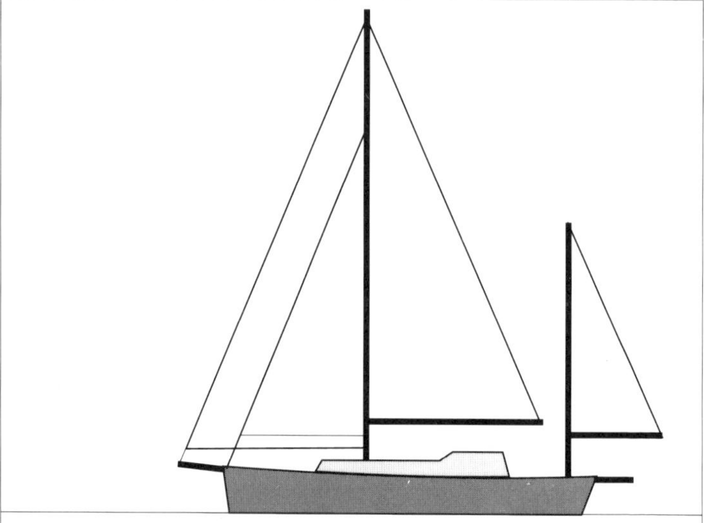

A yawl has her mizzen mast stepped aft of the rudder post, whereas it is forward with a ketch. She is normally cutter rigged with a bow-sprit forward, and a short 'bumpkin' aft to control the mizzen sail.

Fig 67. A yawl.

shore, though we are still short of the harbour entrance. He points out how quickly the background is moving to the right, relative to the town church spire. This rate is even more dramatic when related to the end of Yarmouth pier which is now almost dead ahead. The tides run strongly off Yarmouth and there is a good hour of the ebb still to run.

Two, two-masted yachts have just left the harbour and are now hoisting their sails. They are a **yawl** (Fig 67) and a **schooner** (Fig 68). The skipper draws our attention to the car ferry moored alongside the quay in case it moves off.

We are now about 100 metres north west of the pier and abeam the harbour entrance. Though we are making our approach, the bows are aimed off to the left by about 30 degrees in order to counteract the effect of the tide. Once the end of the pier draws abeam, the tidal stream diminishes considerably, and the yacht is now turned on to a more direct heading. As we approach the harbour entrance on the starboard side, the ferry slips from the quay and looks as though it will fill the whole entrance in a minute or so. Although there is not a great deal of room, there is enough for safety. It may seem a frightening prospect to the novice crew, but in reality it is a frequent occurrence every day at both Yarmouth and Lymington, and one that Solent yachtsmen soon adjust to in safety.

In seconds the ferry is passed and we are inside the harbour, now at much reduced speed. The skipper spots an empty pair of piles and turns right through 'trots' of yachts already moored up in rows, and

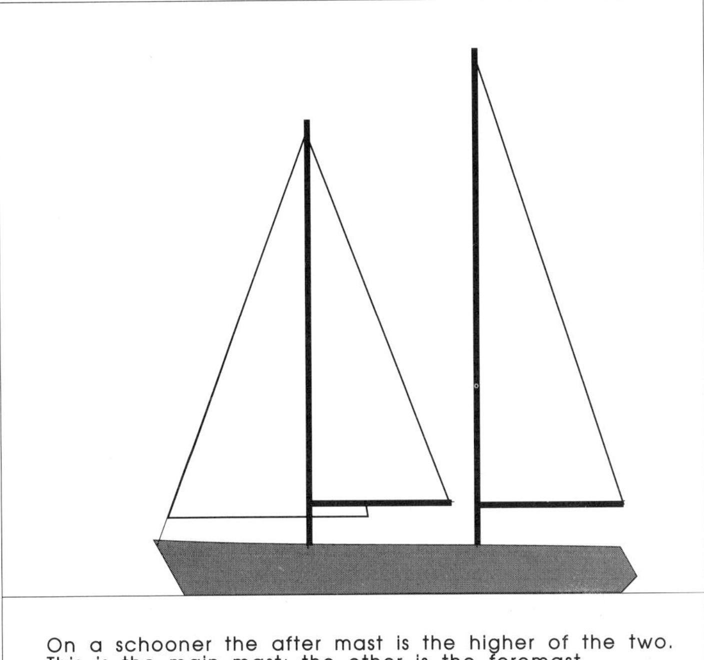

On a schooner the after mast is the higher of the two.
This is the main mast; the other is the foremast

Fig 68. A schooner.

calls 'starboard side approach'. He has already briefed us that the best approach to any mooring is against the wind and the tide so as to retain better control of the boat. Since the wind and tide (a slow ebb) are both from the west, his approach to the piles will be a direct one once the boat has been turned to the west inside the harbour. He has also stated that he will steer the yacht close to the after pile so that the stern warp can be run through as the yacht slowly passes by. He will stop just short of the forward pile for the bow warp to be run through, before dropping back, using the warps, to centre-up.

The fenders are now positioned outboard, more to be out of the way than to 'fend'. You remove the bowline from its cleat on the afterdeck, pass the bowline over the after pulpit on the starboard quarter, then down and back through the fairlead and on to the starboard cleat. Now you carefully lift the open coiled warp from the cockpit sole, see that the coils will run off all right and take the warp forward along the starboard side, outside of everything (mainsheet, foresail sheet, etc) to the area of the shrouds. Turn the coils over neatly to locate the other end of the warp and see that it will run out freely.

The final approach to the piles is now well underway. There is only one yacht on the piles before ours, so the skipper is able to make a very slow and slightly oblique approach to the after pile. Each pile has a parallel stout pole attached. There is a large ring on this pole, to which is attached a chain for pulling up the ring when water depths are high. We are near low water and the ring is easily seen on the end of the chain near the surface. Another crew man is detailed to lift up the ring as we drift slowly by. You pass the end of the warp through the ring and then haul away smartly to take up the slack as you work your way back along the starboard side to the stern, ensuring there is no part of the warp anywhere near the water. The warp tail is then passed inboard through the same fairlead as its other end. As the yacht drifts up towards the forward pile, now under its own momentum, you ease out on the free end of the stern warp. Then, at a signal from the mate on the bow, the skipper says 'check'. You take a turn round the cleat and hold it, thus stopping the yacht. The foredeck crew, with an easier task, soon reeve the bow warp through its ring and now all is ready to centre-up. The skipper asks you to haul in steadily with the stern warp while the bow one is eased out, until the yacht is centred between the piles. The free ends are then secured on their cleats, and the engine switched off.

The sterngland, through which the propeller shaft passes out of the hull, is now examined. There is a slight trickle of water, quite normal, and so the associated grease gun is given a turn or so until the trickle stops. Next the bilges are examined and found to contain a little water. You operate the handle of the bilge pump a few times until the water has gone and the pump sucks air.

Mooring up is now finished. Dinner is already underway for we shall be slipping our mooring at dusk for a few hours of night sailing. Slipping itself should be relatively easy as both warps are doubled-back on board. But now it's time to sit in the saloon and take a few minutes of well-earned relaxation. It has been a hard but very enjoyable day, and it is not yet over!

NIGHT · SAILING ·

Dinner is over, the washing up done and everything stowed. The chat now ceases as the charts of the Solent are opened out on the saloon table for the skipper is about to brief us on the night sail. The wind has backed into the south and has dropped to 10 or 11 knots, the threshold between forces 3 and 4. The tide has turned and the flood (giving increasing depths) will set eastwards through the Solent for the next six hours or so. The visibility is expected to remain good and the weather fine; excellent conditions for some night sailing.

The overall plan is to reach east past Cowes to Mother Bank buoy north west of Ryde, then reach back to Cowes against a foul tide. Despite the reduced wind speed, we shall carry our No 2 genoa which will allow better vision under its higher foot. As a consequence we shall also leave one reef in the main for better sail balance. The skipper had already foreseen the requirement to leave the main reefed as it was lowered for entering a few hours ago.

It will feel quite a bit colder so warm clothing is essential; oilskins serve very well here. There should be little requirement for anyone to go forward on deck from the cockpit, but, just in case, we shall all wear a safety harness. A jackstay made of wire rope runs along each side of the deck from the stern right up towards the bows. Anyone going forward will clip on to the jackstay before leaving the cockpit; the clip can slide all the way forward without hindrance. (In rough conditions, the harness would be clipped on to a stout cockpit fitting before leaving the saloon.) Sailing the yacht will be much the same as during the day, but lookouts become even more important and they will have to be continuously vigilant. Once it is dark, then, what shall we see?

Firstly, it is never completely dark even on overcast nights. Nevertheless we shall not be able to see the outline of ships, yachts, buoys, etc unless they are very close, so we shall have to rely on lights for their identification. The international rules for avoiding collisions at sea lay down precise requirements for every kind of vessel. In a briefing like this it is not practicable to list them all; in any case, they are well described in many dedicated publications. We shall concentrate on the main categories of power-driven and sailing vessels as shown in Figs 69 and 70.

In both diagrams it can be seen that these lights are either visible only from ahead or from astern or, in the case of side lights, they are seen from the one side or the other. But it is not quite as simple as that and here we must pause and explain.

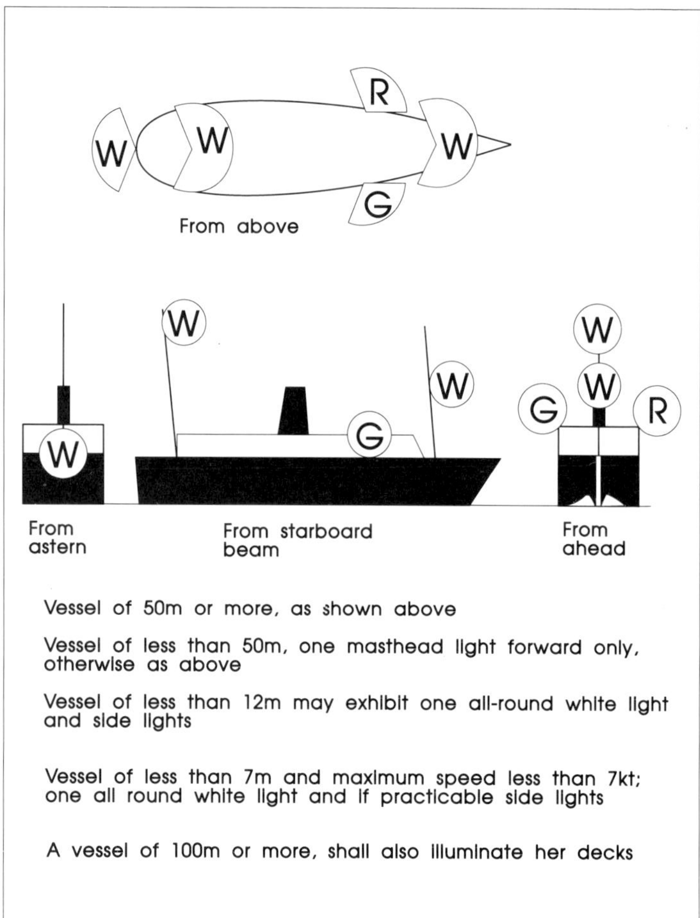

Fig 69. Lights for power-driven vessels underway.

Those lights which are seen from ahead, but not astern, do not 'cut off' on the beam. They cut off at an angle abaft the beam. This angle is 22½ degrees, deriving from 'two points abaft the beam', there being eight points in a nautical right angle. This two point cut-off is important, especially for power-driven vessels. A vessel approaching from more than two points abaft the beam is an *overtaking* vessel and has different rights of way from a *crossing* vessel which, when first seen, approaches from or forward of two points abaft the beam. The difference is shown in Fig 71, page 138.

A crossing vessel can see the masthead and side lights of the vessel she is approaching and therefore knows she is a crossing vessel. A power-driven vessel crossing from the other power-driven vessel's starboard side has right of way. If crossing from the port side it is the give way vessel (Fig 71).

The skipper next talks about lights on buoys. The two systems

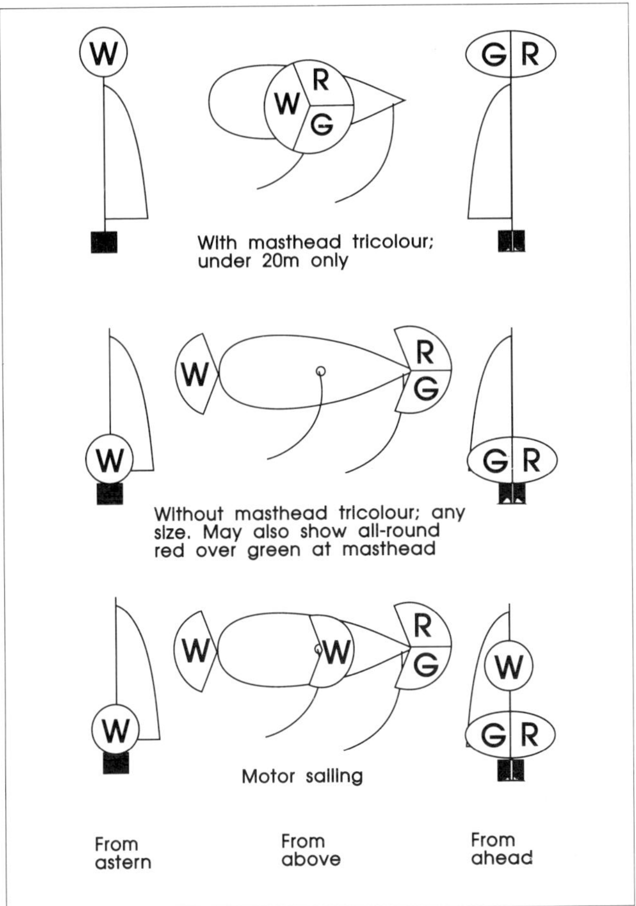

Fig 70. Lights for yachts underway.

(lateral and cardinal) are different. First the port hand buoys of the lateral system show flashing red lights, while starboard hand buoys show flashing green lights. In both cases they are often grouped into two, three or four flashes in order to identify the buoy (see Figs 50 and 51). The lights of cardinal buoys are shown in Fig 72, page 139. The logic here is the clock face. East cardinal buoys are at the *three*, south at the *six* and west at the *nine* o'clock positions. The north cardinal buoy at twelve o'clock flashes uninterruptedly.

As for lighthouses, etc, we can expect to see the light of Hurst Point, west of Yarmouth, flashing red or white according to sector (Fig 51). It is labelled on the chart, Iso WR 6s, which stands for 'isophase', meaning equal periods of on and off (ie three seconds on and three off) every six seconds for the white and red lights. Next, Egypt Point light near Cowes, white flashing every ten seconds, and Calshot Spit light float, flashing white every five seconds.

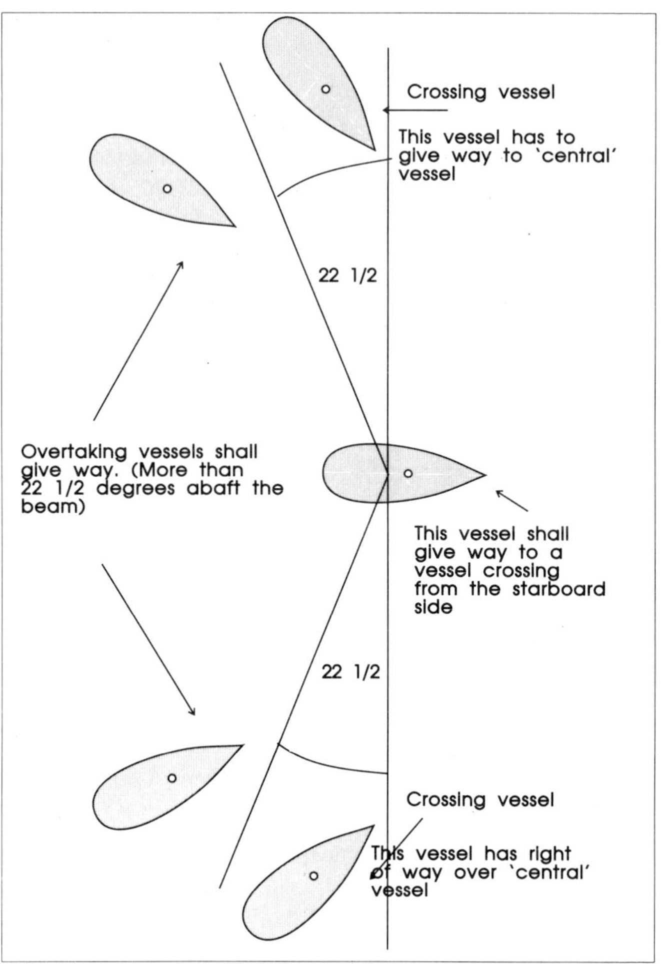
Crossing vessel
This vessel has to give way to 'central' vessel
22 1/2
Overtaking vessels shall give way. (More than 22 1/2 degrees abaft the beam)
This vessel shall give way to a vessel crossing from the starboard side
22 1/2
Crossing vessel
This vessel has right of way over 'central' vessel

Fig 71. Crossing and overtaking vessels, power-driven.

There are numerous buoys, some lighthouses and there will also be a number of sailing and power-driven vessels on the water. All of these must be identified. The task is often made more difficult by a background of town street lighting and, in the case of lighthouses, by cars turning a corner, which can look very similar. A special case is made of very small craft fishing at anchor and showing no lights other than flashing a torch at another vessel which is approaching. This light is often left to the last minute, so the lookouts must be on their toes.

Lastly, we are briefed once again on the use of red and white flares and where they are kept, on the use of the liferaft, and the lifebuoys and sparbuoy, and on the use of torches and where these are kept in the cockpit; further, smoking etiquette is also covered. In short, do

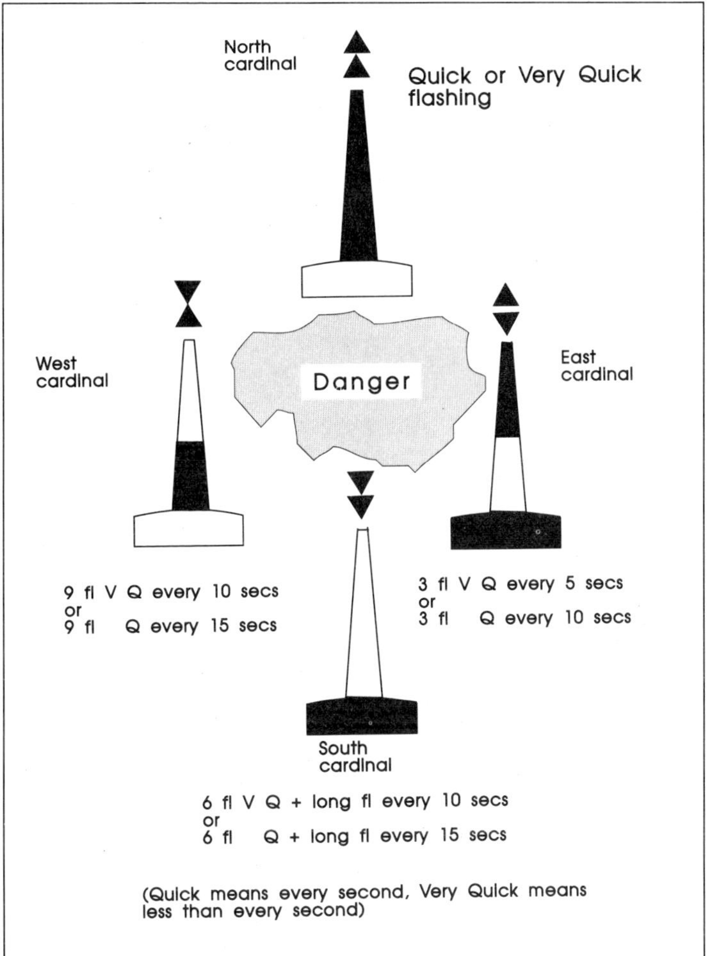

Fig 72. Lights for cardinal buoys.

not 'blind' the helmsman when using torches or when lighting up. In this connection, the cabin light will only be switched on when the main hatch and companionway are closed and similarly will be switched off before these are opened. The navigator will be using a red light over the chart table because this will have little effect on the night vision of those on deck.

Each of us will be required to make several log entries as shown in Fig 73. This is the deck or navigation log which shares its name with the instrument which displays speed and distance run.

Having dressed in appropriate clothing we all proceed on deck to check that our lights are working. We carry a tricolour at the masthead, and this is backed up by red and green lights on the pulpit and a white light on the after pulpit – not only in case of a failure aloft but

Time	Course	Log	Wind	Baro	Remarks
0730					Slipped Cowes marina
0745	290	2366	SW F3	1013	Outside Cowes No1 G, full main
0800	290	2367			Vis good Weather fine
0817	260	2369			a/c 260

Fig 73. Example of deck log entries.

also to be used, with the white light well up the forward side of the mast, if we are motoring. All is well there and also with the compass light in the cockpit and the deck lights. It is a little before dusk. There is enough daylight for our departure and for sail hoisting outside, but it will be dark soon afterwards.

While we were having our meal, another yacht has come alongside and moored up. Besides long warps to the piles, she has bow and stern lines and springs on to our yacht, all of them doubled back. The starting of our engine alerts their crew who come up on deck. They can see by our rig that we are about to slip; our skipper asks if they would let go all of their lines on to us except for their stern line. While this is being done, the skipper asks you to let go the long stern line. You let go the 'free' end, ensuring there are no knots which might snag on the mooring pile ring, and haul away on the bowline end. When all is onboard you coil it up on the afterdeck. Having seen the stern warp clear of the water, the skipper gives a 'chopping' sign with his raised arm, the prearranged signal for the foredeck crew to let go. The other yacht is now asked to haul in a little on its stern warp to us, and when our bow has swung out sufficiently, they are asked to let go. Ahead gear is engaged and we are off. A thank you and a wave are given to the other crew who are already adjusting their long warps to the mooring piles.

The mate is on the foredeck as lookout for smaller craft crossing our bows which may be invisible from the cockpit, while the skipper slowly manoeuvres the yacht round the mooring trots to the harbour entrance. Again, the car ferry slips as we approach the entrance, but this time the skipper waits inside the harbour until the ferry has gone, in order to leave the remainder of the entrance clear for incoming yachts.

Once clear of the harbour entrance and the pier, the skipper alerts the crew to hoist the main and turns the boat round to face south-wards, head-to-wind, before handing over the wheel to you. Keeping the yacht motoring slowly into the wind while the mainsail is being hoist, you note the rapidly changing transits ashore as we are carried eastwards on the tidal stream's conveyor belt.

With the mainsail now up, you are asked to turn left on to a compass course of 050 degrees to take us up the Solent towards Cowes. The compass is a binnacle type, mounted on the wheel pedestal in front of you. You have been shown the compass light switch which alters the illumination on the dial. It is as well that you have a compass course to steer by because your visibility ahead would be seriously restricted as the foresail was being hoist. Whilst you struggle with the course, remembering *when 050 goes left of the lubber line, turn the wheel left to bring it on again, and vice versa*, the foredeck crew have hoist the sail. The yacht heels over as the mainsail is trimmed to the apparent wind which blows from abeam. We are reaching. The mostly unlit large mooring buoys outside the harbour have been left behind on our starboard side, still clearly visible, but it is almost dark ahead and little of the coast there can still be seen, though the land astern is still silhouetted in the remaining twilight.

Time to take stock of what lights can be seen. Hurst Point is visible astern. It is white, and we are in the southern white sector; labelled in the middle of Fig 51. The two fixed red lights (vertical) on Yarmouth pier are clearly seen. They are a useful reference point. Two car ferries, lit up like blocks of flats but still clearly showing the correct lights, are seen on our port quarter: one, showing a stern light, about to enter the Lymington River (and incidentally close to a wooden beacon called Jack in the Basket, which was around in Nelson's day) and the other, showing both masthead lights and a red light, approaching Yarmouth. We can also see the two white mast lights and both the red and green lights of a power-driven vessel steaming towards us, but she is just passing through the Hurst Narrows and so is well astern. It is all clear to starboard except for two small boats showing white lights only on our beam. On the port beam there are several white lights, apart from the ferry, which are probably yachts near Lymington. There is little further of note on the port side, apart from the array of red lights on Fawley chimney fine on our port bow. Ahead there is a single white light. It has been there for some time and does not appear to have altered in distance; the skipper suggests we are following another yacht at the same speed.

'Green, flashing two every five seconds!' is called by a lookout. This is Hamstead Ledge buoy and the skipper asks you to steer for that, finally leaving it close on our starboard hand; this means that we shall pass by the buoy on its northern side, about 30 metres off (about three of our boat lengths). This is much more relaxing on the eyes and gives more time for you to look around, at least through the forward 180 degrees, to see what is going on. You are already aware of a great 'loom' of background lighting ahead, near and beyond Cowes, against which it is difficult to sort out the confusing pattern of lights which is just visible. Whatever vessels are amongst these, however, are some distance off and of no great concern just now.

All of a sudden, Hamstead Ledge buoy is getting much closer. You turn left a little, off the wind, to ensure leaving it to starboard. As you do so you can just make out its outline and 15 seconds later we are romping past it. The tidal 'wake' from the buoy can be easily seen and heard. The skipper is pleased with you. Almost immediately, Salt Mead buoy is sighted ahead (green, flashing three every ten seconds – the timing is from charts of larger scale than Figs 50 and 51). You are asked to keep this very fine on the starboard bow (the intention is to leave it 200 metres or so on our starboard hand) and then someone else is asked to take over the wheel. You pass on what you are steering for, what vessels are around which may soon pose a threat; there appears to be none other than the ship still well astern which is still showing two vertical white lights and both the red and green at a lower level. You take over the duties of port bow lookout, in other words it is your task to keep looking under and around the genoa. Almost immediately you call 'flashing red every five seconds, port bow!' This is identified on the chart as West Lepe buoy which marks the northern limit of the main channel. We are moving in the direction of the flood tide, so red buoys on the port hand and green to starboard mark the channel. We are also keeping well to the starboard side of the buoyed channel.

'Large vessel closing up dead astern!' comes from the stern lookout. Beneath her two white masthead lights, arranged vertically, we can see both red and green side lights (see Fig 69). She is indeed heading straight towards us.

The skipper estimates she is about half a mile away and is about to order a change to starboard to leave her plenty of room, when the mate calls 'she's turning to port!' We all look astern to see the lower (forward) masthead light swing a little to the right of the other. At the same time the red (port) side light suddenly disappears (Fig 74).

In less than a minute she turns on to her original course and is now coming up handsomely on our port quarter. As she draws abeam 300 metres away, she assumes the typical light pattern shown in Fig 69, and we can just see her outline. She is a cargo vessel of fairly modest size. Then, suddenly, as we pass through two points abaft her beam, both the masthead lights and the green side light disappear as the stern light, just as quickly, comes into view. Now this is all that can be seen of her; since the outline has gone, it is impossible once more to judge her size.

This is one of the most challenging tasks of the night lookout. Estimating distance off from other vessels is very difficult, and it is often just as difficult to estimate the size of the vessel within the groups listed in Fig 69.

As we progress further along the Solent the background light from Portsmouth throws the northern tip of the island into a bold silhouette. At its tip, Egypt Point light is now clearly visible. Further left, the background lights around Fawley power station and refinery merge with those of Southampton to throw the mainland skyline into silhouette. Just right of this we can easily identify Calshot Spit light float flashing white every five seconds. Between the two silhouettes there is a noticeably darker horizon; the Solent itself. But even this is not without light, for there are several vessels moving around the Brambles Bank region and some of the lights of the larger buoys there are now just visible. We shall not concern ourselves with these more distant lights just now, but they do provide a 'horizon'. The single white light we have been following for some time is seen to be well above that horizon, supporting the guess that it is the stern sector of the masthead tricolour of a yacht under sail (see Fig 70). It is a little brighter than before so we are steadily overhauling her.

'Red and green lights very fine on the starboard bow!' They are at the same level as the single white ahead so the skipper decides they are the tricolour lights of a yacht approaching us under sail. It is interesting to note that perhaps the single white ahead, elevated a little above the 'horizon', may well have drawn our attention to the approaching yacht in good time, for there is a natural tendency to concentrate visual searching to a thin band along the horizon.

We are on starboard tack, so the approaching yacht must be on port tack (wind from the south). She has already passed the yacht ahead, on its starboard side, and looks set to pass us also on our starboard side. The skipper has two crew hands standing by to ease off the sheets, just in case he is forced finally to turn away, even though she is the give way vessel. Her red light disappears leaving the green only, so she has turned to port to give way. Within seconds she romps past three or four of our boat lengths away; it is sufficient, but at night in relatively open water, only just.

The yacht ahead is now less than 100 metres away; we shall soon overtake her on one side or the other. The skipper directs the helmsman to turn left about 10 degrees and head for Calshot Spit light float

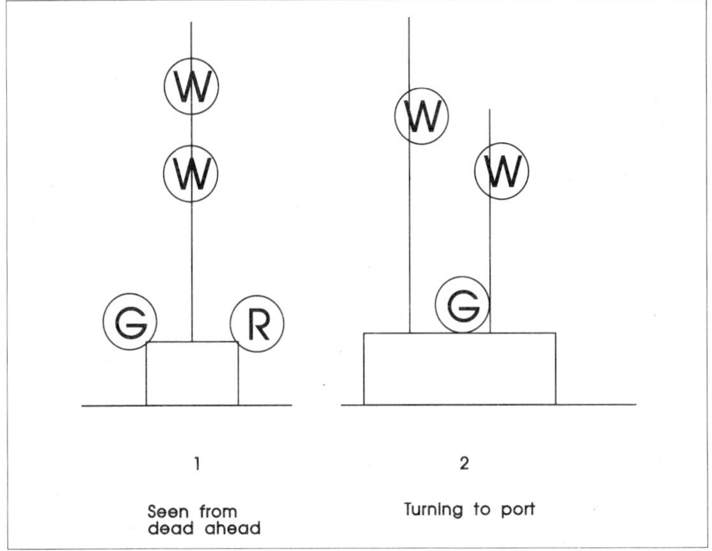

Fig 74. A 'head-on' vessel turning.

in order to overtake to leeward of the other yacht. There are no rules about this situation but, racing apart, it is a long-standing courtesy not to overtake to windward and 'steal the wind' from the slower yacht. A few minutes later we overtake her and, as we do so, Salt Mead buoy comes abeam to starboard at about 200 metres. The next buoy in the chain, Gurnard Ledge, is unlit so the skipper asks the helmsman to maintain his course towards Calshot Spit light float to ensure clearing the unlit buoy.

After about ten minutes, the skipper hands up a small hand-bearing compass and asks you for bearings from Egypt Point and Fawley power station chimney in order to fix the position of the yacht. You place its lanyard around your neck, move to the afterdeck where both objects can easily be seen, raise the compass close to the eye and look through the edge of the flat disc shape to bring the object in line with the sights, then the lubber line in line with the object, then read the bearing from the compass card (it is internally illuminated); see Fig 59. You take Fawley first, whose 'stack' of red lights is fixed; aiming at the top red light you read off the bearing against the lubber line. Do it again as a check, then call out 'Fawley 024'. Now you turn to Egypt Point and take the bearing of its flash; repeat the process and call out 'Egypt Point 081'; total time for the bearings, one minute. The skipper takes a note of the readings and asks you to come down below to see the chartwork, leaving the mate in charge of the deck.

In taking down your bearings, the skipper also noted the time and the log reading. Now he converts the bearings, which are related to the magnetic pole, to true bearings related to the chart's geographical pole orientation. (There is no opportunity here to go into the theory of navigation. The subject is excellently described in books and is also taught in many evening classes.) There is currently 6 degrees westerly **variation** in the Solent. As with most modern hand-bearing compasses, deviation is negligible, but do watch out for spectacle frames; if metallic, they may deflect the compass card to give an incorrect reading. By day, sunglasses may also produce a similar, dangerous deflection.

In converting **compass** bearings to **true** bearings the skipper recommends the ditty: *Compass to true, East is plus and West is minus*. So the bearings become 018 degrees and 075 degrees, respectively.

Next he identifies Fawley power station chimney on the chart, places the centre of a large, square protractor on the chimney, calculates the reciprocal of 018 degrees (198 degrees), measures off this angle on the edge of his scale, makes a pencil mark, then draws a line along this 'back-bearing' from the chimney. At the time of taking the bearing the yacht was positioned somewhere along that line. The process is repeated for Egypt Point (true back-bearing, 255 degrees). The intersection of the two lines gives the position of the yacht at the time of the bearings, which are considered simultaneous. (The chartwork is shown on Fig 51.) The 'fix' indicates that we are mid-channel and therefore some distance away from the unlit buoy.

You both come up on deck to have a look around when 'white, quick-flashing starboard bow' is called by a lookout. The skipper, standing behind the lookout, asks him to point to the light. It is quick flashing (every second) and is identified as Gurnard north cardinal buoy. Almost immediately the same lookout calls 'very quick flashing, close to earlier one'. This is Prince Consort north cardinal buoy about a mile or so further east. The skipper had to satisfy himself that the two similar buoys had been correctly identified. He now asks the helmsman to steer towards Gurnard north cardinal buoy; this track will not only ensure clearing the unlit buoy but will also take the yacht back towards the edge of the channel and clear of any large vessels which may be using it. Both sails are sheeted in a little as the new course is closer to the wind.

You draw the skipper's attention to a vessel head-on some distance away on the port bow. The vessel is in Thorn Channel on the western side of Bramble Bank. He suspects it is a Cowes ferry and would expect it to head south after rounding West Bramble cardinal buoy; its nine very quick flashes every ten seconds can be seen on the vessel's port hand. Very soon the lights show that the vessel has turned to port (the lower white light has moved to the right of the other and the red light has disappeared) and almost immediately the West Bramble buoy light cycle is interrupted after three quick flashes. It has been cut off by the vessel which has clearly passed on the western side of the buoy. Her new southerly course, counteracting the easterly tidal set, is being maintained. The general level of illumination together with her new course confirm she is the Cowes ferry.

The skipper hands you the hand-bearing compass and asks you to monitor her bearing. You take frequent bearings, three or four per minute, on her green light (or any other) and soon notice that the bearings are altering quite rapidly from the direction of the port bow towards dead ahead – they are 'drawing forward'. She is therefore passing ahead and since the outline can only now just be seen, clear ahead. (If successive bearings were noticeably drawing aft, the other vessel would pass astern.)

As she passes clear ahead, her general lighting silhouettes Gurnard cardinal buoy, and we can now see how quickly we are approaching it. The skipper has already asked the helmsman to leave it on our starboard side, and in a few seconds we are past. The buoy itself appears to have charged noisily past us, leaving a long wake which sparkles with phosphorescence. We have cleared it by 30 metres but even so we can appreciate its great bulk. It stands nearly 4 metres high and weighs several tonnes; it must be avoided!

The skipper has asked for a course which will leave Prince Consort and West Ryde Middle buoys on our port hand. As we approach Prince Consort there is a noticeable freshening of the southerly wind, due to funnelling through the Medina valley, which adds another knot to our speed. In this region we have a fair tide of about 3 knots so we soon romp past Prince Consort, and are now sheeting in a little once more as the course is altered to pass West Ryde Middle on our port hand; its nine quick flashes have been seen for some time.

Apart from some shipping movement in the approaches to Southampton Water, some smaller vessel activity astern, and yet another ferry leaving Cowes, it is relatively quiet all round. It's all plain sailing. West Ryde Middle buoy is also left astern, coffee and cake have been passed up as we sail over Ryde Middle Bank where there is always plenty of water. Some chat breaks out amongst the crew for there have been great demands on concentration so far.

'White light dead ahead, close!' from the forward lookout and 'turn right 20 degrees!' from the skipper, in quick succession, shatter the peacefulness of the scene. Coffee mugs are quickly passed below to enable the crew to tend to the sails which are now flogging a little. The white light was a torch operated by a lone fisherman in a small boat at anchor on the bank. The torch was only switched on when he saw our yacht bearing down on his boat. The lookout saw the light as soon as it was switched on and since he almost immediately saw a 'back-lit' face, he added 'close'! The time interval between sighting and passing was no more than ten seconds; the distance about 40 metres. The new course is maintained as the skipper wishes to head towards Mother Bank buoy. Coffees are back up, and the situation is discussed and the value of the emphasis at the presailing briefing is firmly driven home. All are impressed, including the skipper.

'White light dead ahead, close!' once again immediately followed by 'turn right 20 degrees!' This time the skipper was facing astern. By the time he has turned round to see the second small boat at anchor, the yacht is already turning to clear it. This time the lit warning is given in better time, and some 20 seconds from first sighting, the danger is clear. 'Turn left 20 degrees to keep Ryde Pier lights fine to starboard' is given to the helmsman who brings her back on to the original course.

'Two white lights, port bow' is reported. They are separated horizontally, the left being higher than the other. There could be a number of solutions here so, since they appear to be still some distance away, the skipper asks you to take frequent bearings of them both. You call out the bearing of the left light, then the right, and repeat these every 15 seconds or so. They are drawing aft steadily, and simultaneously the angle between them is widening. The skipper concludes it is a vessel at anchor, facing west as she rides to the east-setting tide (Fig 75).

'Red and green masthead lights dead ahead!' is called some minutes later by the starboard lookout. He can see these lights above the general glow from Ryde which also defines a horizon, so he has usefully amplified his observation with 'masthead'. Since these are the only lights showing, she is a port tack sailing vessel dead ahead. This is another opposite tack situation and we are still on starboard tack. Once again the skipper has two crew hands on the sheets in case the other yacht hasn't seen us. She hasn't and is too close for comfort.

'Turn right sharply; sheet in on both!' is ordered. Seconds later the other yacht storms past, about 10 metres from our port quarter. A rather useless apology is heard – and ignored. Once back on course, the skipper explains that if the other yacht had given way, finally, he would probably have turned to his starboard. Had we turned left, to port, at the same instant we would have made a collision inevitable. It

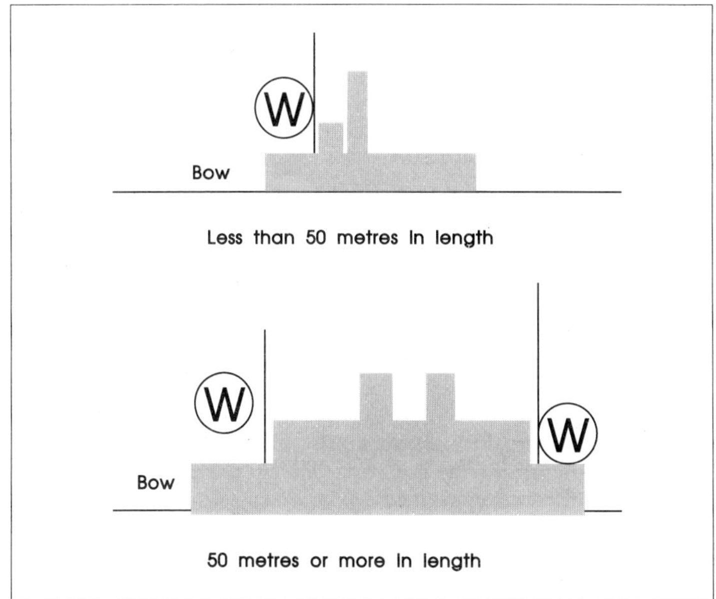

Fig 75. Anchor lights.

was clear that the skipper's turning order alerted the other yacht to our presence; an excellent example of not taking anything for granted at sea, especially by night.

Northeast Ryde Middle, Southeast Ryde Middle, Peel Bank and Mother Bank buoys have all been called and correctly identified. The skipper has sketched in a 'fix' on the chart based on these buoys and timed when the first two were in line; it is adequate under the circumstances. The course has been altered to leave Mother Bank buoy close to port. The two white lights seen earlier are now abeam to port. The configuration confirms that it is a vessel of 50 metres or more at anchor (Fig 75).

Mother Bank buoy is now closing fine on the port bow. The skipper takes the wheel and calls 'ready to gybe!' You haul away at the mainsheet as the skipper begins to turn downwind. He checks that you are all but sheeted in, that no one is in the way of the boom then calls 'gybe-oh' as he turns the stern through the wind. You let out the mainsheet after the gybe, while others haul away on the foresail sheet to set it on the other side of the yacht. With the sails now set on the new course, the skipper hands over the wheel to you and asks you to steer towards Peel Bank buoy to leave it close on our port side.

Whereas on the eastbound trip the buoys came up quickly as we sailed through the fair tide, averaging 8 knots and sometimes more than 9 knots over the ground, it is already apparent that it will take much longer going west against the tide. Though yacht speed is similar at about 6 knots, the tide is running at 2 knots, and later we will have nearer 3 knots against us, so that speed over the ground is halved at least. But Peel Bank comes abeam eventually and, after a cup of soup all round, Norris buoy, the next port hand one, is approaching. (The East Solent channels are buoyed as though the flood tide sets in from the east instead of the west.)

'Very large vessel dead astern!' is reported. You take a quick glance astern to see, still at a safe distance, the usual configuration of a head-on vessel (Fig 69) plus three red lights arranged vertically from her yardarm. She is a 'vessel constrained by her draught' to which we must give way – 'sail over steam' and overtaking rules notwithstanding. The skipper asks you to leave Norris to starboard and then to keep Old Castle Point (easily seen against the 'loom' from Cowes) very fine on the port bow. The coast is 'steep-to' (see depth contours on Fig 50) and we are near the top of the tide, so there is plenty of water close in, at least as far as the point.

Norris buoy has come and gone, the distance to the very large vessel has decreased considerably, Prince Consort is well in sight and so now are the nine quick flashes from Gurnard buoy. The skipper has just asked you to steer for Gurnard buoy when, 'red and green masthead light, dead ahead, closing fast!' is called. 'Turn left, sharp' from the skipper, and with our sails gently flogging, the other yacht passes our starboard quarter at about 30 metres. We are the port tack boat and with the large vessel closing astern, the only safe avoiding action was to turn to port.

With the yacht now back on course for Gurnard buoy, the large vessel coming up through the deep water channel is catching up fast. We can see something of her outline, at least the forepart and she is huge. She is now almost abeam and about 400 metres distant and though her decks are illuminated we can see little of this due to her vast freeboard. It is only when she is abeam that we are able to see most of her outline. Her bridge, carrying her red and green side lights, is not near the stern but appears to be only a little abaft halfway. Further, the main mast, carrying the higher masthead light, is immediately abaft the bridge so that masthead and side lights do not define her overall length; neither are they required so to do. It is only when she has drawn forward and when her steaming and side lights cut off, that her stern light comes into view to confirm that there is a very long afterdeck abaft the bridge, almost as much as forward of it. She passes 100 metres north of Prince Consort buoy steaming north west and, on approaching West Bramble's very quick flashing nine, she sounds one blast on her horn to indicate that she is turning to starboard around West Bramble buoy for Southampton.

While most of the crew have spent the last few minutes looking at this ship, you call 'what are these objects in the water dead ahead?' The skipper informs you that they are yacht mooring buoys in long trots stretching away from us (they are mostly empty) and asks you to turn right a little to pass on the outside of them all, keeping Gurnard buoy fine on the port bow. He asks the port lookout to watch for a buoy, flashing red every second on our port bow. This is at the entrance to the Medina river. We shall be mooring up at Cowes Marina about one mile from its mouth.

The engine is started, and when the buoy has been identified, he asks you to bear away a little to allow room to round up to hand the sails; the wind is still southerly but even with a fair wind it would be unseamanlike to attempt to sail up the river by night.

The skipper takes two crew forward, all harnessed to the jackstays, to hand the foresail, leaving the mate to supervise in the cockpit. At the skipper's signal you round up head-to-wind, engage forward drive and use just enough throttle to hold her there. The foresail is soon down and tied to the lifeline under the skipper's direction, and with it out of the way the skipper calls for the main halyard to run. You apply a little more throttle to keep the boat head-to-wind, using the relative wind direction dial as the only practical aid, while the deck crew struggle gallantly to contain the lowered mainsail. That handed, and tied over the boom, the sail handling crew come aft to the cockpit where the skipper asks you to increase the revs a little and turn to starboard a touch so as to leave the red buoy to port and steer for the buoy flashing green every three seconds which marks the starboard side of the channel. The yacht is moving around a lot in the lumpy sea which always exists off Cowes while the tide is running, then suddenly all is quiet as you enter the channel and turn up river.

The skipper points out the line of red buoys on the port hand. There is no complimentary line of green buoys on the other side. Instead, the west bank of the river is the starboard side of the channel and you should keep your present distance off the west side. He also states that there is a chain ferry at the bend in the river about half a mile ahead.

The mate and the remainder of the crew meantime have been detailed to rig mooring warps fore and aft, as well as three fenders on each side, kept inboard meantime. They have also been instructed not to obscure your view as they carry out these tasks.

Apart from a couple of yachts ahead, which are already turning right into West Cowes Marina, all seems quiet in the river. The Southampton car ferry is still moored up at East Cowes, and though there are some small craft astern, they are not overtaking. The skipper points out that the chain ferry has just left the west bank, and that this should mean that it should be safely 'between trips' by the time we reach the bend in the river.

'Am I going to be allowed to take the yacht that far?' you ask yourself, but the question is answered by the skipper who says 'keep her as she is'. He draws the attention of the whole crew to the little 'bridge' structure at each end of the ferry, from which a flashing white light will be hoist when the ferry moves off (black ball by day). We are now close enough to see that the cars are still rolling on and that there is no one on the bridge.

He asks you to increase the revs so as to accelerate the yacht through the gap while it is still safe to do so. The river opens out a little as you turn the bend past several boatyards and mooring piles. The skipper points out the pontoons of Cowes Marina on the port hand still a few hundred metres ahead and, just as you are about to break out into a sweat at the prospect of taking her alongside, he says

'I've got her. Take over the bow warp.'

All hands are called to the cockpit and the skipper says that he will drift past the marina as slowly as he can with the tide still with us so that the mate, using the big torch, may be able to spot a free berth, preferably with an uptide approach. When one has been located, he will turn the yacht round in a broad circle so as to give the crew time to rig the warps on the appropriate side and slip the fenders outboard. He has appointed you to the bow warp and someone else to the stern. As the yacht stops alongside the pontoon, the success of the mooring depends on the warp hands who must take the lines to their nearest pontoon fitting, taking care not to slip or trip, keep some tension in the warp, get a round turn on the fitting and then hold it until further directions are given. You, especially, have a great responsibility, since, with the tide still running, the yacht will soon drift back with the tide unless the bow warp is secured to prevent it.

'Row E, second slot in, starboard side to, mooring cleats' says the mate as he comes aft to the cockpit. From now on, day or night, there are to be no raised voices on entering harbour, except in an emergency. You have all been briefed what to do and what signals the skipper will use.

You go forward, rig the bowline end of the bow warp through the starboard fairlead from outside and slip it on to the nearest cleat. Then, tidily holding the loose coils, you walk aft to the starboard shrouds where you are joined by the stern warp hand. As the yacht angles in towards the end of the pontoon you both face forward, take the coils in the right hand, then holding on to the shrouds with the left hand, you step over the lifelines to stand on the toerail.

As soon as the gap is small enough, you lean out and jump ashore; the yacht is still edging slowly forward. Taking care, you go forward, ahead of the bows, maintaining tension in the warp, locate the most suitable cleat and take a round turn to hold her. The yacht is just stopped, using astern power, as you do so. Meantime a third crew member has leapt on to the pontoon to ensure that the fenders remain in the gap between it and the hull. The stern warp is temporarily secured at the same time, so the yacht is nicely under control from the warps.

The skipper requires the yacht to move a metre or two along the pontoon, so asks the stern hand to ease out slightly as you haul in gently until he is satisfied. He then signals 'make-up' to you both, using a figure of eight rotation of his hand. You apply two such turns over the cleat and then finish off with a half hitch on the horn nearest to the yacht. Now you coil the tail tidily and place it near the cleat and out of the way.

The mate is already supervising the rigging of the springs from cleats on the fore- and afterdecks to a pontoon cleat midway along the hull. The skipper checks it all over. It will do nicely; she is moored. Just the ensign to lower and the sterngland to check; anything else, like tidying up the furled main using a 'slab stow' and also folding the No 1 genoa into slabs before restowing it in its bag, can wait till the morning. It's time to relax down below.

The skipper quickly runs through the day's events as he pours out a generous tot all round. You have learnt about tacking, gybing and heaving-to; running under poled-out foresail and running under spinnaker; gybing the spinnaker and man overboard; anchoring; mooring on piles and alongside a pontoon. You have also learned of the importance of lookouts as well as something of navigation and the collision avoidance rules. In all, a great deal of seamanship with an understanding of the 'command decisions'.

You are also all very tired, and more than a little uncomfortable in places, but the level of chat and the smiling faces indicate that today will be long remembered. It is the first in what will probably become a long and enjoyable sailing career for many of you.

INDEX